Contents

Acknowledgments 9
Introduction 11
Zbydniów, My Birthplace 13
My Fateful Dream 23
Our Garden 24
Father's Family 28
Cousin Genia's Wedding 34
Another Memorable Wedding 37
Uncle Leibish's Engagement 39
First Grade 41
My Dyslexia 48
School 50
Chronic Battle with Cravings 54
Zbydniów 57
Fall in Zbydniów 60
Winter in Zbydniów 62
Summer Vacation and Cheder 70
My Parents Decide to Move to Rozwadów 75
Last Yom Kippur Holiday in Rozwadów 77
WWII Comes to Zbydniów 79
Bombing of Zbydniów 82
My Father 93
The Matchmaker 98

Unforgettable Visit to the Big Mansion	100
My Tonsil Saga	108
Aunt Genia and Susan's Visit	117
The Town of Rozwadów	119
Mother's Family	121
Mother	132
Expulsion	134
Janów	159
Gypsy Forecast	163
Mother's Journey Back Home	169
Mother Back in Janów	195
On the Way to Siberia	202
We Have Arrived!	206
Siberia	235
My Brother David	244
The Package	250
Discovery of Zakavrashyna	253
Mother in Jail	276
Freedom at Last	284
Tashkent	293
Southern Republics	302
Kolkhoz Life in Turkmenistan	307
Dzhambul	315
Oblava (Roundup) in Dzhambul	327
Dzhambul, Our White Puppy	334
The Reason I Fear Dogs	338
School Project: Stamp Collecting	346
Dzhambul: Typhoid Epidemic	349
Life in Dzhambul	356
Mother's Fur Cape	360

My Sister Leah's Evil Eye 362
Doing Business in Dzanbul 364
Our Melamed 370
Another Episode with the Meat Business...374
The KGB...377
Skimming Food from My Sister 381
Baking Passover Matza 386
The Meat Business Continues...388
Second Typhoid Epidemic...391
Arriving in Poland...408
Far away from home...412

ACKNOWLEDGMENTS

First and foremost, I am indebted to my dear mother who acted on my suggestion and undertook this project. The whole chapters which are incorporated here she so ably wrote in Yiddish and I was able to translate.

To my dear cousin Rachel, who left us at the age of 92, who had a phenomenal memory almost to her last days and filled the gaps when needed.

The first run of language corrections, where needed, was ably done by my daughter Daphne. When technology became a factor, Sandra lent a hand, but the bulwark of technological work was willingly and expertly provided by a true gentleman, Olivier.

I am grateful to all those relatives and friends who urged me to continue and not give up.

This project was about 30 years in the making.

INTRODUCTION

My photo for train pass-1937

While I visited my mother in the late 1970s, we had a discussion about a certain event in our lives that took place during World War II.

The actual subject of the conversation eludes me, but I remember that our recollections differed.

It occurred to me then that my younger sisters, Leah and Sarah, might not know much about our family's past, the war years, and probably very little about their own background, so I asked my mother to write down some of the things she remembered. At first she laughed but later agreed that it was a good idea. After all, she had plenty of time.

I instantly realized that such a project would occupy her, exercise her mind, and give her an opportunity to record some family history for future generations.

Whether anyone would be interested in the past or would read it was of no concern at the time.

During my next visit a year or two later, my mother presented me with a shoe box filled with written scraps of paper of various sizes. I was moved to tears. She had written about her life, her siblings, and other members of the family. She wrote about her childhood, young adult life, education, marriage, the war years, and much more. It was all in Yiddish, her favorite language and one she was most familiar with. She agreed that families owe it to their descendants to inform them about their past.

While reading those sheets of paper, I discovered fascinating information about the family including myself that I had no knowledge of or had forgotten. I complimented her on the great accomplishment and urged her to continue. It was not a literary gem but a sincere account of her life and ours.

When I returned home, I thought about the assignment I gave my mother and the important work she was doing for our family and thought to myself, *Why don't I do the same?* Though our lives were intertwined, I might remember certain things she didn't, and vice versa.

Several of my relatives expressed an interest in the project and urged me to go on. My story may not be chronologically accurate, but it's what I remember.

Some of my relatives also contributed information I didn't have, and I am grateful. Some relatives requested to remain anonymous, so their names may have been changed in some way or omitted.

The Internet was also helpful with some of the statistics. Please keep in mind that this narrative is what I remember. Geography and some places, people, events, or names may also differ. I did make every effort to stick to the truth. If any of my relatives remember things differently, that's their prerogative.

Zbydniów, My Birthplace

I was born in a small village called Zbydniów, situated in the southeastern part of Poland called Galicia. The nearest town, Rozwadów, today's Stalowa Wola, was about eight kilometers away. The closest villages surrounding Zbydniów were Majdan, Zaleszany, Turbia, and Kotowa Wola. The village took its origins on the banks of an old tributary of the river San.

Zbydniów has been in existence about eight hundred years, not necessarily always under the same name. The name Zbydniów was taken from Zbygniew Horodynski, the great-grandfather of the last owner of the Horodynski estate. Centuries ago, most of the land in Poland belonged to the kings and was in turn leased or awarded to the Polish gentry for favors granted to the kings.

Poland was often attacked by neighboring countries, and the kings needed cash in order to outfit the army. The king's coffers were often empty, so that was when they turned to the nobility for loans. Many of these loans were returned in the form of farmland and other properties. That was how, in the early nineteenth century, the nobleman Mr. Zbygniew Horodynski acquired the whole village including much of its surroundings.

In the middle of the fifteenth century, Zbydniów had only fourteen residents, and as time progressed, the population of the village grew, especially after the arrival of the Horodynski family. The enlarged estate of about 1,200 hectares that Mr. Horodynski received consisted of orchards, forests, fertile-soil farmland, and riparian rights to the San River—in itself a very valuable asset. Now that he owned this vast estate, he was in need of workers; thus, he attracted many farmhands and other skilled laborers from neighboring villages as well as other parts of the country.

Eventually, some professionals also found employment and settled in the village.

The majority of the inhabitants, including my father, worked for the local squire, Dominic Horodynski, the heir and great-grandson of Zbygniew Horodynski. At the beginning of the twentieth century, there were over several hundred inhabitants in Zbydniów. The religious composition was 99.9 percent Roman Catholic and forty-eight Jews (must have been my father's family). In 1939, only eighteen Jews lived in Zbydniów.

Before World War II, the Horodynskis, in addition to all the land, owned a flour mill, a sawmill, a brewery, livestock, horses, carriages, and a black Ford—the only car in the village. One of the squire's great passions was horse racing, and he owned and bred many of them. Most of Horodynskis employees lived in his properties, as did we. Everyone paid rent or provided services.

Several professional residents of Zbydniów come to mind: the postmaster, the trainmaster, a blacksmith, a shoemaker, a butcher, a carpenter or two, some teachers, and the Catholic priest.

The Horodynski family occupied a most opulent mansion situated on many manicured acres of luscious gardens. The mansion was enlarged, modified, and modernized several times over the years. In addition to the main building, there was an orangery, a hothouse, stables, a garage for the master's Ford, and a carriage house. All this was surrounded by a high concrete wall with trees growing along the inside. The top of the wall was strung with barbed wire and shards of glass imbedded in the concrete. The interior must have been as impressive as the exterior, if not more; though I had seen only one room in the mansion once, the impression remains with me to this day. I will describe this memorable visit later.

The multifamily house we lived in was directly across the road from the squire's estate. Diagonally across the street from our house stood an old wooden hut where the blacksmith shoed horses. Behind it was a large stagnant pond full of plants, frogs, and other creatures. In the summer, white and yellow water lilies covered the surface of the pond. On certain summer nights, the frogs entertained us with their croaking. At the far end of the pond were two rows of shabby barracks called *czworaki*, where the poorest employee families lived. These long wooden one-story structures were divided into individual rooms, and each room was occupied by a family with several children. The men worked for the squire, as did many of the women. The children ran around half-naked and dirty while their parents worked. Some of the children did not even attend school. In those days, school was not compulsory and illiteracy was commonplace. There was only one paved cobblestone road in the village, running east to west from one end to the other. The shorter unpaved roads crisscrossed the village and were covered with mud after each rain or melting snow.

Most of the homes along those side roads were constructed by their original owners and handed down through the generations. Many housed two or three generations together. The predominant building materials were wooden logs, thanks to the abundance of forest in the area, making wood the most economical building material. The sizes of the homes varied according to need, but most consisted of two to four rooms. There were also some brick homes, including the one we lived in. Indoor plumbing was nonexistent at that time, except possibly in the Horodynskis' mansion.

Everyone had a well that supplied fresh, clean water and an outhouse in the yard. Very few had electricity. Most villagers had gardens adjacent to their homes, and a chicken coop, and those who could afford it owned a cow or two and a horse and wagon. A horse and wagon were an absolute necessity for farming and transportation.

As I mentioned, the village was founded on the banks of a small tributary of the San River. This river was a vital asset and had many beneficial uses. An old wooden bridge straddled the river, enabling the connection between Zbydniów, the nearby village of Majdan, and beyond.

Zbydniów, as well as the whole area, came into prominence in the 1880s, when the railroad tracks were laid and a one-story train station was built (which still stands in total disrepair). Before the war, trains passed several times each day and some still stopped once in a while. In its heyday, the station was full of life. It contained a spacious waiting room with a wood-burning heating oven and several benches, a small office for the stationmaster, and a tiny ticket office.

Until the railway came through the village, the main means of transportation were horses and wagons. But the railroad opened many new opportunities for the population in the region.

Zbydniów was a small village. It most likely looked like many others and most inhabitants knew one another, and there was an amicable atmosphere. Nonetheless, the Jews were considered outsiders and were looked upon with suspicion and envy.

But that did not prevent me from having friends among the Christian children.

Among the many valuable contributions of the Horodynski family to the village was the construction of an elementary school in the beginning of the twentieth century.

The elementary school, built and completed in 1905, in use up to this day, was a two-story building large enough for several classrooms, a library, and administrative accommodations and a recently added gym.

The building we lived in was centrally located, so it landed itself to many uses. It was a long and narrow one-story brick structure. It housed three families, a small business enterprise, and the village post office. It had a fairly large fenced-in backyard with a water well in the middle, a barn for two cows, a chicken coop, an outhouse, and plenty of room for the foul to roam and for us kids to play. The outhouse was a small wooden structure with three separate stalls, each one with a door and a small window for ventilation. In the summer the stench was oppressive, and in the winter it was too cold to sit there. The fence surrounding the yard was mainly to keep the chickens, ducks, and geese from wandering away. Adjacent to the left side of the house was a garden of considerable size enclosed by a picket fence, which we shared with Aunt Reizl.

The house residents were our family of five, my aunt Reizl, her husband and three children, and there was a small room that was the post office, with separate quarters for the postmaster and his wife.

Each family had a separate entrance from the outside, but the whole building was accessible and connected on the inside.

Our apartment consisted of three rooms: a bedroom, kitchen, and another separate room across the hallway, which we called the summer kitchen or storeroom. This room was whitewashed, with a cold slate floor. It had no heating oven, but it did have a cooking stove used primarily in the summer. It was a space for storing produce and other perishables in the winter.

My aunt and her family also occupied three rooms, one of which was used as a bar / grocery store, nicknamed Karczma, the Inn—hence the name for the building, which remains to this day. In the largest room in the front was a bar with high stools, where my aunt served her customers liquor, mainly vodka, the preferred drink, and snacks. She also sold some grocery items. This small enterprise was her source of income. Her husband, I am told, was not the best provider; his job was to buy supplies for the business.

About two years before the war broke out, my parents, in partnership with Aunt Reizl, acquired a billiard table. This new game table was a novelty in the area, and men came on Sundays after church to try out the new game of billiards. It was an additional source of income for both our families.

My aunt Reizl; her husband, Yitzchak; and their three children, Rachel, Israel, and Esther, lived in two rooms: the all-purpose kitchen and the bedroom. The kitchen had a brick oven / hearth and an additional bed, where my cousin Israel slept when he came home from school (in Rozwadów), usually for Shabbat and holidays. That oven was where Aunt Reizl and my mother did their weekly baking.

My aunt would rise each Friday at the crack of dawn and start the yeast dough in separate large bowls, from which she created the most delicious cakes, challah, and breads. I loved the cracked end-crust of my aunt's round loaves of bread, which she would slice for me while still warm, then my mother would smother it with fresh, sweet butter. I loved to watch the butter melt and disappear into the little crevices.

Mother would also prepare her dough and bake bread, challah, and cakes for the Sabbath and the rest of the week. I must admit that my aunt's bread tasted much better than my mother's. Today, a good, fresh slice of freshly baked bread and butter reminds me of those childhood days.

Our bedroom was a square room with two tall windows facing the main road. They were adorned with white eyelet curtains on the inside and wooden shutters on the outside. The walls were covered with white wallpaper with a tiny rosebud pattern. The wooden floor was painted maroon, which the maid polished with a special paste every Friday. A large bed with a very thick mattress and two small night tables on each side occupied most of the room. Above the headboard hung a large wood-framed painting of a colorful pastoral landscape. My brother David's cradle was situated close to the bed, against the outside wall. The cradle was moved once a year during the Christmas season, when my mother put up a small Christmas tree for our nanny. She never wanted to go home for Christmas, or other holidays—she preferred to stay with us—though mother never objected to her taking time off for the holidays. Eventually, we found out the reason that she didn't want to go and be with her family.

During the year, we kept the Christmas ornaments in the attic, but we always added more, made by us and our nanny. Christmas was a very busy and happy time for the Christian residents. Some Jews also got caught up in the festive atmosphere, when Chanukkah coincided with Christmas. Many evergreen trees growing in people's yards added aroma and color to the white blanket of snow. Groups of people went from house to house, singing Christmas carols. After they sang for us, Mother would reward them with hot tea, cakes, and coins. Our nanny taught us Christmas songs, and I still remember one or two.

Back to the bedroom.

Against the left wall stood a large mahogany wardrobe with a mirror in its middle panel. Everything, from the crochet bedspread to the eyelet curtains and many other decorative items in our home, was hand-made by my mother. She knew how to crochet, needlepoint, knit, sew, embroider, and do other handicrafts. Mother had many talents, and some of them came in handy especially during the war.

The entrance to the bedroom was from the multipurpose kitchen, where we spent most of our waking hours. It was the center of our daily activities. I vividly remember all the furnishings and where they were located. In one of the corners, near the window and the door leading to my aunt Reizel's kitchen, stood a floor-to-ceiling, white-tile, wood-burning heating oven. A white wooden credenza with upper glass doors occupied most of the inside wall, dividing the two kitchens. It stored all our kitchen utensils: dishes, pots, pans, etc. Two drawers, dividing the upper part from the lower, stored the meat and dairy cutlery separately and small cooking utensils. To its right, in the next corner, was a large wood-burning stove with four burners. Then came the door to the bedroom, and at the opposite wall was our maid/nanny's bed. Above the bed hung an enlarged framed photograph of my maternal grandfather, Zecharia Leib. This was the only photo of him we had. I still have a smaller version of it now.

In the middle of the kitchen stood a heavy oblong wooden table with a bench on each side and an armchair at both ends. Father always occupied the armchair at the head of the table. The table could accommodate six to eight comfortably. Above it hung a kerosene lamp, our source of evening light. This wooden table served as a surface for all the activities in our household, starting with Mother's food preparation, ironing, my homework, Father's bookkeeping, and everything else requiring a flat surface.

The Sabbath was my favorite day of the week. It was a joyful day. It began Friday after sundown and was especially festive. The table was covered with a white cloth. The gleaming silver candlesticks and Father's kiddush cup (wine goblet) were polished every Friday morning, and the challah breads were the centerpieces of the table. The freshly baked challah was covered with a square coverlet. It was forest-green wool embroidered with pink and red roses and green leaves. It was part of Mother's trousseau, which she herself embroidered. Over the years, moles have eaten holes into the wool fabric and it is now full of stains. Maybe it can be dry-cleaned, but the fabric is very fragile, so I keep it as is. Mother gave it to me many years ago, and I treasure it. Eventually I found the courage to part with it and donated it in 2016 to the Yeshiva University Museum.

Mother always prepared special foods for the Sabbath. We always had gefilte fish and chicken soup for Friday-night dinner and other delicious dishes. The chickens, ducks, and geese came from our own coop.

During and after meals on Fridays and Saturdays, we would sing special songs called Z'mirot. Both my parents had beautiful voices and loved to sing. This gift was handed down to all of us.

Saturdays, when Father came home from services in Zaleshany, we had the main meal then Father would take his weekly nap. In order not to disturb him, weather permitting, Mother would take us for a walk. She dressed us in our finest, and we would take long walks. We would go visit Grandma Leah or to the river or just walk on the main road.

Mother wore the latest fashions. Even though we lived in a small village, she kept up with the fashion world and made her own clothes in the latest styles. She was envied by all who saw her. Mother was particularly fond of large-brimmed hats.

Most inhabitants knew one another. Very few traveled beyond the area, except to a wedding or other special occasions. I would not be surprised if things still remain pretty much the same, though the Internet may have contributed to some changes.

Summer, though hot at times, was my favorite season. The tall trees gave the desired shade, and the gardens displayed a profusion of color and fragrance. Summer provided an abundance of fruits and vegetables.

I loved to go to our garden and pick fresh vegetables for the day's menu. It is still one of my favorite tasks. Mother would go to the woods with our nanny and pick pails of mushrooms, blueberries, strawberries, and whatever else was in season.

Mother wearing
fur cape, 1938

Father at 17

Father's passport
picture 1949

With my mother and brothers David and Israel in 1937

My Fateful Dream

One hot summer night in August 1939, I was restless in my sleep. Suddenly I woke up frightened, covered with perspiration, and sobbing. As I sat up in bed, I immediately felt my mother's arms around me and her soothing whisper trying to console me. She asked me what happened. I related to her the terrible nightmare I had. I dreamed that our neighbor's house across the yard was engulfed in flames, black smoke rising to the sky. Villagers were standing around helplessly, unable to put the fire out. We all stood there and watched the house being consumed by flames. I never forgot that horrible dream.

On September 1, Germany invaded Poland.

On that fateful day, our lives changed forever.

Our Garden

Adjoining the left side of the house was a large fenced-in piece of land. It came with the house, and we and Aunt Reizl had permission to use it. This was my favorite place in the summer and still holds fond memories.

In the spring and summer, Mother spent countless hours in the garden, tilling the soil, fertilizing, watering, weeding, and anything else the plants required. My aunt did the same. Their hard work produced an abundance of vegetables that we enjoyed long into fall and winter. Barrels of pickled cabbage and cucumbers were stored in the cold cellar, which was accessed from the backyard.

Mother used to lose herself among the plants, forgetting the rest of the world. I remember that on sunny days, Mother always wore a wide-brimmed straw hat. She had a fair complexion, and she knew even then that the sun had damaging effect on the skin. I don't recall Mother ever having a tan. The wrinkles on her face as she matured were a result of a difficult life.

Spring was a busy season in our household. That was when the preparation of the soil, seeding, and planting took place, and later, the watering, feeding, and weeding. The main plant food was compost and cow manure.

Mother created oblong raised beds for each vegetable and designed a very effective irrigation system that saved her many trips to the well. Weeding was a tedious job, but a necessary one. Her tender loving care was evident in the abundant crops the garden yielded every year. Mother taught me about the different plants she cultivated and how to care for them. Through years of practice, she learned a lot about gardening, and it showed.

We grew every vegetable available in Poland, except potatoes. To grow potatoes, which were the staple of the Polish kitchen, Father leased a parcel of farmland from the squire and planted potatoes there.

A profusion of multicolored blossoms grew on the periphery of the surrounding fence, adding to the hues of the blossoming vegetables. It was a sight to behold. The most difficult chore was watering when there was not enough rain. Every pail of water had to be drawn from the well and carried by hand to fill the conduits between the rows, which were an ingenious maze of canals surrounding each garden bed. Some of the watering was done by hand with a watering can. Mother loved flowers, and every Friday, there was a vase of fresh, colorful blossoms on the table in honor of the Sabbath.

During the season, the varied fragrances filled the air.

Summer was a happy time, and also a very busy one. Then came fall, when Mother preserved many fruits and vegetables that lasted long into the winter months. My aunt's half of the garden was similarly cared for and produced great results.

During the summer months, fruits ripened on the vine. The green beds of different plants were interwoven with reds, yellows, and oranges. Oh, but the taste! The taste of the vegetables can only be appreciated by someone who has tasted freshly picked produce straight from the garden. We did not appreciate it then, as it was an integral part of our lives. In midsummer, when the tomatoes and cucumbers began to ripen, Mother made a scarecrow from a broom and some of Father's old clothes, topped with an old hat, thus protecting the vegetables from hungry birds.

Even city folk enjoyed the freshness of the fruits of the earth, because they could buy them twice a week at market and they would buy directly from the farmers.

In later years, wherever we lived and had a piece of land nearby, no matter how small, my dear mother found a way to cultivate the soil, and we enjoyed whatever she was able to grow. Maybe that is why I love nature. I enjoy trips to the market or into the countryside, stopping at fruit stands. I truly enjoy going to a market and doing my own picking.

Later, even in Siberia, Mother worked a small patch of land adjacent to the forest where it was cleared of trees. Other people who knew how to garden followed suit, and many would seek Mother's advice. The little patches of land were fenced in to keep animals out. Some people even hung little name tags so everyone knew whose property it was.

One day, in that harsh wasteland, Mother sent me to the garden to pick some cucumbers. I opened the wooden gate and went over to the cucumber patch. As I picked up a leaf to pluck a ripe large cucumber, I had a scare that will haunt me for the rest of my life. A snake was underneath that leaf. It raised its head and hissed at me. I let out a loud scream and ran home as fast as I could. I ran into our room screaming and crying, my whole body shaking. I frightened my mother so that she could not speak. She grabbed me by the shoulders and shook me with all her might. Hearing my screams, neighbors began to gather at the door. I yelled at the top of my lungs, "A snake, a snake!" Mother finally understood what happened. She tried to console me by saying that these were harmless garden snakes and they didn't bite. But even then, it took me a long time to calm down. I knew there were snakes in the forest, but I had never seen one before.

For days after this encounter, I refused to go to the forest to pick blueberries for our daily meals. Mother had to take the pail with her to work and pick blueberries while she worked. Ever since that incident, I am deathly afraid to even look at a picture of a snake. As I write about this incident so many years later, a shiver goes through my body.

I revisited my mother's beloved garden on a dreary day in November of 1989.

It looked abandoned, messy, and gray, the house in disrepair. It was a sad sight.

My second and most recent visit was in October 2010, seventy-one years later, almost to the day I left it. The new owners were renovating the house, and there was a grocery store where my aunt's bar used to be. Though some walls were removed, I was able to point out to my daughter where each room was and what purpose it served.

The outside was more or less intact—even a red mailbox, the sign of the post office, was attached to the front wall. A very sad feeling came over me, and tears welled up in my eyes.

Father's Family

A Short Synopsis

I know my father's family better than my mother's because we lived in close proximity for many years and spent the war years together.

I never knew my paternal grandfather, Israel. He passed away long before I was born. There is conflicting information about his death. One story tells that he died during World War I, and the other story is that he passed away during a typhoid epidemic. I vaguely recall a photograph of him hanging in our kitchen, showing his bearded face and a large skullcap on his balding head.

My paternal grandmother, Leah, was a wee bit of a woman, small of frame, probably under five feet, bent over from the burden of a hard life and possibly osteoporosis. I was told by relatives that her mother passed away when Leah was still a child. Her father remarried, but the stepmother was not kind to Leah and wanted her out of the house. Leah went to live with an aunt in another town and stayed there until she was married to my grandfather Israel at a tender age of thirteen or fourteen. Very little was spoken about my grandfather.

My grandmother Leah, this little wee woman, gave birth to thirteen children. I finally learned their chronological sequence. They were Chaim Layzer, Chana Golda, Esther (we called her Etky), Reyzl, Mali, Chana, Heshl (my father), and Leibish. Leibish had a twin brother, who also died during a typhoid epidemic. Then came Regina (Rivtche) and Genia. The last child was Simah (who died in infancy). The family lived in poverty in a small hut in Zbydniów.

There were plenty of mouths to feed. After the head of the household died, the three surviving sons, Chaim Leizer, Heshl (my father), and Leibish had the responsibility of providing for the family.

Chaim Leizer, the eldest son, soon married and moved to a village by the name of Bojanów. The two remaining sons, Heshl and Leibish, assumed the responsibility of breadwinners. They had no professional skills, but circumstances forced them to learn things quickly.

My aunt Hannah was sent to the neighboring town of Rozwadów to learn how to sew, and she worked as a seamstress. This skill served her well all her life. In Rozwadów, she met her future husband, Baruch Borger, also a tailor. They married and had one daughter, Fayga (Zipora), who was born in 1936 or 1937 and died of lung cancer in 2006. She was a heavy smoker most of her adult life. Fayga married Abraham Altman and had two sons, Baruch and Israel, who are married now and are raising the next generation. Zipora lived to welcome and enjoy her first grandchild.

Chana and family remained in Rozwadów until the Germans evicted them in 1939.

My father's two elder sisters, Molly and Esther, left home in the early 1920s in search of a better life. They first went to Switzerland and stayed there for several years. In Switzerland, Esther met her future husband, Joseph Brauner, who was also a tailor. (It looked like tailoring was a popular profession among Jews.) They married and remained there for several years. From Switzerland they went to Palestine. Life was hard, and the climate harsh, so they soon joined Aunt Mollie in the United States. They also had three children, Rose (Shoshana), who was born in Palestine, and Bertha and Israel (Izzy), who were born in the United States.

They settled in Philadelphia, Pennsylvania, where they opened a dry cleaning store in the downtown area, with Uncle Joseph doing the alterations. That was their source of income until Uncle Joseph died and Aunt Esther had to sell the business. By that time, all three children were grown up, married, and out of the house.

Aunt Mollie landed a job in Switzerland as a nanny with a Jewish family and continued her journey with that family from there to America. She first settled in Rhode Island, where she made many friends. She saved every penny she could and sent money home to help the family. I was told that she also invested in the stock market, a daring venture for a young woman in the 1920s, but Mollie was a brave and daring woman. In 1929, she came home to visit the family, and at that time, a match was made between her and Israel Kofman (Srulek, as we all called him). He was born and lived in the nearby town of Ulanów, which was about twenty kilometers from Zbydniów. He became the love of her life, and she was his. They married in 1929 and moved to America permanently.

While Aunt Mollie was visiting her family in Poland in 1929, the big crash of the stock market occurred and wiped out most of her hard-earned savings. Communication in those days was not as swift as today, so my aunt did not know about her financial ruin until she returned to the United States. The newlyweds were shocked when they heard the news but took it all in stride and started a new life in the new land in poverty.

They had three children, Harriet, Joan, and Chaim Yossel. Uncle Srulek once told me that in the beginning, he took any job he could get. At one time, he worked at a pepper packing company. The pepper made his eyes tear and burn, but it was an honest living that helped put food on the table. No matter what financial difficulties they were in, there was always food for the needy and help for the family.

SoonAfter some years of hard work, their financial situation has improved, but they lived modestly and continued to help their families back home. They were generous philanthropists in their community and beyond all their lives.

After some years, Uncle Srulek, with two of his brothers as partners, went into the cardboard box business and kept it for many years. This business was more profitable, and their life became easier.

As their children grew, my aunt and uncle decided that their children needed a more-extensive Jewish education, which was unavailable at that time in Providence, Rhode Island. They saw potential in the New York area, namely Brooklyn, where there was a larger Jewish population and more Jewish schools. So they decided to move the family to Brooklyn, New York. My uncle kept his business in Rhode Island and traveled back and forth every week for many years to come. He spent the weekdays at the factory and rejoined his family in Brooklyn for the Sabbath.

My dear aunt Mollie died in 1984 after a long bout with leukemia. Uncle Srulek lived to a ripe age of one hundred years. Though his body showed the ravages of age, his mind was crystal clear till his last day.

These two wonderful people took me in when I came to the United States. They were my benefactors and mentors as long as they lived. I will always be grateful for their wisdom, teachings, and material help.

Aunt Chana Golda (we called her Cha Golda for short), one of father's elder sisters, married Hersh Yitzhak, who came from a well-to-do family of farmers and horse breeders. His parents owned land, cattle, and horses. After the wedding, she joined her husband and in-laws in Pierunka, a village not far from Rudnik and Nisko. This must have been somewhere between 1915 and 1920. They had two sons, Victor and Aaron. (I will write more about this family in a later chapter.)

My father's two youngest sisters, Genia and Regina, had gone to Switzerland too. That was in the mid-1920s. After some unsuccessful trials at making a living, they left Switzerland and eventually settled in Paris, France. They both learned the fur business, sewing tiny pieces of fur together that eventually became a pelt. They worked primarily with mink.

When I visited my aunt Regina in Paris many years later, she still did the same thing in her apartment, part of which was a makeshift workshop.

Aunt Regina visited the family in Zbydniów in the early 1930s. At that time, a match was made for her with a Mr. Sol Schmidt, a local young man, and they married within a very short time. The couple went to Paris and remained there. They had no children. Her husband died a few years later of tuberculosis.

On my first visit to Paris, I met aunt Regina's second husband, Shlomo Shwinger, whom she married after World War II. He was a tall, slim man and was well educated, especially in Jewish subjects, and made sure everybody knew it. He was a difficult, selfish man and did not treat my aunt kindly.

Aunt Genia married handsome young Jack Wechsler in Paris also in the early 1930s. They had a daughter, Susan. Just before the war, her husband left for Venezuela as a stowaway on the *Queen Mary*. When the war broke out, he could not return and his wife and daughter could not join him, so they were both stuck on different continents.

Both my aunts Regina and Genia and daughter Susan survived World War II in the south of France. They obtained false ID cards and posed as Christians. They bleached their hair blond and looked very Aryan. They worked on a farm as hired hands, while Susan attended a Catholic school in a local convent. Thus they escaped the Nazi death camps. When the war ended, both sisters returned to Paris.

Since there was no communication between husband and wife for six years, Jack Wexler surmised that his wife and daughter perished in one of many Nazi death camps. He remarried in Venezuela. After the war, Aunt Genia and Susan came to the United States. Somehow, Aunt Genia found out about her husband's second marriage, and she felt she was free to do the same.

Aunt Genia remarried. Her second husband, Sol Mohl, was of German Polish ancestry. He was the kindest person and most devoted husband one could wish for. He adored my aunt Genia. They resumed the fur business in the United States, and she dressed elegantly wherever she went. She loved sipping coffee in a sidewalk café in Manhattan—it reminded her of Paris.

She was stricken with Alzheimer's disease and suffered for eight long years until she passed away.

Uncle Sol survived her, but he missed her terribly. He lived to the ripe old age of one hundred.

Aunt Regina remained in Paris. Her second husband, Shlomo, passed away in the 1980s and was buried in Israel. After she retired from the fur business, she came to visit the family in the United States several times.

With time, her Parisian friends died and she remained alone. The family tried to persuade her to move to the United States to be close to the family, but my aunt Regina was a great patriot and did not want to leave France. She died in a Paris hospital of an uncertain illness. It could have been malnutrition, as the nurses told us she had refused to eat.

My cousin Leah and I flew to Paris and saw her on her deathbed in the hospital the day before she closed her eyes for the last time. It was April 1995. Her body was flown to Israel and was buried next to her husband.

Aunt Reizl remained at home in Zbydniów until she married a man by the name of Yitzchak, from a nearby town. That must have been sometime in the 1920s. The newlyweds needed a place to live in, so my father solicited the help of Mr. Horodynski, who relinquished several rooms in his Karczma for them to live in.

So after the other siblings dispersed, three remained in Zbydniów: Grandmother Leah, Reizl, Leibish, and my father.

Everybody somehow found their niche and a way to support themselves.

This is a short synopsis of my father's family. I will certainly refer to some, or all of them, when the opportunity presents itself. The sequence of events may not be 100 percent accurate, but the events, as I recall them, heard from my parents during their conversations and gathered from my cousins, are factual.

Cousin Genia's Wedding

And Other Celebrations

Itche Kofman, Uncle Srulek's brother, who was married to cousin Genia's aunt, became a widower in the mid-1930s. He and his deceased wife, Zlata, had a little girl, Nushia. (I just found out that Nushia was her nickname and her real name is Chaya Gitl, but we always called her Nushia.)

On her deathbed, Zlata asked Itchi to marry her young niece Genia, the eldest daughter of Chaim Layzer.

Genia was a meek, soft-spoken person. She was petite, with and cream-white complexion encased in wavy jet-black hair. She was very nearsighted, and I never saw her without her dark-rimmed glasses.

Itche, one of the four Kofman brothers from Ulanów, was a man of medium height, slim, with a receding hairline and a typical Semitic nose. He had a terrific sense of humor, was a wonderful storyteller, and was the most loving, devoted husband and father anyone could wish for. This is how I knew him. He wore his hats to one side and usually had a cigarette in his mouth or between his fingers. Religion to him was more of a habit, an integral part of his childhood upbringing. He brought up his two children as religious and law-abiding Jews.

Itche had very little formal education, just as most of his contemporaries did, but that did not stop him from reading the daily newspaper or having long discussions and arguments about politics and many other topics. He was a man who would fit in most groups of people, religious as well as secular. Genia was a stay-at-home mom, bringing up her two children.

Well, the night of their wedding was a memorable one for me. I was about four or five years old.

Most Jewish weddings consisted of two parts: before and after the *chuppa* (nuptials). Very little food or drink was served before the chuppa, which made it the cheaper portion of the wedding. Only guests of utmost importance, like rabbis, prominent businesspeople, close relatives, and other important members of the community, would be invited to the main meal following the chuppa.

This bride and groom were not prominent or rich, so the wedding was modest. It took place in Genia's home in Bojanów, and only the closest relatives were invited.

I am told that the year was 1935, so I must have been about four years old.

My brother Israel and I and another child were put in a crib to play together so as not to disturb the festivities in the adjacent room. The idea was to keep us away from the crowd. We must have had some toys to play with, or maybe not. In those days, most children improvised their games. Toys were a scarcity and a luxury that only the wealthy could afford.

Sounds of music, singing, and laughter came from the adjacent room, where the wedding was taking place. Mother looked in on us once in a while, and at one time, she brought us cake and candy.

I wanted to join the wedding party, and Mother promised to take me there, and eventually, she did for a few minutes. She told me that we were better off staying where we were, listening to the music. The celebrants might trample us while dancing, and she could not watch us because she had to help with the serving of the food. I was not too convinced or too happy with the arrangement, but I had no choice. She left the door open a bit so we could listen to the music and singing.

We were not completely alone all the time, because every once in a while, someone would come in and remove a platter or some other dish from the wooden cupboard and take it to the guests at the wedding party.

At one point, a man with a black beard, a black coat, and matching hat came into the room. He looked at us sitting in the crib. I guess he did not expect to see us there. He put a finger to his lips, signaling us to be quiet, and looked around. When he spotted the closet, he swiftly walked over, pulled out a cake, and walked out through another door, closing it behind him.

At first, I did not pay too much attention to this episode; it happened very quickly. Other people, men and women, came in before him and removed all kinds of things from the cupboard and took them to the guests.

A while later, an elderly woman came into the room, went directly to the cupboard, opened it, and began looking for something. She asked me if I saw anyone take out a cake. I told her that I saw many people come and take all kinds of plates or cakes. I was not watching them.

She realized that I would not be of much help, and she left the room, returning with another woman and my mother. All three were looking for the cake. I looked like a cat that swallowed a canary, but I did not say anything. The man had asked us to be quiet, and I was. This was exciting. I felt like I was playing a grown-up game that looked like fun; otherwise, it would have been a dull evening. Two more people came in looking for the cake but found none.

My brother was getting cranky; he was tired, and so was I. I told my mother I wanted to join the festivities or go home. Mother loved music, dancing, and all kinds of entertainment and was not eager to leave. My brother and the other boy fell asleep a short while later. At that point, Mother took me out of the crib, and we both entered the crowded, noisy room full of smoke and perspiration odor. People were dancing, singing, and having a good time.

I must have been sleepy, too, because after a short while, I asked to return to the small and quiet room. The next thing I remember was Mother waking me up to get ready for school.

Eventually, I told Mother about the man who took the cake. According to my description of him, he was identified as one of my father's relatives. I begged her not to disclose to anyone that I told her about it. I don't think she ever did.

Though today it sounds like an irrelevant incident, it was a big deal then.

Another Memorable Wedding

When I lie awake, unable to sleep, as it happens quite often, my thoughts occasionally take me back to my childhood and I recall events of those days.

It was a warm Sunday afternoon, and I was on the main road of our village, heading toward my grandmother Leah's house. I heard music and singing and rushed to see where it was coming from. As I was nearing one of the village houses, I saw a large gathering in the front yard. The house stood on an incline, and the whole yard was visible from the street. The people were dressed in their finest. Some were standing, singing, dancing, and some were sitting at tables, eating and drinking. At the end of one of the long tables, the bride and groom were seated. They were the cause of the celebration. A wedding was in progress. I stopped across the road, watching the party, and even sang along one of the songs I knew.

Suddenly, there was a loud scream. I looked in the direction of the commotion. Two young men were in the middle of a fistfight. One of them must have been the groom, as he was dressed in a white shirt. The music and singing stopped abruptly. Other guests were standing around, yelling at one another, pushing and shoving. The two young men were arguing and shouting and punching each other. Due to the screaming all around, I could not make out what the fight was about.

I, as well as some other onlookers, observed the commotion from across the road.

Suddenly, one of the young men, holding a bottle (probably vodka) in one hand, hit it on the table and lunged toward his opponent. The other man raised his hand to protect himself, and while his hand was in the air, the attacker hit his palm with the broken bottle. Instantly blood began gushing from his palm, spraying him and the people around him. Everyone was horrified. Some of the guests lunged toward the fighting men and separated them.

They took the bleeding man into the house. The music stopped, but not the arguing.

I forgot my original destination and, instead of going to my grandmother's, ran home. I was so horrified that I didn't wait to see the outcome of the fight or find out the reason for it. I ran into the house as though someone was chasing me.

It was Sunday, and my father was home, working at the kitchen table. As I pushed the door open and flew into the kitchen, he turned his head toward me. I could hardly catch my breath and started blurting out the horrible scene I had just witnessed. Father told me to calm down and repeat the story because he did not understand anything I said. He sat me down next to him and asked where I saw all this. I told him the name of the people. He said the daughter of those neighbors was getting married to a young man from another village. They must have had too much vodka, and he said drunk people sometimes don't know what they are doing. They must have been arguing about something, and it's common for drunk people to fight. "But," I interjected, "why did he have to hit him with a broken bottle and make blood gush out of his hand?"

"Well," Father said, "as I told you, some people, when they are drunk, cannot think rationally and at times become violent."

"But," I said, "I've seen you drink vodka sometimes too. How come you don't become violent?"

He smiled and answered calmly, "It depends on the person's character and how much he drinks. I drink a small glass when I have a cold, and that's it. Those people must have drunk a lot more."

I said to my father, "I will never drink vodka!"

And I never have.

My errand to my grandmother's that day was never accomplished.

Uncle Leibish's Engagement

Since I am on the subject of weddings, I will mention yet another that took place a few years later.

It is not the wedding of Uncle Leibish that I recall, but his engagement, which is still vivid in my memory. It took place in our home in Dzhambul, Kazakhstan. It was what they called a *vort* or agreement, the first and only one of its kind that I witnessed or attended.

Uncle Leibish was already thirty-plus years old when he got married. All other siblings had married. There were valid reasons that he did not tie the knot earlier, one of them being that he was the youngest male to remain home and take care of his mother. Zbydniów had no eligible brides to choose from. Matchmakers apparently did not discover him. Then the war broke out and we were on the road. It was not a time to think of marriage, so Uncle Leibish remained a bachelor until 1944.

The engagement ceremony was in our house, and it was something I had not seen before or since. It was an arranged marriage, but the bride, Adela, and groom knew each other from Siberia. Maybe I am getting ahead of myself, but I figured, since I am on the subject of weddings, I will include this one too.

Adela and her family were from Przeworsk, Poland. The father was a Bible scholar, a pious man. His eyes were red from too much studying by insufficient light. His spouse, Nechama, was a gentle, soft-spoken, kind soul, and I loved her dearly. As the custom prescribed, she always wore a kerchief on her head. I can still see the freckles on her kind face.

Our families were not only united by marriage, we also became lifelong friends.

I remember the evening when the two families and guests gathered in our home. They were seated on chairs and benches at a long, extended table. Many guests were standing for lack of chairs. My mother baked cakes and prepared other dishes. My aunts also brought food, and of course, the bride's family contributed their share. The room was full of people, and there must have been a rabbi or two. To me, any man with a beard was a rabbi, which I later found out was not so. There were toasts to the bride and groom and their families. There was singing, but there was no room for dancing. As was the custom, the groom was supposed to show off his knowledge of the Holy Scriptures.

My uncle must have passed the test with flying colors, because there was a lot of applause and toasting after each recitation of Dvar Torah, explanations of passages from the Holy Books.

The wedding took place shortly thereafter because both were not youngsters, it was wartime, and there was no time for long engagements. I heard that one of my father's sisters was not happy about the match. She was a widow with a child, and Leibish was one of the major breadwinners in the family. She was afraid that after he was married, he would abandon his widowed sisters and only take care of his own family. But Uncle Leibish did no such thing. The families lived together in one house, and it was incumbent on everyone to carry his or her weight.

The newlyweds moved into a tiny room with a separate entrance attached to the house.

First Grade

In Poland, as in many countries, children start attending school at the age of six. I do not recall the availability of a nursery school or kindergarten, especially in a small village like Zbydniów.

Mothers, or grandmothers, usually stayed home and took care of the children. Most of my friends were older and began attending school before me. I had no one to play with during school hours, and I was bored. I began pestering my parents to enroll me in school so I could be with my friends. Mother thought I was too young and would not be accepted, but I persisted. My parents knew the school principal personally. I intimidated them into cashing in on that friendship and persuade him to make an exception and enroll me in school on a trial basis. I promised that if I could not keep up with the rest of the class, he could dismiss me.

The school year had already begun. It was a cunning proposal since I knew exactly what the class had learned—because my friends used to show me what they did in school—so I was sure I would be able to keep up. So one morning in late September 1937, Mother and I got dressed up and went to school. We were admitted to the principal's office. It was a small room with a large wooden desk in the middle of it. A portrait of the current Polish president hung on the wall in front of us, and the Polish flag stood in the right corner of the room. A bespectacled, square-faced, stocky man jumped up from his chair, flashed a friendly smile, and stretched out his hand to Mother. He kissed the back of her hand, typical European custom, and showed Mother to the only other chair in the room. I stood next to her, slightly flustered. I was a shy and insecure child. I grew out of some of these traits, but never entirely. The room was whitewashed.

A few framed diplomas hung on the wall in front of us. The principal asked Mother a few polite questions about the health of our family and then turned to me, smiling. "And what brings you here, my child? As far as I can see, you are too young to attend school."

I blushed and raised my eyes to Mother. She looked at me and said, "Why don't you tell the principal what you came for?"

I pulled her down close to me and whispered in her ear, "I thought you already told him the reason and all we came for is to register?"

Now the man spoke. "Is it polite to whisper secrets in front of other people"? He looked at me quizzically. Now I was really embarrassed, and I was getting angry at Mother for putting me in that embarrassing position. I was red in the face, and tears began welling up in my eyes.

The principal saw what was happening and made an attempt to put me out of my misery. He exclaimed, "Oh, now I remember speaking to your father, and he told me that you are ready for school. Is that true?"

"Yes," I answered, trying to calm down. I knew I could not show him that I was still a child. I had to demonstrate my maturity.

His voice calm but authoritative, he quizzed me in some simple arithmetic. He gave me a paper and pencil and asked me to write my name or anything else, if I knew how. I approached his desk; it came up to my neck, but I raised myself on my toes, wrote my name on the paper, and began writing the alphabet, which I already knew. He stopped me after the third letter, took the paper, and pretended to examine it. He turned to Mother and said, "Madame, I see you have a very smart girl here. She knows quite a lot for her age. The school year has just begun, so I think she can catch up with the class if she tries hard enough. I see that she is eager to learn. We will give her a chance. We will make an exception and admit her despite her tender age. But"—he turned to me—"I am warning you in advance that if you lag too far behind the other pupils, you will have to wait till next year, when you will reach the appropriate age to enter school."

I was thrilled. Now I'd be together with my friends. I'd go to school with them and learn what they did. I could not contain myself; I jumped up and kissed Mother on the cheek and thanked the principal, but Mother thought that he deserved more than just a thank-you. Mother suggested that the principal deserved a kiss too. At that moment, I was so happy I would have kissed a monkey. I ran around the oversized desk and placed a loud smack on his cheek. I was to start school the next day, Tuesday, which Mother always considered a lucky day. He wrote a short note for the librarian with instructions to give us two books, one math, the other for reading. He also told my mother what other materials I would need and to report to him at 7:45 a.m. the next day.

All I needed was a briefcase and a pencil case. Mother promised that Father would buy those two items for me next time he went to Rozwadów.

I had to wait until two o'clock, when school was over and my friends would be coming home, so I could share my good news with them.

And so began my formal education at the age of five and a half.

That night, I could hardly sleep in anticipation of my first school day. I was up at the crack of dawn and asked Marysia to help me tie my shoes, comb my hair, and tie it in a red ribbon. I insisted on wearing my best holiday dress, which my mother made for me to wear on holidays and special occasions. This certainly was a special occasion. Mother was an excellent seamstress, and she made most of our clothes. I got two dresses a year—one in the spring, for Passover, the other in the fall, for the High Holidays—and I wore them until I grew out of them. Since I had no younger sister at that time, Mother would give them to one of the poor children in the village.

Marysia went out to milk the cow. I wanted to come along, but she would not let me. She argued that I might soil my pretty dress. Father walked into the kitchen and was surprised to see me all dressed up, sitting at the table, waiting for breakfast. "What kind of a holiday is today?" he asked. "Why are you dressed up so bright and early?"

"I'm going to school!" I answered happily.

"Is that so?" he said with a knowing smile. "And what will you learn in school?" he asked.

"Everything they teach me!" I answered quickly.

"That's my girl," he said. "That's what schools are for."

After a while, Marysia came in with a pail of milk and a basket of eggs. She poured some milk into a white enamel pot, started a fire in the stove, and put on the milk to boil. We were not allowed to drink raw milk as it might contain bacteria and cause illness. Father put on his prayer shawl and his phylacteries and faced the eastern wall, murmuring his prayers. Marysia was busy preparing breakfast.

Mother eventually woke up and joined us in the kitchen. She came in wearing a robe. I asked her why she was not dressed, but she assured me that she would be ready in time to take me to school. Father asked why I didn't go to school by myself since I was old enough to be accepted into first grade. Mother interjected by saying that she would only go with me the first day and, thereafter, I would go with my friends. The school was about one-quarter kilometer away, not a very far walk on the paved cobblestone road.

Mother helped Marysia with breakfast while Father finished his prayers, and we all sat down to eat. Mother fried some eggs—we always had fresh eggs from our own chickens—but I did not have too big an appetite that morning. I was too excited and nervous, but Mother insisted that breakfast was very important and I needed strength to learn. I ate as much as I could, finished my glass of milk (that was a must), and was ready to leave.

It was only seven fifteen in the morning. Mother went into the bedroom to get dressed, and as she opened the door to the bedroom, my brothers came running. They sat down at the table, ready for breakfast, but first they had to wash their hands and recite their morning prayers. This was our morning routine. The boys whispered something to each other and, once in a while, gave me a quizzical look.

Father was ready to leave for the office, but before he picked up his heavy briefcase, he came over to me, placed a kiss on my forehead, wished me luck, and jokingly said to me, "Make sure you learn your math well so you can help me with my bookkeeping." I promised that I would, and then Father walked out. It was seven thirty, and I was getting nervous.

I called out for Mother to hurry up. She called back, saying that she'd be ready in a few minutes. Soon she came out dressed very nicely and had put on lipstick. She always wore lipstick whenever she went out among people.

I was ready and waiting.

As we were leaving, Marysia yelled after us, "Make sure you listen to the teacher!"

As we approached the main road, we met other children going in the same direction, carrying their briefcases or knapsacks. I was the only one accompanied by a mother. Farther down the road, we met one of my friends who also attended first grade. We embraced. We were good friends, and she was happy I was accepted and we would be classmates. Others envied me and showed their dissatisfaction. Mother was tempted to send me off with my friend, but I insisted she come along. Firstly, I wanted to make sure all went well, and secondly, there were some boys who used to throw rocks at me and yell, "Zydowka!" Jewess. I wanted to be sure that nothing went wrong on my first day of school. We walked at a brisk pace and, within fifteen minutes, walked into the school building. The doors of the classrooms were marked, so it was easy to find my classroom. It was the first door to the right. My friend was our guide. She walked with us into the classroom and introduced us to the teacher. The teacher did not look surprised, because she already knew she would be receiving a new pupil. She knew exactly who I was—everyone in the village knew us. We were the Jews. There were only four Jewish families in the village.

I curtsied, greeting the teacher. She complimented me on my proper behavior and showed me to the desk I would be occupying. The classroom was a very large square room with tall windows facing the front of the building. My desk, which I shared with another girl, was the third one in the right row. There were three rows of desks, two pupils at each one. When I recently visited my school and walked into my class, a nostalgic feeling came over me. The room had not changed much, except for some pictures on the walls and several bookcases filled with books. I was told the classroom now doubles as the school library.

The teacher assured Mother that all would be fine and that she could go home. The bell rang a few moments later, and the pupils began filing in and taking their seats. Some passed by me and gave me a condescending look; others greeted me with a smile. One boy stuck out his tongue and made a face. But I took it all in stride. I didn't know exactly what to expect and later learned that some considered me a stranger, an alien, and that I had no right to be in school together with them.

I was the only Jewish child in the whole school.

My cousins were older and had attended that school a few years earlier. Now they were in higher grades and attending a different school.

Most girls accepted me, but I did have problems with some boys, though. At that time, of course, I did not understand why. I used to complain to my parents that some boys hit me, threw rocks at me, called me Zydowka, and so on.

My father, when I told him who the boy was, would say, "Ah, this family is anti-Semitic. Just don't pay any attention to what they're saying." I asked him what it meant to be anti-Semitic, but he said I was too young to understand. He promised that when I grew up, I would know. It was not easy to ignore getting beaten up or being verbally abused. I knew I did not provoke them in any way—I didn't even talk to those children—so why did they hate me so much?

Mother also reassured me that I would understand when I grew up and maybe they would grow up and understand more and possibly change their ways. Her prediction came true sooner than she or I thought.

The teacher began the day by taking attendance. She read the names in alphabetical order, and when she read my name, she told the class I was a new pupil and asked the children to welcome me.

Then she asked everyone to rise and sing the national anthem. After that, everyone put their hands together and began the morning prayers. I did the same. Though I was Jewish, I knew the Christian prayers well. My friends taught them to me. I am not sure the teacher noticed, because she did not say anything to me. Then we all sat down, and the teacher instructed the class to copy into our notebooks what she wrote on the blackboard. All was quiet, save for an occasional disturbance by one of the children, usually a boy. The girls behaved well. The teacher now passed between the rows, checking what we were doing.

She approached my desk and my body stiffened, but I continued to write. She stopped next to me, looked down at my notebook, and corrected one of the letters I had copied wrong. I had to watch myself and make sure I was writing with my right hand, and that was not easy. She instructed me to copy this letter ten times at home and the other letters only five times.

I nodded. My face turned crimson red, and I continued to write. After everyone finished, she explained all about the letters and instructed the class how to do the homework. She also reviewed the work from the previous day. This first day of school was so important and new to me that I remember every detail.

The bell rang, and a commotion started instantly. Everyone headed for the door. I followed my friend and stayed very close to her. The play area was in the front of the building. There were children everywhere, running in every direction and playing all kinds of games.

I did not want to run around—I was afraid to soil my pretty dress. I stood near the wall and observed what the others were doing. Two boys started to fight in one corner of the yard, but one of the teachers went over and stopped them immediately. One little boy was teary-eyed, but another teacher calmed him and held him by the hand. A short while later, the bell rang and everyone rushed inside.

The pupils returned to their classes, and the next lesson began. Discipline was very strict. Everyone was quiet—you could have heard a pin drop. I sailed through the math class. The teacher asked questions, and I raised my hand several times to answer them. She was surprised by my knowledge of basic arithmetic. I knew everything the class had learned so far from my friends. She complimented me again, to the displeasure of some pupils. I tried to ignore them, but it bothered me. I thought they would be happy that I knew some things.

My Dyslexia

I forgot to mention my disability, which I had no idea I had then, or the reason for it.

I was always a slow reader, even though I am an avid reader, but had no idea why. I only recently found out the reason, by sheer coincidence. It turns out that I was meant to be left-handed, but in those days, it was considered a serious defect. Mother even warned me that if I continued to predominantly use my left hand instead of my right, I would not be able to get married. No young man would want to marry a lefty. In my mother's opinion, it was a serious disability. So every effort was made to force me to use my right hand for every task, especially writing.

Mother made sure that my teacher was aware of my problem and asked her help in correcting it. The teacher was happy to oblige. Whenever she saw me write with my left hand, she would come over to my desk, call my name out loud for everyone to hear, and order me to put my left hand behind my back and write only with my right. If she noticed my transgression more than once or twice the same day, she would come over to my desk, tell me to put my left hand on my desk, and hit my fingers with a long ruler.

Writing with my right hand apparently went against my nature and brain, and it was difficult to stay within the lines. My handwriting was a disaster.

This made it difficult for me to concentrate on the lessons, as I was busy worrying about which hand to use. It was a distracting factor the first and even the second year in school. I was forced to do many other things with my right hand, and over the years, I mastered it. I guess Mother's strategy worked, but only where writing was concerned. All other functions remained in my left hand. I can hold a spoon or fork equally well in both, but everything else, I do with my left hand. Despite this difficulty, I was a pretty good student.

After the math class, which I sailed through, we had calligraphy and drawing.

At the end of the last class, the bell rang, and it was time to go home. As anxious as I was to come to school that first day, I was just as anxious to get home and share my impressions of that memorable day.

School

Bullies and Anti-Semites

As two of my friends and I were leaving the school building, a boy classmate ran past us, pushed me, and yelled, "Jew show-off!" One of the girls caught me by the hand and saved me from falling down the stairs.

"Don't pay attention to him," she said. "He's stupid and a bully. He envies anybody who knows something." Then my friend added, "He is ignorant, so he envies others who know."

I accepted the excuse. This certainly marred the happiness of my day, but I was already looking forward to the next. We ran in the direction of our homes, and I stormed into the kitchen breathlessly, as though someone was chasing me. Instantly my mouth went off like a machine gun. Mother picked her head up from the stove, asking what had happened. She asked me to sit down at the table, calm down, and then start talking. I was so eager to share this day with everyone that Mother was not able to stop me for a moment to catch my breath. When I finally stopped, she asked me to repeat everything, this time slowly and in sequence, just as things had happened. When I came to the part of morning prayers, Mother stopped me and asked, "Are you telling me that you were reciting Christian prayers?"

I nodded.

"You will not do this again! You are Jewish, and you recite Jewish prayers. Christian people recite their own."

"But the whole class recited these prayers, and I am also a pupil now," I protested.

"Yes, you're a pupil now, but you follow your own religion as they do theirs."

"That will make me different from the other children, and I don't want to be different. Some boys throw rocks at me as is because I am Jewish, and this will give them another reason to do so."

By now, Mother was upset and declared that she would have to speak to the teacher or principal about this. Now I was afraid that she would spoil everything and I would be expelled. This would be disastrous.

"By the way, where did you learn Christian prayers?" she asked. "Did Marysia teach you?" She was referring to our nanny.

"No!" I protested. "My friends did, and I taught them mine."

"What a silly thing to do!" mother declared.

This prayer discussion certainly put a damper on my otherwise happy and exciting day.

I changed my clothes and did my homework, and then Mother sent me out to check on the boys. I saw them playing in the yard, went to report to Mother, and went out again, hoping to see any of my friends, but the streets were deserted. It was harvesttime, and most children helped their parents with their chores.

Then I heard Marysia calling me from the garden, where she was working. She was anxious to hear all about my school day. I repeated everything to her, but her reaction to the prayers was quite different. She didn't see anything wrong with it. The first few days of school went by quite well despite the occasional harassment from some boys. I was more or less used to their hostile behavior from before.

The big surprise came on a Friday, and it had nothing to do with the boys.

During the last hour every Friday, there was Catholic religious instruction, which was conducted by the local priest. The priest came into class as usual and took attendance, and when he finished, I raised my hand and told him that he did not call my name. He asked me my name, and I told him. He smiled and said, "You must be Hershek's daughter who works for the local squire."

"Yes!" I answered.

He added my name to the student list and began quizzing some pupils about the previous lesson. All this was foreign to me, but I concluded that it was a Christian religious lesson and that it did not concern me. I sat quietly and listened.

Toward the end of the lesson, the priest asked the class, "Do you know anyone in this class who has not been christened? All fingers pointed at me. I did not understand the question and did not know what *christened* meant.

My face got red, and tears welled up in my eyes. I had no idea what I was accused of. I was hoping that the priest would stop the children from pointing at me, but he did nothing. I got up from my seat and ran out of class straight to the principal's office. By the time I reached his office, I was crying hysterically.

It took a while to calm me down, and when I did, I told him what took place in class. He apologized to me and said that from now on, I would not have to attend religious classes on Fridays. He kept me in his office until the bell rang and classes were over for the day. We waited until everyone was gone from my class, and the principal then went with me to pick up my books and asked one of my classmates to walk me home.

Since it was Friday, my father was home from work early. When Mother noticed my red eyes, she began questioning me. I was glad that Father was home too, so I could tell them both what embarrassment and anguish the priest had put me through. Father was very angry. He knew the priest well as they often discussed politics and even religion, so why would he hurt his child? Father promised to go to the church and talk to him. He did go and ask the priest why he had done that. His answer was evasive and not even to the point. He explained that he wanted to know which of the Christian children was not christened.

This surely was a ludicrous answer, since he was the one who did the christening in the parish and knew everybody on a first-name basis.

I never attended religious class again in that school. Many times I would meet the priest coming up the stairs as I was going down on the way home. Once or twice he even asked me, "Anna, are you going home now?"

My answer was a curtly "Yes."

Chronic Battle with Cravings

A couple of incidents that are attributed to my cravings stand out in my mind.

One day, I was walking with my mother on the main road of our village. It might have been a Saturday, because we were both dressed up. It was a warm day, and a slight breeze rustled the leaves in the trees. Suddenly, the breeze carried toward us a very strong scent of salami. I took one whiff, and my cheeks turned red and my whole body was in heat. I felt that I must have a piece of that salami, or else . . . As it turned out, we were passing the local nonkosher butcher shop, and apparently, the salami (Polish kielbasa) was in the process of being manufactured/smoked.

I am sure that Mother also smelled the aroma but did not pay attention to it.

I didn't want to take another step and told her that I wanted to go back home. Mother was surprised and asked me what happened to make me want go back so suddenly. I didn't want to tell her because I knew that the salami aroma was coming from the nonkosher butcher and I was not allowed to eat it. She urged me to continue, but I refused and finally told her that I had a stomachache and wanted to go home.

She allowed me to return home alone, and she continued on her way. By the time I reached the house, I felt like I was getting a fever and went to lie down. My nanny came in to inquire about the reason for my return alone and why I was in bed. Since she was Christian and was allowed to eat pork, I figured I could tell her that I wanted a piece of that nonkosher salami very badly but implored her not to tell my parents.

By that time, I was really burning up with fever. My nanny saw my red cheeks; she touched my head and darted out of the room to get the thermometer. It turned out that in a short time, my fever had shot up to forty-two degrees Celsius! She wet a small towel and put cool, moist compresses to my forehead.

My mother returned about an hour later and found us both in the bedroom. The nanny told her I had a fever, and I tried to reassure her that it would pass. My nanny took Mother by the hand, and they both walked out of the bedroom.

Father woke up from his Sabbath afternoon nap due to the commotion and saw me holding the wet compress to my forehead. Both women returned a few moments later, at which time Mother asked my father to go with her while Marysia remained with me in the bedroom. The door was slightly open, and I overheard my mother telling Father to go to the butcher and get a piece of salami for me.

He objected but was convinced by my mother that I was still young and she would absorb my sin for eating nonkosher salami. She argued that my craving must have been so intense that it caused me to get a fever. She also reminded him that Jews were allowed to do all kinds of forbidden things for health reasons or to save a life.

It was getting dark and the Sabbath would be over soon, and Father went. The shop was already closed, and the butcher was surprised to see my father knock on the door, asking to buy nonkosher salami. My father told him the reason. The man opened his store and cut a large piece of salami, wrapped it in paper, and gave it to my father. He said he was happy to hear that his salami was so popular.

When Father returned home and unwrapped the large chunk of salami, I immediately recognized the strong, smoky aroma, and my eyes and mouth flew open. The butcher had cut it into several pieces. I received the largest slice, but Mother insisted I eat it with bread. The rest went to Marysia for taking such good care of me.

I was extremely happy that I recovered almost instantly. My fever was gone by morning.

One late afternoon, after visiting one of my friends, I returned home and told Mother that I was hungry and would like a slice of bread with vinegar. Mother was quite smart and realized that I had probably seen someone eat bread with vinegar or some variation of it. Having prior experience with my cravings, Mother did not object and gave me what I asked for. I began eating the bread soaked in vinegar and almost choked. Mother instructed me to take small bites to help me manage the strong taste. She saw I was struggling with the concoction, so she told me that I didn't have to finish it if I didn't want to. I was thankful to her for letting me off the hook. After a while, she asked me where I had been and where I saw people eat bread with vinegar. I told her which friend I had visited and that her mother had given the children dark bread with lard and put some drops of vinegar on it. It was dinnertime, so they sent me home to have my dinner. I knew very well that I would not get lard in my house, so I settled for bread with vinegar.

Over the years, I wasn't able to shed some of the cravings. To this day, I crave chocolate/mocha ice cream and salami with lots of garlic.

Zbydniów

I've mentioned our village several times, so I feel it's time to describe it in greater detail.

Zbydniów was situated along the banks of one of the tributaries of the river San. The main and only cobblestone paved road cut through the middle of the village. This road, leading in the easterly direction through another small village called Turbia, led to the nearest town, Rozwadów. The opposite direction, going west, led to the railroad station, and three kilometers hence was the village of Zaleshany. At the end of the village in that same westerly direction stood, in a small roadside (*kaplica*), a statue of the Virgin Mary, and a short distance farther, at the very end of the village, was the church. Across the road was a very important landmark: the train station.

Crossing that paved road, going north to south, was a dirt road that began at the mill and ran along the fence of the squire's estate, along our house, and hence through the old wooden bridge over the river all the way to a village called Majdan. Other shorter dirt roads and alleys branched out of these two crossroads to the hamlets of the village. Many of these homes housed two to three generations and were handed down from parent to child. Each home was built according to the owner's needs, taste, and financial ability. Brick homes were rare due to the high cost. Wood and logs were in abundance and much cheaper since the whole area was surrounded by forest. Selling a home to a stranger/newcomer was a rarity. Occasionally, they were enlarged to accommodate additional members of the family. Our village was surrounded by farmland, orchards, and forests, most of which belonged to Mr. Horodynski. Some of the villagers also owned some land. Those who did not own any land, like my parents, could lease some acres from the squire and grow their own crops.

Though narrow, the river flowing on the periphery of the village was an important asset. The water was cool and clean, and it served mainly for irrigation, transportation, recreation, and fishing. The old wooden bridge was strong enough to withstand the weight of heavy wagons filled with crops and other goods going to neighboring villages and towns.

One of my uncle Leibish's businesses was fishing. The river supplied a variety of fish, mainly carp, the main component for gefilte fish. Many housewives took advantage of that fact. Uncle Leibish would catch the fish with a net suspended from a small boat and store his ketch in specially constructed wooden cages submerged in the water right near the bridge. On Thursdays, he transported the fish to his customers in Rozwadów.

We enjoyed the river especially during the summer—it was a great place to swim in. In the winter, when it froze solid, we went sled-riding on it. There were reeds growing on the very deep opposite bank, and some people went there by boat and cut the reeds for basket-weaving and other creative objects.

Most of the place's inhabitants were farmers. Zbydniów had a nonkosher butcher. He made kielbasa, which filled the whole village with the most incredible aroma. Though one of my cousins had mentioned that Mr. Perlmutter might have been a part-time kosher butcher. There were only a handful of people in Zbydniów who ate kosher, so there was no need for a full-time kosher butcher business.

Among the other professionals were a blacksmith and several carpenters, even though most men were familiar with that profession. There must have been a shoemaker or a shoe repair business in the villagein town. Shoe repair was a common thing. These are the professionals I remember. There must have been others. My grandmother Leah had the tiniest grocery store in her home, where she sold sugar, salt, yeast, flour, and possibly a few other items. I remember going there to buy yeast.

Most inhabitants knew one another. Very few, if any, left the village or traveled to any big city. Their lives were concentrated around the village perimeter, except on special occasions, like a wedding.

The majority of the inhabitants were born, lived, and died there.

I would not be very surprised if little had changed in Zbydniów in the past fifty to sixty years, though it is probable that the recent generation had ventured out into the world , whatwith the arrival of the Internet.

Summer, though hot at times, was my favorite season. The tall trees gave the desired shade, and the gardens were in bloom. The flowers, growing profusely everywhere, filled the air with a wonderful fragrance. It was a time when I loved to stay outdoors and play with my friends or run freely in the fields, picking flowers. Summer provided an abundance of fresh fruit and vegetables from our garden. Mother used to send me out into the garden to pick some green onions, dill, or parsley (whatever the dish she was cooking required). I loved doing that. Not only did she make me feel that I was helping with the food preparation, but at the same time, I also learned a lot about them. I liked picking fresh vegetables from the garden, and I still do, whenever I have an opportunity. There is no equal in taste and nutrition to a freshly picked produce. The aroma, the crispness, and the taste are truly special.

When the blueberry-and-mushroom season would begin, Mother used to go with our maid into the forest and pick baskets full of mushrooms and pails of blueberries and wild strawberries. She was an expert at making delicious jams for the winter and cooking delicious pierogi (a cousin to ravioli) filled with blueberries. She would string mushrooms and hang them up to dry for future use. During the cherry season, Mother would fill five-gallon bottles with cherries, top them with sugar, and store them in the attic under some straw. When it fermented, it became the most delicious cherry liquor.

Fall in Zbydniów

The fall season had its own beauty and excitement. The weather would get cooler, and the rain usually returned to soak the parched soil. It signaled that harvesttime was coming to an end. The trees would display many colors. It was time to return to school. Yes, I did like school very much. It was a time of gathering the fruits of our labor in every household as well as in ours.

My father had leased some farmland, from Mr. Horodynski, on the outskirts of the village, and we planted a lot of potatoes, cabbage, onions, and other staples that could be easily preserved during the winter months. We used to hire locals to help us with the harvest. I loved to accompany Mother into the fields when she took lunch to the workers.

I specifically remember fondly one such outing. I went along with Mother to help her carry the food. She had cooked potatoes, smothered them with butter, and a jug of milk (yogurt) as a cool chaser. When we arrived, the men and women gathered around us eagerly, awaiting their midday feast. There was a small bonfire burning nearby, and I put some freshly dug-up potatoes for roasting.

One of the women gave me an ear of corn, and I put it on the fire to roast too.

When the potatoes were done, I peeled the blackened, crisp skin and enjoyed the most delectable baked potato I had ever had. The roasted corn was even more delicious.

After the workers finished their repast and had had a short rest, they returned to their potato-picking. Mother put a few potatoes in her empty basket, and we walked home. It was still quite hot, and we returned home exhausted.

This ritual was repeated several times a week; whenever people worked for us, Mother made sure they ate well.

Autumn was also a time of preparing and preserving produce for the winter. Whatever we did not grow ourselves, we bought from the local farmers. The pickling season was a very busy time in our household. Even my grandmother Sarah used to come from Rozwadów to help with the chores. This was serious business.

The perfect and appropriate storage area for the barrels of cabbage, pickles, and the like was the cellar, which was situated under the house, with an entrance from the yard. There was a trapdoor and about six or seven steps leading to what resembled a dug-up cave.

This was hard work. The vegetables had to be picked, examined for imperfections (only the perfect ones would do), sorted, and cut/trimmed if necessary. Small cucumbers would be arranged in a barrel or other vessels, salted, added with spices (garlic and dill), covered with the appropriate amount of water, and a few weeks later, were ready for enjoyment.

I can recall Mother having a large cutting board for shredding cabbage. When the barrels were filled, sealed, and ready for storage in the seller, Mother would hire two to three men to help transfer them to the "cellar."

At times, our kitchen resembled a small factory with the aroma of dill and caraway seeds filling the air.

We enjoyed the fruits of my mother's labor all winter long.

Winter in Zbydniów

Memorable Trip to Tarnobrzeg

There was lots of snow during winter in our village, and at times, everything came to a halt. I do not recall any mechanized snow removal. The main road was cleared manually as much as possible. All able-bodied men would come out with shovels and work long hours until the main road became passable. The narrower streets and paths leading to individual homes were the last to be cleared by the residents of the area. Everyone had to pitch in.

Most peasants switched from wagons to horse-drawn sleds. After a big snowstorm, the accumulation could be a few feet and the school would be closed for days.

The river San and its tributaries froze over, and we would go sleigh-riding whenever the ice was safe and thick enough, which was during most of the winter months. The banks of the river were elevated, and we would have a great time sliding down.

Unfortunately, I could not indulge in these childhood pleasures very often because I got frequent earaches, sore throats, or bronchitis and would spend days or weeks in bed. That was every winter and sometimes during warmer season.

When I would cough, Mother would apply suction cups to my back and chest to help me recover. The suction cups hurt, and I could hardly breathe while they pumped my blood to the surface, creating dark-blue, almost-black circles on my skin. Mother was happy to see the black balls on my body, for that meant that the blood had circulated and my inflammation would be gone quickly.

A fever would usually accompany my infections. I had enlarged tonsils, and Mother would say that they were at the root of all my problems and one day they would have to be removed.

That did not happen until I was twenty-two.

One freezing winter night—I might have been six years old—I woke up crying with pain in my throat and a high fever. Mother touched my head and yelled for my father to wake up. She took my temperature, and it was over 43.5 degrees Celsius. That is considered extremely high even for a child. She applied a cool, moist compress on my forehead, which made me feel a little better.

She urged my father to call Mr. Horodynski and ask if he would let us borrow his car with the chauffeur or a horse and wagon. We had to see a doctor as soon as possible. Father objected, saying that it was the middle of the night and he wasn't going to wake the squire at this ungodly hour for his sick daughter.

Mother would have none of his excuses and threatened to make the call herself if Father refused to make it.

Mother woke our nanny and told her what was going on. She came over to my bed, wrapped me in a blanket, put me on her lap, and was holding the moist, cool compress to my forehead, turning it every few minutes so the cooler side touched my skin.

Father put some clothes on and went out to the hallway to call his boss. In the meantime, Mother told the nanny to dress me while she herself was getting ready. Father returned from the post office (that was where the telephone was) and announced that the chauffeur and car would be here shortly to take us wherever we needed to go.

My parents decided to take me to a well-known ear, nose, and throat specialist in the town of Tarnobrzeg. They had conferred with him in the past about my problem, and he agreed to see me. Apparently, the doctors in Rozwadów were of no help, so they looked far and wide until they found out about this specialist.

Father had not called the doctor in the middle of the night to tell him of our arrival, but this was an emergency and they were hoping he would not turn us away. Mother decided it was time once and for all to see this famous doctor in the hope that he would give me the magic potion and end my suffering.

It was not easy to get an appointment with this doctor. He was affiliated with the military hospital in Tarnobrzeg and saw only special cases privately.

Father had once asked Mr. Horodynski if he knew a good specialist who could help me. Mr. Horodynski answered that he knew many good doctors in the country and abroad. Father had asked him once if he could arrange an appointment for me. He promised that he would, but there was no concrete date set. This would be the night Father would cash in on Horodynski's promise.

I was dressed to the hilt—I could hardly breathe. The driver arrived in Horodynski's black Ford and tapped lightly on the bedroom window. We were ready. Mother gave Marysia instructions on what to feed the boys, and we left. A cold gust of wind pushed us back as we stepped outside. It felt rather good. My whole body was on fire. We entered the luxurious car, and the driver asked where we were going. My father told him, and he took off. It was a bright, starry night. I could see the moon and a myriad of stars through the window.

This was the first time in my life I ever rode in a car. It was a weird feeling, gliding on the icy road. It was a smooth ride compared to a ride in a bumpy horse-drawn wagon. I had traveled by train many times, but this was very different from riding in a horse-drawn carriage. I liked it a lot. I told my mother how much I liked the ride, and she smiled.

I forgot about my pain and the fever. I was totally absorbed with the car and the brilliant sky. The journey took a couple of hours, and at one point, I fell asleep. I woke up when the driver stopped the car in front of the hospital. It was a gray, freezing morning. I opened my eyes and saw the facade of the military hospital. In front of us stood a tall gray wall two or three stories high, full of dark windows. The double-entry door was also very large. It was midmorning.

The chauffeur opened the door of the car, and we walked out into the freezing air. Before we left the car, Mother was sure to bundle me up so only my eyes were visible. The driver told my father that he would stay nearby in case he was needed. There were some people rushing to and fro and horse-drawn wagons passing us by. I had very little time to look around because we entered the large double doors and were inside the hospital. Straight ahead, a wide, high staircase was looming before us. I looked up in amazement.

I had never seen such a big staircase before. Suddenly, another amazing thing happened. A nun in a gray uniform and funny-looking white head cover appeared at the top of the stairs and ran down with the agility and swiftness of a cat. In the blink of an eye, she was in front of us, asking questions. Mother told her the reason for our visit. The nurse ushered us into a small waiting room on the ground floor. There were some chairs and a small table in the room and a tall tile-heating oven in one corner.

While the nurse was still talking to us, a loud crash of broken glass and a man's shouting voice were heard from upstairs. The nurse explained that this must be the famous doctor, probably dissatisfied with something. She turned to me with a reassuring smile and said that he did not shout at children. The damage was already done, and I decided that I did not want to see this doctor, no matter how famous he was. I wanted to return home right away. My parents tried to reassure me that he was my only hope. He was the best, most experienced throat specialist. If I ever wanted to get well, he was the one who could help me. The nurse returned to the top of the stairs with the same agility when she came down. This doctor was known as a great specialist in the ear, nose, and throat area. He had gained a lot of experience while serving in the Polish Army. He was also known for his great temper and love of vodka. When he got drunk, there was no telling what he might do. This must have been one of those mornings.

We began peeling off some of our clothes. The ceramic heating oven emitted a pleasant warmth with a slight scent of pine. It was a welcome difference from the harsh winter day outside.

An elderly man was sitting on one of the chairs and was dozing. He opened his eyes for a moment when we entered and returned to his previous position. We waited about half an hour, and then the door opened and a different nun came in and asked for us by name. She told us that the doctor would see us now.

We followed her up the big staircase, and she ushered us into an examining room. The nun told us to sit down while she got busy registering me and preparing all kinds of instruments.

I asked her if all those gadgets were for me. She turned to me with a disarming smile and said that some of them were needed to help the doctor with the examination. To me they all looked scary. I'd been to many doctors' offices before and had never seen such scary instruments.

As time passed, I became more and more nervous and began to cry. Mother tried her best to console me and tried to reassure me that this famous specialist would heal me once and for all.

Wasn't that what I wanted? Wasn't this the reason we came all this way? The sobs made my throat hurt even more so a few minutes after I stopped crying, but my fear did not go away. We waited in silence a little longer, then the door opened with great force and the famous doctor walked in and closed the door with equal force.

He was tall and very thin and had a receding hairline. He was wearing a white coat, with a stethoscope bulging from his pocket. Eyeglasses in very thin frames were hanging on the bridge of his nose. His face was pale, and he appeared nervous. He greeted us curtly and said to me, "So this is Horodynski's protégé."

He asked my name, and I told him reluctantly but immediately added, "Doctor, please don't hurt me!"

"Don't worry one bit," he said, rushing to reassure me. "If you cooperate and do what I say, you will not feel any pain."

He told my mother to sit on a big examining chair and hold me on her lap, facing him. He placed a shiny round object resembling a mirror on his forehead and told me to close my eyes, open my mouth wide, and say "Ahhhhhh" as loud as I could. This was nothing new to me. Every time I went to see a doctor, I had to do the same. He examined my ears, my glands, and asked, "Well, did this hurt?" I shook my head. It truly did not hurt. He smiled at me and said I was a brave girl and that I was free to leave. He prescribed medicine that would make me feel better in a few days. He asked one of my parents to remain in the examining room.

My father stayed behind to pay the doctor and get the prescription. A few minutes later, he joined us.

I was bundled up again, and we walked out onto the street. The cold air felt good on my face. There was a lot of hustle and bustle in the street as townspeople went about their business. Father noticed that the car was parked nearby, and we walked toward it. I was glad my eyes were not covered up so I could observe the unfamiliar street scene.

There were tall buildings on both sides of the street. By tall I mean three to four stories high. Most of them were attached. We passed a shoe store, and I jumped up to look at the window display. There were women's shoes, some with high heels. I thought they were very pretty, and Mother agreed with me.

As we approached the car, Father asked the chauffeur if he had eaten breakfast. When the man answered in the negative, Father pointed to a small restaurant across the street, and we all went inside. The first thing I did was peel off some of my clothes. It was warm and pleasant inside.

I think this was my first restaurant experience. Apparently, it was not a kosher establishment, so we only had tea and rolls. Father told the driver that he could order anything he liked. He ordered fried eggs, rolls, and butter and also tea.

I had no appetite and had difficulty swallowing, but Mother urged me to have some tea. I had a few sips, which Mother cooled for me in a spoon. A wood-burning stove stood in the middle of the room and spread warmth throughout the establishment. There were a few square tables with chairs. Several other customers were also having breakfast. They could have also been visitors like us or businesspeople. They were all men. I was curious about everything and examined my surroundings very carefully.

The man and woman behind the counter were busy preparing the orders. The glass shelves on top of the counter were laden with rolls and cakes. I was getting hot and removed some more of my clothes. Father took all our coats and hung them up on the hanger stand. We all relaxed, and for a short while, I even forgot about my pain and the famous angry doctor. We finished our repast, and it was time to start our journey back home. Father paid the proprietor, and we all bundled up and went back to the car. I was excited, anticipating the ride in the car again. After all, this was not a daily experience for me.

The wind had subsided, and the air felt somewhat warmer as we walked. I was allowed to remove my scarf and breathe freely. Every time the cold air hit my throat, I felt pain.

As I mentioned, my parents were told that my tonsils must come out as soon as possible. The doctor recommended a very experienced surgeon in Kraków. Of course I knew nothing about this.

In the meantime, he prescribed medication for me to take until this flare-up was completely gone. I had to be perfectly well for the operation. My parents did not even hint anything to me about an operation.

As we traveled home, people stopped to look at the car and at us. Even in a large city like Tarnobrzeg, chauffeur-driven, expensive cars were a rarity. At one point, I asked Father if we would also own such a car when we got rich. He answered in the affirmative, knowing quite well that it was a pipe dream. I guess he wanted me to feel good and not ask too many questions. At that time, he could not even imagine that one day this dream would come true.

I constantly looked out the window, observing what we were passing and recording all I saw. Occasionally, I would ask for an explanation of some unfamiliar objects.

My parents were glad that I was distracted and I did not complain about my throat.

We passed through small towns and villages I had never seen before.

Though there were great similarities between them, still, each was different in size and appearance.

I wanted this journey to go on endlessly, but we arrived home in the late afternoon and I immediately began recounting to my nanny the adventures of the trip. Sharing my experiences with Marysia and the boys kept me busy until dinner.

Father went straight to the office, hitching a luxury ride in the chauffer-driven car. Mr. Horodynski's home was on the way to Father's office. The chauffer lived in the compound, so he didn't have to make any extra trips.

Summer Vacation and Cheder

Hebrew School for Boys

The school year passed quickly. Unfortunately, my attendance was poor as I was sick more often than not. I was plagued with frequent sore throats, bronchitis, earaches, and the like. Mother used to dress us to the hilt during cold winter months in the hope that we would not catch a cold. Well, it must have worked in reverse. We were sick very often, but my good friend and classmate would bring me the homework and show me what they had learned each day. I kept up with my studies pretty well and advanced at the same pace as the rest of the class. Despite my poor attendance, I finished first grade with good marks, and the whole first year in school was an interesting and happy experience.

Summer arrived, and school was over. My parents decided that I needed some Jewish education.

Since the Bet Yaakov Hebrew School for Girls was also closed for the summer, they decided to send me to a cheder—a Hebrew school for boys. Rozwadów was the nearest town that had Jewish schools, so I spent most of my first summer vacation in Rozwadów with my grandmother Sarah, aunt Beila, and her husband, Itchale Kanarek. During that summer, I also got to know my other relatives who lived in Rozwadów.

I was enrolled in a cheder, the only girl with thirty-two boys. Cheder was open twelve months a year, and one could join at any time.

My brother Israel did not join me. He was supposed to start his Jewish education in September or October of 1939 full-time. That was supposed to occur after we moved to our new home in Rozwadów.

Since I was a beginner and only a part-time student, I was placed together with the youngest group. The rabbi (teacher), whose name escapes me, was nicknamed the Red One. This name came from his reddish beard and ruddy complexion. I actually felt very good being the only girl among all those boys. The classes were repetitious and boring. Since I was older than most boys, I learned much quicker. The rabbi was satisfied with my progress and showed me off to the rest of the class. He pointed out that I, a girl, knew my lessons much better than the boys did.

Apparently, the age factor was not considered—it was girl versus boys. The cheder was a one-room classroom in a small one-story wooden house on a side street in Rozwadów not far from the railway station. It was gray on the outside, with a sloping straw roof. The house also contained an additional room, the living quarters of the rabbi and his wife. The largest room was the classroom, which was whitewashed and had a cool slate floor that was in desperate need of repair.

A very long wooden table extended almost from one end of the room to the other, and we sat on both sides of the table on long wooden benches. The rabbi sat on a rickety chair at the head of the table so he could see all of us. In one corner stood a basin on a stool and, next to it, a pitcher filled with water and a metal cup. A towel, which was once white, hung on a nail nearby for drying our hands. On one wall there was a long row of nails that served as hangers for the boys' coats in the winter. The nails were low on the wall, unused and dangerous in the summer. Otherwise, the room was cool and smelled of sweat. When the odor became unbearable, the rabbi would open a window to let some fresh air in. Sometimes the noises in the street disturbed us and he would not allow us the luxury of breathing fresh air.

There was a fisherman's net repair shop next door. In the summer, the entrepreneurs took their work outdoors, into the street, where there was more room and the air was much fresher. During recess, we all went outside to watch fishnet repairmen at work.

The only light that came into the classroom was from the two not very clean large windows. On cloudy or rainy days, a low-hanging kerosene lamp supplied the meager light.

The rabbi's wife stayed mainly in their living quarters, which was in the back, busy with household chores. Occasionally, we would get a whiff of something delicious cooking in the back. The only times the rebbetzin (rabbi's wife) would interrupt us would be when she came to ask the rabbi for money before she went to the market or to bring him a glass of tea.

The rabbi did not raise his voice much when someone disturbed him or got out of hand. He carried a leather riding whip and did not hesitate to use it when the opportunity presented itself.

Class began at 8:00 a.m., and we studied until twelve noon, with one short recess. Many boys went home for lunch, but some would bring a sandwich and had their lunch in the classroom. Occasionally, some would not bring a sandwich and stayed hungry. The older boys who already knew how to read started earlier in the morning. They would first pray and then study.

This free time was used for play outdoors or to go to the bathroom, which was a tiny wooden hut in the back of the house. The rabbi would rarely allow us to go to the bathroom or get a drink of water during the lessons. Years later, my father told me that the rabbi actually did not want to accept me. Girls simply did not go to a cheder, together with boys. They went to the all-girls school, Bet Yaakov, instead of public school. The nearest Bet Yaakov was in Rozwadów. My summer stint in the cheder was preparation for Bet Yaakov.

Father paid the rabbi double the amount the boys' parents were paying, and I was accepted and treated like a VIP. After a week or so in my aunt's house, I missed my home and family and didn't want to stay with my grandmother anymore. There was a daily morning passenger train passing Zbydniow to Rozwadow óóat seven or seven thirty and a train back at about 2:00 p.m. going to Zbydniów and beyond. My parents bought me a monthly pass, and I started commuting even though I had to get up an hour earlier. It was a short ride, and I liked riding the train. It made me feel all grown-up, riding the train full of adults. The train station was nearby, and I went directly from the train to the cheder and at twelve noon. When classes were over, I either went to my grandmother Sarah's for lunch or took the train home. I think I was the only child on that train without an accompanying adultan yg. My and my mother's monthly passes, these are the only documents that remained with us throughout the war. I still have the pictures which were attached to the monthly rail pass. Mine is marked 1937. Mother is wearing her beloved black fur cape.

I met some girls in Rozwadów during that summer, but these were not lasting friendships. Though Grandmother and my aunt wanted me to stay with them—and they spoiled me and even let me eat ice cream, which was a forbidden treat (Mother claimed it caused my sore throats)—I still preferred to go home and be with my family and friends. I also wanted to tell my friends about the big city. Some of them had never ventured beyond our little village or ridden a train. They wanted to know all the details of my adventures.

I was only too glad to oblige.

During the two short months at cheder, I learned the Hebrew letters, how to read a little, some Bible stories, and I memorized some prayers in addition to the ones my mother had taught me. The school year was approaching again, and I was eager to return to a more normal way of life at home. I missed regular public school and being with my family and friends.

What interested me most in the cheder were the stories of the Bible. I did not understand very much of what the rabbi was teaching because he taught in Yiddish and my knowledge of Yiddish at that age was minimal, but I listened attentively and caught a few words here and there. I did commit to memory the names of our biblical ancestors, and when I came home, I asked Father to repeat the stories in Polish. He happily obliged. One of the Bible stories we learned was about Joseph being sold into slavery by his brothers.

This particular story bothered me very much. I could not understand how one brother could sell another or do him harm of any kind. I had asked the rabbi, but he grappled with answers that did not satisfy me.

My father also had some difficulty explaining jealousy and favoritism.

After numerous examples of that phenomenon, I still could not grasp the full meaning of it. Father finally told me that I would understand what jealousy was and no doubt experience it myself when I grew up. I had to leave it at that. Sure enough, Father was right. Whenever such a situation arose in real life, I always remembered my father trying to explain it to me. Now I understand that anyone can experience it, but I also believe that it's in one's power to overcome it and not allow it to rule one's life.

At that time, I did not realize how important my Jewish education would be in my future life.

My education came in dribs and drabs during my formative years because of the war and moving from place to place. I am sorry that I didn't pursue it more intensively afterward. There are valid reasons for that, too. But despite my insufficient Jewish education, I was always committed to my Jewish heritage and its values. I did everything possible to perpetuate its teachings, to live by its precepts, whenever possible, and to hand them down to my children.

My Parents Decide to Move to Rozwadów

In the spring of 1939, my parents made the decision to give their children, especially the boys, a solid Jewish education and move to Rozwadów, where there were a variety of Jewish and Hebrew schools. Father would have to commute to work to Zbydniów, but the train made it easy. It was a ten- to fifteen-minute ride and a short walk to and from the train stations. Mother would be close to her family again.

It took a while to find a suitable and affordable house. I remember, when my parents discussed purchasing a home, they often used the word *hypoteka*. Many years later, I found out it meant "mortgage." Nevertheless, they finally found a home in Rozwadów, on a side street, 20 Trzeciego Maja Street. It was spring of 1939. We had to wait until the purchase was finalized, and the house needed some modification, painting, cleaning, etc. This was supposed to have been accomplished during the summer. My mother often traveled to Rozwadów to supervise the work. Since the work was not completed during the summer, our move to Rozwadow was postponed 'till after yearthe High Holidays.

One summer day in 1939, Mother took all three of us by train to Rozwadów to see the new house. It was removed from the center of town, on a narrow, unpaved street. The exterior was painted a pale yellow, topped with a gray roof. The property was surrounded by a white picket fence enclosing a good-sized, overgrown, and neglected yard. There was a back door that led to a small patio and a narrow path leading to the outhouse. Though it was Rozwadów and there might have been indoor plumbing in some homes, it had not reached our house yet.

A gray entrance door was partly open. I asked Mother if we could change the gray to red. She did not react. There were men working inside the house. As we entered, one of the men asked Mother some questions. While the two were talking, the maid led us through the house. I was impressed with the enormity of it compared to our present accommodations.

The first room was enormous, and it was instantly evident that it was the kitchen. We proceeded to another good-sized room, which I was told was my parents' bedroom. There were two additional rooms, one for my brothers and the other for our nanny and me. She could also sleep in the kitchen if she chose to. I persuaded her to sleep with me, and we were both happy about the arrangement.

We were all happy about all that space, which we were not used to.

The idea of living in the city was alluring and held a promise of excitement.

The man promised Mother that all would be ready by the middle of October.

In all the excitement, I forgot that I would have to leave all my friends, whom I had known all my life. This thought came to me on the train ride back home.

I confronted Mother with that question. "How and when will I see my friends?" Mother reassured me that I would make many new friends and that I would be able to visit the old ones whenever possible, especially during the summer. She told me that Father would be commuting to work daily and there would be times when I would be able to join him or even take the train by myself. From that day on, all we talked about was the new house. A whole house all to ourselves!

That was a new and exciting feeling.

It was not a Horodynski mansion but it was a great improvement to what we had.

Last Yom Kippur Holiday in Rozwadów

It must have been 1938, during the High Holidays. We were staying, as we often did, with my grandmother Sarah and aunt Beila. It was Yom Kippur (the Day of Atonement), a day of prayer and fasting and a day when the Yizkor prayer for the dead was recited. It was customary that children leave the synagogue while this prayer was recited.

All the Jews were at the synagogues, praying. The synagogue was a whitewashed two-story building with a wide staircase in the front, at the end of which was an enormous double wooden entrance door adorned with the Star of David on each side. As was customary, the men occupied the first floor, where the Torah was placed on the eastern wall. Somewhat removed was the wooden pulpit. The balance of the spacious hall was filled with benches (pews). Women prayed on the second-floor balcony.

This was the first building the Germans burned when they entered Rozwadów.

On that Yom Kippur day, a festive yet somber mood prevailed. Everyone was dressed in their best. I was upstairs with my mother as well as other female relatives. I wanted to impress my parents and fast at least half a day. I didn't have breakfast that day. When the Yizkor prayer was announced, all the children left the synagogue.

My aunt Chana (Father's sister) asked me to watch her daughter Feyga, who must have been two or three years old at the time. Aunt Chana gave me a large piece of sponge cake wrapped in paper to give to Feyga in case she cried.

The minute we left the building and Aunt Chana returned to her seat to join the congregation in the solemn prayer, Feyga did not stop screaming. I gave her a piece of cake, which she threw on the dusty ground. She wanted her mother, and no cake or anything else pacified her. It must have been about ten or eleven in the morning, and I was getting hungry myself. I was very tempted to eat the sponge cake. About twenty minutes later, the prayer ended and Aunt Chana heard Feyga's screams inside the synagogue. She came rushing down the stairs to calm her daughter. She scolded me for not taking good care of my cousin. I was very hurt and hungry and ran inside to look for my mother. Mother apparently realized that playing grown-up games was doing me no good, so she went to get my brothers, who were downstairs with my father, and we all went to Grandmother Sarah's house and had a good lunch. Father remained in the synagogue.

Naturally, Mother did not touch any of the food.

This was my first encounter with my cousin Feyga. I had seen her before but had never babysat for her. Over the years, Zipora (her Hebrew name) and I became very close. At one time, we even attended school together for a short time. After the Jewish state was established in 1948, she moved there in 1950, attended a teacher's seminary, and became a teacher. In the early 1960s, she married Abraham Altman. They had two very talented sons, Baruch, named after her father, and Israel, named after our grandfather.

Both her sons are married and have children. Zipora lived to welcome her first grandchild. She was a heavy smoker most of her adult life and died of lung cancer in 2005.

WWII Comes to Zbydniów

There was a lot of uncertainty and worry in 1939. Hitler was flexing his muscles, and the threat of war was in the air. On September 1, 1939, he dispelled all the doubts and speculations by attacking Poland.

It was a swift action on land and in the air, and Poland, being outnumbered, unprepared, and out-equipped by the enemy, was overrun in a very short time. Poland was first hit from the air, eliminating all the strategic installations that could impede Germany's swift occupation of our country.

One of my classmates had lived in France with her family for a few years prior to Hitler's war plans. When they returned to Zbydniów, they brought with them some very interesting objects, among them a radio and a record player. Very few people in Zbydniów had them in those days or even knew what they were.

I certainly didn't.

I liked going to this friend's house. They were interesting people, and they even spoke French. My friend even had her own bicycle. I was always fascinated by new things.

My father used to visit them on occasion, listening to their radio and discussing politics with the man of the house. I'll never forget the evening I went with my father to their house and listened to the radio for the first time. The war had already begun, and everybody was anxious to know what was happening on the front and in the rest of the country. Their radio was a large wooden box with a carved-out grill in the front. It stood on a low table near the wall in their living room. The man of the house turned a knob, and a man's very excited voice seemed to be coming out of the box. They all listened attentively. Through the translator we understood that some Polish soldiers fell in battle and that the enemy was advancing at a rapid pace. I soon lost interest in what the man was saying. What interested me more was where his voice was coming from. How could a person fit into such a small box? My fascination was with the phenomenon of a midget being hidden in that box and that his stories excited so many people. I examined the box from all sides but saw no sign of a human being.

Seeing the concerned look on the men's faces, I knew it was not the time to ask questions. About fifteen minutes later, the broadcast was over. Another turn of the dial and the radio was silent.

The proprietor and my father began a heated discussion about the war, which I didn't really understand. I didn't think it would affect me in any way, so why did I need to know? This was grown-up stuff.

I do remember a name that was mentioned several times: Hitler.

Little did I know how much this cursed name would affect me and the rest of the world.

We stayed a while longer, and my father decided it was time to go back home. On the way home, Father was pensive, and I really didn't want to bother him. But the radio fascinated me. I could not wait for a more appropriate time to find out about it. When I finally asked him, Father tried his best to dispel the mystery of the invention, telling me about airwaves and the like. All this was above my head, beyond my comprehension, and it still is. My curiosity did not diminish with time—I am still fascinated by it as well as by many other new inventions.

The next time I actually saw a radio was after the war, when we bought one in 1946. It looked very similar.

It was a sunny September Sunday morning, my friend's long-awaited birthday party. She had promised that one of the highlights of the party would be music coming from the radio or the record player. The party was scheduled for noon on Sunday, when everyone would be home from church. My mother helped me put on her newest creation, my beautiful pink dress, which she tried her best to copy from my cousin Susan's Parisian-style one. She made it for me for the approaching Jewish High Holidays.

Though the fall season did not call for a summer dress, I begged her to make it for me, so I can wear it next spring on Passover. She purposely made it bigger so I would not grow out of it in six months. She made sure I realized that the fabric was expensive and to take extra care not to soil or stain the dress. I put on white socks and my first pair of shiny black patent leather shoes. I usually wore simple brown lace-up oxfords by Bata. My deal with Mother was that the patent leather shoes would be worn on the Sabbath, holidays, and other special occasions. Birthday parties in those days were not very elaborate, but they were special occasions and a reason to get dressed up. I was lucky then to have more than one dress and more than one pair of shoes, unlike some of my friends. This was not always the case.

That same morning, my cousin Victor arrived from Pierunka.

Bombing of Zbydniów

My cousin Victor was born in Pierunka, a tiny village near the town of Nisko. Victor's grandparents, parents, and younger brother, Aaron, all lived together in a large house on a farm. Victor's mother, Cha-Golda, was my father's sister. She had married a close relative, possibly a cousin, whose name was Hersh Yitzchak. The newlyweds moved in with the groom's parents and began their married life on the farm.

Hersh Yitzchak's father was a well-to-do farmer and a horse breeder. The whole family worked on the farm.

While Hitler was bombing other parts of the country, Pierunka and its surroundings enjoyed peace and quiet. Victor, the older of the two boys (eighteen or nineteen at that time), was sent by his parents to fetch my grandmother Leah and our families from Zbydniów and take us all to *safety* in Pierunka, supposedly for a few weeks, until the war was over.

Victor told us that where they lived, it was very quiet. He stated, "What would the Germans be looking for in our small godforsaken village?"

Adjacent to Rozwadów, in the nearby town of Stalowa Wola, there was a recently erected munitions factory. The reasoning was that this munitions factory would be targeted. Since Pirunka was pretty far away, we would not be bothered by the bombing of the Stalowa Wola factory.

While Mother was weighing the idea, I was allowed to go to my friend's birthday party for a short while. Mother walked over to the post office (in the same building), where there was a phone, and called my father in his office to discuss the matter. Though it was

Sunday, my father was at work. He concurred that it was a good idea to keep the children safe but said that he could not join us right away. He would try to join us on Friday. He also had to discuss the matter with his employer the next day. It was Sunday, and my father was respectful of his boss's day of rest.

Mother returned and told the maid to begin packing some of our clothes and other necessities, enough for a week. It was decided that a week would be enough time for the bombing to stop and for quiet to return to the area.

I went to the party, and Victor was going to get Grandmother Leah ready.

The rest of our relatives were to follow (later, my aunt Reizl changed her mind and refused to go).

My friends and I had a wonderful time at the party, and I completely forgot about Victor, the war, and all the other problems. We were played games, danced, and jumped to the rhythm of the music coming from the mysterious radio.

The record player my friend had was the other wonderful invention I could not understand.

While we were having ice cream (which I was allowed to have only on rare occasions), Victor appeared. He had come to fetch me. I was having fun and didn't see any reason for leaving the party. He informed me that these were Mother's orders.

He waited until I finished my ice cream, and I reluctantly said good-bye to my friends. As we walked out of the house, we heard a zooming noise. It started low, but it quickly intensified, and when we reached another neighbor's yard, we heard a crashing, thunderous noise very close by. People came running outdoors to see what the loud noise was. As we looked up, we saw five German bombers flying over our heads in the direction of the railroad station. My friends father said that the planes were probably going to bomb Stalowa Wola.

My cousin Victor grabbed me by the hand, and we began running home. We took a shortcut through the fields, but the terrain was very rough and uneven. These were potato fields after the harvest, and the earth was dug up. While we were running through those fields, my shoes were sinking into the earth, my white socks full of dirt. I felt pebbles in my shoes. This slowed my pace considerably. The airplanes were coming back in our direction, and I was so scared I could not speak.

I would not dream of complaining about my discomfort. Victor pulled my hand with force, and we doubled our pace. The airplanes were right above our heads, very, very low. We were the only ones in the open field. I'm sure the Germans saw us.

At this time, we changed direction away from the house and ran toward the railway station. There was a deafening sound of an explosion. Victor sought to seek shelter in a ditch. Suddenly, I was being pulled down to the ground. The ditch was about one to two meters deep. Victor and I were lying in the ditch, watching from afar as the railroad tracks flew in the air. Though I was terribly frightened, my curiosity won out and I picked up my head to see what was going on around us. We saw large chunks of rails, concrete, and dirt flying in the air and falling in every direction. Some pieces fell not too far from us with a loud thud. The whistle of the bombs repeated itself again and again as loud explosions followed and debris fell all over the place, covering us with dirt.

I started screaming. Victor covered my mouth with his hand and ordered me to shut up. I could see that he was also terribly frightened. In all this commotion, I covered my head with both arms, trying to shut out the world. I cried because I lost my beautiful new shoe, and Victor tried to explain to me that our lives were in danger. He promised to go back and find my shoe.

There were four explosions in all. After each one, debris flew everywhere, and some of it landed on us. We could see long chunks of railroad tracks flying in the air. We were hit with pieces of wood and rocks and covered with lots of dirt. Our big mistake was running toward the railroad station.

We mistakenly thought that the planes were heading in the opposite direction. The bombers approached their bombing target from a different direction each time they returned, and that confused us.

Victor and I remained in the ditch until all was quiet. I finally opened my eyes to the horror surrounding us. Now I was *really* scared. Victor stood up first and brushed some dirt off. We could still hear the faint hum of the departing bombers. Victor noticed a bleeding scratch on my arm and tried to clean it with his handkerchief. Ordinarily, I would cringe and cry at the sight of blood, but for some reason, I did neither. Suddenly, I was very calm. I must have been in shock.

All this happened so suddenly, so unexpectedly, so quickly that I did not know what to make of it. I was covered with dirt, my new, beautiful dress was completely ruined, and one of my very first patent leather shoes was lost. Those were my primary worries, and only half an hour before, I was singing and dancing at my friend's birthday party.

My eyes began to sting and I raised my fist to rub them, but Victor stopped me just in time. He tried to clean my eyes with the other side of his clean handkerchief. I began feeling pain in my arm, head, and legs. I looked down and only then noticed two small rivulets of blood streaming down my right shin. I had scratches all over my arms and legs. Seeing the extent of my injuries and the sorry state of my holiday dress, I envisioned my mother's reaction. She would be very angry and probably give me a spanking, but I also knew that Victor would protect me. He would bail me out. I began crying again, rubbing my sore eyes, which were getting redder and more painful. I wanted to go back and find the other shoe, but Victor protested. He said he would bring me home and, while I was getting cleaned up, he would go find my shoe. He pulled my hand, and we stepped up our pace.

As we approached the house, a few neighbors were standing in a group, talking about the bombing. When we entered our kitchen, I found Mother visibly upset, holding a crying David in her arms. Upon seeing us enter, she rushed toward us, yelling, "Thank God, thank God!" She put down David, and I ran into her arms, crying loudly. Suddenly, I felt safe and was no longer afraid of the bombs, the explosions, and the loud noises. She pulled me away from her body and examined the sad state I was in.

Tears choked my throat; I could not utter a word. She raised her questioning, tear-filled eyes at Victor, and he explained what had happened. Mother also heard the loud explosions, and she thought they were in Stalowa Wola. She didn't realize they were that close. She was busy preparing for the trip to Pierunka. She called the maid and asked her to take over, to clean me up and tend to my wounds. She scolded Victor for taking me in the wrong direction, and an argument ensued. Suddenly, Mother stopped in her tracks. She had realized that the railway station was very close to my father's office and Horodynski's mansion. She ran to the post office to call my father in order to find out if he was all right. Upon seeing Mother run, I wiggled myself out of the maid's arms and followed her.

When Father's voice was heard on the phone, Mother's expression changed from horror to pure contentment. Her lips turned up in a smile. Father reassured her that he was fine, that he'd seen it all, but that nothing happened to him or the mill. He was just about to call her to find out if we were all right. She did not tell Father about my adventure, which surprised me, and I asked her why. She explained that there was no need to worry him at this time. He would find out everything soon enough. I was a little disappointed but let it go at that. Mother and I returned, and the maid proceeded to clean me up. There were many wooden splinters in my hair. She tried very hard to remove them without causing me too much pain. When I was all cleaned up, my wounds and scratches tended to, I sat down at the kitchen table with a warm cup of milk. Mother promised Father that we would all be ready in an hour and asked him to be home by then. Mother realized the danger we were in and speeded up the preparations. She now knew Victor's parents' idea had merit.

Mother continued to gather and pack our belongings into numerous bundles. We used sheets and blankets to make bundles. Suitcases were a luxury. We might have had one or two suitcases then, because Father traveled on business occasionally and he would not carry a bundle with him, but they were too small to hold what we needed for the whole family. We did not travel far from home, and there was no need for suitcases or trunks.

Now that I think about it, I recall that Mother had a small wicker trunk. Once or twice, she went to a spa in Rabka or Krinica and used that wicker trunk. Years later, she was still talking about the good times she had there and how beneficial those baths were.

Now Mother told the maid to get busy with lunch. Our daily main meal was in the early afternoon, except on Fridays. Victor cleaned his clothes as best as he could and washed up, and Mother gave him one of Father's shirts to wear. He then joined us at the table.

As I may have mentioned, the kitchen table was the center of our home. All plans, conversations, discussions, entertainment, kitchen chores, and of course, meals took place on or around the kitchen table. It is my favorite place in the home to this day.

Victor went next door to Aunt Reizl's apartment to try to persuade her to join us on this trip to Pierunka, but she refused. He argued that if God wanted her and her family safe, He would keep them safe wherever they were. Additionally, her husband, Yitzhak, was away on business.

Father finally came home, and Mother put food on the table. This was, you may say, a ritual in our home. Dinner was served upon Father's arrival. The trouble was that we hardly ever knew when that hour was. But Mother had to adjust her schedule to his erratic hours. This was not easy, because Father expected dinner to be ready whenever he walked in.

Father and Victor were conversing. It began with the usual inquiries about the family's health and other stuff. Then the conversation turned to the war and today's bombing. Only then did my father find out what happened to Victor and me. He looked at me and noticed the scratches on my face and arms. He asked if I was feeling all right and began eating. I expected a little more sympathy from him as, after all, I went through an ordeal and I was hurting, but Father was never a sentimentalist.

When I grew older, I learned that Father was not very big on expressing sympathy or other emotions. He kept most feelings to himself, but not anger. He was quick to disapprove and quick to be angry.

We finished dinner, and the maid cleaned up while Father went to try to convince my aunt to come with us. She still refused. Her two older children were in Rozwadów, in school, and her husband was not home either.

Victor began loading the wagon. Since my mother did not know how long we would stay in Pierunka, she packed quite a lot. She even took kitchen utensils and dishes. Mother understood that extra people in a household would require extra kitchen equipment.

Father had to stay put as he had too much work. Since the war began, he worked long hours and conferred with Horodynski very often. Mother and Victor tried to convince him to come along, but his sense of duty and responsibility prevailed. This is no idle statement. He was always responsible and conscientious about his work and business.

Father's sense of responsibility and loyalty to his employer was apparently inherited by me. Since I entered the workforce, I adhere to the same standards. My work ethics are of a high standard and will remain so as long as I work for others. I am happy to say that the same bug has bitten my daughter. She is extremely conscientious and loyal to her employers.

Mother could not understand this way of thinking. For her it was family first and foremost, and my parents often argued this subject. As an adult, I understood my father's logic and usually sided with him. Mother would be very hurt by me taking Father's side and would fight with me too.

Now back to Zbydniów.

Father hastened our departure. He did not want us to travel in the dark. These were not normal, peaceful times. Even in peacetime, traveling at night could be dangerous. The roads were full of deserters, thieves, and other such characters. It was dangerous to travel anywhere in Poland.

The distance to Pierunka was about thirty kilometers or so. A horse-drawn carriage loaded with baggage and people was a slow way to travel. Nevertheless, we said our good-byes and started out on the road. The boys and I were excited about the journey. To us it was an adventure. Mother sat in the front, with Victor, and we sat on top of the bundles in the back.

We stopped at Grandma Leah's house and picked her up. Leibish stayed home. She only carried one small bundle. Victor helped her onto the wagon, and she sat with us in the back.

Our interest began to intensify after we left the familiarity of our village and saw new and unknown sights. But for the first couple of hours, our journey was uneventful.

We had just left Nisko, a small town between Rozwadów and Pierunka. The sun was low, and the air was getting cooler. We were told to wear our sweaters, and I helped David with his.

Mother heard a strange humming noise and asked Victor to stop for a moment.

The wagon stopped, and we could all hear an uninterrupted hum that was growing in intensity and coming in our direction. There was a young forest on the right side of the road. At this point, we realized that the noise was coming from German bombers heading in our direction. Mother grabbed David. Victor took Israel and me down hastily and then helped Grandmother off the wagon.

We all ran as fast as we could into the forest.

There were some peasants on the road, walking home from the fields, and they did the same. The horse neighed, jumped up on his hind legs, and started galloping. He veered off the road and also ran into the forest. Victor left us with Mother and ran after the horse. He soon caught up with the horse and tried to calm him by putting a rag over his eyes.

While all this was happening, the bombers were over our heads, spraying the road and the forest with bullets.

After a short while, we heard loud explosions rip through the Stalowa Wola factories. This was the third time the munitions factories were bombed.

We stayed in the forest for a long while and listened to the bombers unload their cargo. When all was absolutely quiet, we all began emerging from the forest. We, the children, were very frightened and cried during this whole ordeal.

My morning encounter was still fresh in my memory, and now I had a new one to deal with. We cuddled close to Mother, and I could feel her body tremble. Victor brought the carriage around and put us back in, and we started out on the road again.

This whole episode took maybe twenty minutes, but it was enough to leave a scar for the rest of our lives.

Israel and I returned to our seats, but David was still frightened and would not leave the safety of Mother's arms. Mother began arguing with Victor about the *safety* of Pierunka, which he had promised. "Well," he said, "after all, we are at war, and who is to tell what the Germans are up to at any given time?"

The sun was setting, the sky was darkening, and Victor was urging the horse to speed up his trot. We arrived at their home after dark. It was a large wooden hut, not much different from thousands of other prewar village homes. We walked into the main room, the kitchen. My aunt Cha-Golda ran toward us, thanking God for our safe arrival. We were all asked to sit at the table. My aunt had hot potato soup ready for us, and we ate it with great appetite. The kitchen is the only room I remember in Victor's house, possibly because we spent most of the time there. It was a large square room with whitewashed walls and small windows. Maybe that's why I remember it being dark even during the day. It contained the usual kitchen equipment—a large wooden table, chairs, stove, and possibly other items that I do not recall.

A very large square fenced-in yard surrounded the one-story house. Chickens, geese, and ducks ran around freely. The water well was in one corner of the yard, and there were several cows in the cowshed.

I remember going with Mother the next morning to milk the cows. The horses were in a separate stable and were cared for by the men.

This household was up at the crack of dawn. I remember my uncle Hersh Yitzhak putting on his tallit (prayer shawl) and phylacteries and praying early in the morning; he made his sons do the same.

The German bombers kept coming almost daily in search of new targets. They flew over Pierunka several times while we were there but did not throw any bombs or shoot at us. I recall, one morning after breakfast, we were playing in the yard and a squadron of German bombers flew very low over our heads. The loud noise of the engines scared David, and he began to cry. I tried to console him, pointing out that they were not shooting at us, but David kept screaming and shaking with fear. When the bombers were gone and the zooming noise subsided, Mother heard David cry. She came out and took him inside. Israel and I became used to the sound of the bombers and didn't cry anymore.

After a few days, Mother realized that we were not much safer in Pierunka than in Zbydniów and wanted to go home. My aunt and uncle persuaded her to stay through the Sabbath day. My father arrived late Friday afternoon, and the family was reunited.

He took the train from Zbydniów to Nisko and hitched a ride to Pierunka. Victor and Aaron entertained us whenever they were free from their chores. They let us ride a pony, gave us rides on the wagon loaded with hay, and played games with us.

Early Sunday morning, we reloaded the wagon and went back home. Victor joined us on the trip back so he could take back the horse and wagon. We returned to our "normal" life, as normal as life could be in wartime.

I went back to school. Some boys in my class jeered at me, accusing me of starting the war. They were saying that the Jews started the war so they could become even richer. One of them even accused me of pointing out to the Germans where the strategic targets were so they could bomb them. When I protested their accusations, they said they knew all about the Jews. They reminded me that our family fled so we would not be home the day of the bombing and thus saved our skins while leaving everybody else vulnerable. My girlfriends didn't say anything in my defense, but they did not protest either. These were eight- and nine-year-old children. Now, fifty years later, I understand how deeply rooted anti-Semitism was in Poland, and I am not so sure that much has changed for the better over the years.

I came home from school crying, asking my parents all kinds of questions about these unfounded accusations. Both tried to explain that they were vicious lies and that I should not pay any attention to what the boys were saying. It was not an easy task, but I learned not to react to their accusations.

After a few days, they really stopped bothering me. I knew my parents hurt inside but didn't show it. I guess they were used to anti-Semitic remarks and learned to live with them. Most Jews lived with anti-Semitism for centuries. This seems to be an incurable sickness.

On October 10, 1939, German soldiers came and very politely told us to leave our home.

People say that our lives are predestined. Is it fate that has prompted me to write this chapter about Victor on this particular day? It must be, because I received a phone call from his daughter Carol telling me that my dear cousin lay gravely ill in a Florida hospital. I took the next plane and went to see him.

In that hospital bed I saw a sad shell of a man whom I hardly recognized. I knew my cousin Victor as a man full of life, spirit, and joy. I realized that his end was coming but that it was much too soon.

I wanted to make sure that it was known that Victor probably saved my life in that ditch during the bombing of the Zbydniów railway station and by dragging us to safety into the forest on the way to Pierunka. I wanted to record that chapter in his life about which few people know.

Today, on a bitter, cold, snowy, windy Thursday, December 30, 1993, my dear cousin Victor completed his life's journey at the age of seventy-three. He passed away two days earlier in Florida and was buried today at Beth David Cemetery in Elmont, Queens, New York. May his memory remain in our hearts forever.

My cousin Victor was a very important part of my life, and I will write about him further.

My Father

My dear father was born in Zbydniów in 1899, one of thirteen children, of whom only ten survived, three boys and seven girls. Two males died during a typhoid epidemic in 1922 along with my grandfather Israel. The youngest girl, Simma, died in infancy for reasons unknown. The surviving children were Chaim Layzer Heshl, Leybish, and females Etky (Esther) Reyzl, Molly, Chana-Golda, Chana, Rivci, and Genia

Father was short, about five feet five inches, but he made up for it in brains. He was of slight built and had always been slim. His back was hunched, just as Grandmother Leah's. It might have been hereditary or from long hours of study and constant paperwork as an adult. He always worked, if not physically then mentally—he always had his thinking cap on. He read the daily newspapers and loved discussing politics and religion. Father was mainly self-taught; he only finished first and second grade of the local elementary school. He loved numbers and taught himself the basics of math—I should say memorized it—which served him well in later years.

He was bald at a very young age, but never completely. When I once asked him why he had no hair on his head, his answer was "Stupid hair doesn't grow on a smart head."

His younger brother, Leibish, was also bald at a young age. His sisters had very thin hair, and so do I. I was always reminded by my late mother that I inherited my father's family genes. I never figured out if it was good or bad. One thing I know about my fathers family:

They were hospitable, generous, smart hard working no-nonsense people.

Father's nose was too long for his slim face, and he had closely set, very expressive gray eyes that could say more than words, and he used them effectively when he wanted.

He was a no-nonsense man and did not tolerate laziness or incompetence.

He had been a chain-smoker since his teenage years but didn't smoke on the Sabbath or on Jewish holidays, when religion forbade it. On the days when he could not smoke, he constantly drank tea. He sweetened his tea and coffee by sucking on a lump of sugar. Father never put sugar into his hot drinks and always drank it piping hot from a glass. It was not until a few years before his death that he drank coffee from a mug that my sister Leah gave him as a gift. He didn't want to hurt her feelings, so he broke his habit and drank coffee from that mug. But his tea was still poured into a glass.

My father never cared about clothes; to him clothes were a necessity, not a fashion statement, and he tried to carry over this idea to my mother and us, but not very successfully.

His mind was always preoccupied with something, whether it was family matters, work, business, or world affairs. All those subjects were constantly on his mind during his waking hours. I am sure that this state of mind contributed to his constant irritability and nervousness. He tried to excel in whatever he did.

He only finished second grade but, over the years, acquired a vast amount of knowledge by reading and learning from others. All his life, he was limber and quick. Even when he was much older, he still walked very fast and very few people could keep up his pace.

My father had a very good job before the war. He was general manager of a large estate that belonged to the local squire and landowner, Mr. Horodynski.

As I learned from other people's stories, my father became a *businessman* at a very tender age. Being the older of the two remaining sons at home, after the eldest brother, Chaim Layzer, married Sima and moved to Bojanów, my father assumed the responsibility of the breadwinner for the family. He must have been in his teens or early twenties. There were two or three younger unmarried sisters still living at home, his younger brother (Leibish), and of course, my widowed grandmother (Leah).

Word got around that my father was an able businessman. Soon, people gained confidence in his knowledge and ability, and they trusted him and sought him out to engage in business ventures.

The area was surrounded by forests, and the construction industry boomed after WWI. The railroad passing through Zbydniów gave a great boost to the development of commerce and trade. He would buy trees, cut them to order at the lumber mill that belonged to Mr. Horodynski, and send the wood on rafts down the river San to his customers.

When Mr. Horodynski heard about this young man's business acumen and what a hard worker he was, he decided to hire him. At first, he asked him to manage the *tartak*, a lumber-cutting plant. After a while, when my father proved to his employer how capable and efficient he was, Mr. Horodynski entrusted him additional tasks, including bookkeeping. Eventually, my father became Mr. Horodynski's right hand.

After a while, Father leased the flour mill from his employer and processed grain into flour for the local farmers and other customers. The family income increased, and things began looking up.

The squire traveled frequently and needed someone reliable to manage the affairs of the estate in his absence. When he found and hired my father, his worries were over, especially when he saw my father's mathematical ability. There were no computers or calculators in those days. This was not an easy load to carry for a young man, but my father, wanting to prove himself and needing the income, took on this great workload. I think my father invented workaholism. And I may have inherited some of those genes.

Mr. Horodynski loved my father, respected him, and trusted him implicitly. In those days, that was a rare relationship between a Christian and a Jew, an employer and an employee, but it served them both well.

Mr. Horodynski was married. His wife also came from a rich, aristocratic family. She was tall, slim, and not very pretty. There were rumors that she was very frugal. I saw her once or twice passing our house in a horse-drawn carriage. She was wearing a black outfit with a white collar.

Rumor had it that black was her favorite color.

The couple had three handsome sons and a daughter. The sons, Dominic, Zbygniew, and Andrew, attended private schools, and one of them studied at the Sorbonne in Paris just before the war. The youngest child was a daughter. Her name was Anna, and she was a year or two older than me.

His thinking cap was always on. He loved numbers and taught himself basic math, which served him well all his life. He was bald at a very young age, but not completely. When I once asked him why he had no hair on his head, he answered, "Stupid hair does not grow on a smart head." His brother Leibish was also bald, and the sisters had very sparse hair.

Father was a no-nonsense man and didn't tolerate laziness or incompetence. I don't remember the color of his eyes, but Leah tells me they were light hazel/gray and very expressive. He had been a chain-smoker since his teenage years but abstained on the Sabbath and Jewish holidays. On those days, he drank lots of tea. He sweetened it by sucking on a lump of sugar. Clothes to him were a necessity, not a fashion statement, and he tried to instill the same idea in my mother and his daughters, but not very successfully.

His brain worked 24-7. He was occupied with family matters, politics, business, and world affairs. I am sure that this state of mind contributed to his constant nervousness and irritability.

He tried to excel in everything he did, and he supplemented his lack of education by constantly reading and learning from others.

Father was conscientious, diligent, and a hard worker. These attributes must have landed him the lucrative and prestigious job with Mr. Horodynski, who also helped my uncle Leibish make a living, as well as many other people in the village. Uncle Leibish received permission, for a fee, to milk some of Horodynski's cows every morning.

My grandmother Leah churned the milk into butter, made farmer cheese, and other byproducts, and Uncle Leibish delivered the finished products to town and sold them. After a while, he acquired a steady clientele. Naturally, Mr. Horodynski got paid, and everybody was happy.

With the additional income, my grandmother's poor household could breathe easier. Leibish would rise daily at dawn and, with one or two of his sisters, would go to Horodynski's barns and milk the cows. On the Sabbath, the peasants would do the job and keep part of the milk as payment. The balance of the milk went to Horodynski's household. Mr. Horodynski owned many cows, so there was enough milk for everybody.

The Matchmaker

My father was already nearing thirty, and it was time to take a wife and start his own family. He heard about this pretty, educated, and eligible young lady, Noemi, who lived in Rozwadów. He sent a matchmaker to inquire about her. This was the custom in those days, though in certain circles of orthodoxy, the custom still prevails.

My mother was the youngest of her siblings and was still single, but twenty-three was not considered too young for marriage. All her brothers and sisters had been married, and most were raising families.

The matchmaker described my father as "the rich comptroller of Horodynski's vast estate" who was well versed in languages and the Holy Scriptures.

Horodynski was famous for his wealth, but among the Jews, he was also known as a friend and benefactor. My mother was intrigued hearing all these accolades about this eligible bachelor. Though the matchmaker never told her that he was short, bent-over, and a chain-smoker.

Smoking was not frowned upon in those days, but Mother always had difficulty tolerating it. Coming from a fairly poor home of modern orthodoxy, my mother went to school. I am told that she even attended high school. She loved to read and did so all her life. Even after the invention of television, Mother read the daily newspaper and an occasional book.

Though my mother was born in the small village of Pławo, she spent most of her teenage years in Rozwadów, which was walking distance. She went to school in Rozwadów and had many friends there.

The general atmosphere of education and enlightenment in the town had a profound influence on her. For an orthodox girl, to attend public school in those days was a rarity and a great achievement. She was proud of it, and it boosted her self-esteem. She was a beautiful young lady with a slim figure, and since she knew how to sew, it was easy for her to follow the latest fashions.

I was told that Mother had many suitors who were interested in her before she met my father, but she picked my father. I am sure it was his brain, not his looks, that drew her to him. They were married in 1930. I know no details about their wedding.

My father received (not for free) a three-room apartment in one of Horodynski's houses, and after the wedding, my mother moved to Zbydniów. Though she was born in a small village, she spent her youth in the city. When asked where she was born, the answer was always Rozwadów.

Zbydniow or Plavo, by comparison, was primitive, like going back in time.

I don't think my mother was ever happy in Zbydniów. Every opportunity she had, she went into town. The fifteen- to twenty-minute ride by train made it very convenient. My parents had monthly train passes, and eventually, I got one too.

Every so often, a Yiddish theater troupe would make the rounds and stop in Rozwadów. My mother never missed a show. Once, she even took me along and we saw the renowned Yiddish actress Molly Picon perform. The show was *Yiddl mitn feedl*. My knowledge of Yiddish was very limited at that time, but Mother explained everything on the way home on the train. I enjoyed it immensely.

Many years later, possibly in the late 1970s, I saw Molly Picon perform in the Catskills.

After the show, I went to see her backstage and told her about my attending my first Yiddish show with my mother with her starring in it. She autographed the program and wrote a lovely note to my dear mother.

Unforgettable Visit to the Big Mansion

Mr. Horodynski's youngest child was a girl. Her name was also Anna, but she was lovingly called Haneczka. She was a year or two older than me. She was taller than me, with a peaches-and=cream complexion, curly blond hair, and blue eyes. Being an aristocrat had its advantages.

A French-speaking governess brought her up. Haneczka spoke fluent French, Polish, and possibly other languages. I met her once and will never forget that encounter.

It was on a warm September day, I recall. My father had some business to attend to and was going to meet with his boss at the mansion. The Horodynskis had just returned from their summer vacation in France, and rumors had it that Haneczka had brought back a talking doll. My curiosity was enormous. To meet the girl who was the envy of us all was almost impossible, but now the talking doll was an even greater incentive and challenge. Any doll was a prized possession, but no one had ever even heard of a talking doll then.

It was a Sunday. There was no school, and my mother was glad to send me away for a while. She had enough to do with my younger siblings, so she persuaded Father to take me along. The estate was nearby; actually, the fence of their backyard was across the street where we lived. It was an enormous estate situated on many manicured acres.

The mansion was surrounded by formal gardens, which Mrs. Horodynski personally supervised. Rumors had it that the chief gardener and chef were imported from France. There were several gardeners tending to the myriads of flowers and exotic plants. Mrs. Horodynski was particularly fond of roses, and the house was surrounded by every type, color, and fragrance. When the roses were in bloom, the scent was intoxicating. We could smell them in our house through the open windows.

There was a hothouse on the property, where hearty winter plants and flowers grew. A gravel road led from the iron gate to a circular driveway in front of the "big house." In early spring, lilies of the valley and violets of every color grew on both sides of the gravel path. There were many species of trees and lilacs, and Father told us that cherry trees grew on the perimeter.

Where there were no flowers or bushes, there was grass.

The big house, as we called it, was a stuccoed two-story, colonial-style white structure covered by a red tile roof. Several steps led to a large, wide portico flanked by four white columns. Heavy, carved wooden double doors led to a large vestibule. We used to see the roof.

My unforgettable visit to the big mansion was through the iron gate, and it looked very big, but when I came closer, it looked enormous. I had been to Rozwadów, the nearby town, where there were quite a few two-story buildings, but nothing prepared me for this. Without question, Horodynski's mansion was the biggest, most beautiful, and most enchanting house I had ever seen.

Somewhat removed from the house to the left was the garage for his black Buick. To me, it was the most magnificent machine known to man, and it moved faster without the aid of horses!

The stables, sheltering the beautiful stallions, were in the far corner of the estate.

Mr. Horodynski was an avid hunter and loved breading racehorses. There were horse-drawn carriages, riding horses, and horses to work in the fields.

Some house servants also lived in the compound. The whole estate was surrounded by a ten foot concrete wall that was capped with red tile and barbed wire.

All visitors had to ring a bell at the gate, and a servant would come out to inquire about the nature of the visit. If it was an unexpected visitor, the servant would return to the mansion with the information where the decision was made whether to admit the visitor or not. My father was a frequent visitor and was admitted without question.

My father often expounded about the opulence of the mansion and the people in it. He knew most of the house and its owners very well.

(When I saw the mansion again in 1989, my heart sank. The building was partially destroyed, probably bombed, and never rebuilt during the Communist era.)

Father let me ring the bell, and a short while later, an elderly man came toward us, dragging his feet along the gravel road. He looked tired and somewhat bent over. He made a crunchy noise with his shoes.

When he recognized my father, a broad smile appeared on his pale face, and his eyes fixed on me. The servant inquired who I was. Father introduced me and explained the reason for our visit. The man opened the gate and admitted both of us, saying that he was happy to meet me. As we walked toward the mansion, my father instructed me how to behave, mainly not to disturb him and not to touch anything. I fully understood and agreed. We followed the servant to the house, and he opened the heavy door for us, bade us good-bye, and disappeared through a side door. Another man, taller and younger, in a black uniform with shiny gold buttons came out and escorted us to the library, situated on the right side of the vestibule. He opened an ornate wooden door to reveal a spacious, enchanting room. The servant announced us to the proprietor as we entered the room.

Mr. Horodynski stood up from behind his enormous desk, shook hands with my father, and turned his attention to me. "And who do we have here?" he asked. My father introduced me again, this time by name. "Anna must be a popular name," Mr. Horodynski said, "because that's also my daughter's name. Would you like to meet her?" I blushed and shook my head in the affirmative.

Mr. Horodynski stated that since he and my father had some business to discuss, which would not interest me, I might as well enjoy myself. He walked out of the room and left the door open. Father and I sat down on a large chesterfield sofa upholstered in luxurious brown leather. It felt cool to the touch of my thighs. I was wearing a short dress made by my mother. It was white cotton with tiny rosebuds. As a child, I always wore short dresses. My mother made sure I was properly dressed for this historic visit.

My eyes roamed along the walls, taking in the most unusual sights. The wall to our left was lined with books, which filled two floor-to-ceiling, glass-enclosed bookcases. The other two walls were paneled with expensive wood and filled with paintings, stuffed birds, animal heads, and horns. A deer's head with enormous antlers hung high right above the large desk. At first I was frightened, thinking these animals might hurt me, but my father reassured me that these were dead animals and could not hurt anyone. I had many questions, but I was afraid to ask at that time. I didn't want to concentrate on any particular thing in order not to miss anything.

My eyes roamed along those mysterious walls, consuming every inch. I distinctly remember two large paintings, both hunting scenes. One was rather gory, depicting a wounded dear, dogs barking all around him and a hunter pointing his gun at the dead deer. The other was of flying birds and hunters pointing their guns at them. The paintings were very explicit and in vivid colors. I was in awe of all these artifacts.

There were other stuffed chairs in the room, but the focal point was Horodynski's enormous desk, laden with papers, books, an elaborate (probably marble) inkwell, a couple of richly framed family photographs, and many other objects. His similarly upholstered large armchair was placed directly under the enormous stuffed head of a dear with gigantic antlers. The deer's eyes were open and looked directly ahead.

For a moment, I stiffened, thinking, *What if he looks at me?* Quite a bit of time must have passed since Mr. Horodynski left the room, for I was able to absorb many details of that opulent library.

Father was getting impatient and began saying something to me, but just then, Mr. Horodynski returned with his daughter. Anna was a very pretty girl. She had an oval face with alabaster skin and blue eyes, and light-blond curly hair framed her angelic face. Haneczka, as she was lovingly called by her family, was taller than me and slimmer.

She was wearing an organdy dress of pale blue to match her eyes, black patent leather shoes, and pretty white socks. It was said that her wardrobe, as well as her mother's, was made in Paris. (In those days, *Paris* was an abstract word to me, except for the fact that two of my aunts lived there.)

In her arms she carried the most enormous and beautiful doll I had ever seen. I was completely overwhelmed. At that point, I just wanted to hold that doll. There was no smile on the girl's face, and I could tell that she was not very pleased to see me or make my acquaintance. Nevertheless, for properly bred nobility must keep appearances, she came into the room, stretched out her hand to me, and curtsied to my father. She motioned for me to follow her, and I did instantly. We stepped out into the sunlight, but she immediately went under a tree, seeking protection from the hot sun. We walked on a patch of grass in front of the house. She finally relinquished one arm of the doll to me, and we both walked the doll on the grass. She asked me if I would like to hear the doll talk. "Yes please!" I rushed to answer.

Haneczka pushed a button on the doll's back, and the doll said very clearly, "Mama."

I could not believe my ears. I was in ecstasy. "Does she say anything else?" I asked.

"Yes," Haneczka answered, "but I don't feel like tiring her, so let's put her to sleep."

She laid the doll down on the grass, and the doll actually closed her eyes. I was in awe of the doll, of the girl, of my surroundings. I asked Anna If I could come back some other time to play with her and the doll.

She said no very definitively. She added that her governess would not allow her to play with the likes of me. Today her father gave permission. It was his idea, but there would be no other time.

Though I was hurt by her answer, I did not want to lose any time or dwell on the rejection. The doll was the object of my interest at that moment. I wanted to know what she called the doll and what other tricks the doll did. The answer I received was an angry retort, that it was not any of my business. This nasty remark clouded my joy and brought tears to my eyes. I wanted to run inside, get my father, and run home as fast as I could, but I knew I could not disturb my father, and I also knew that I would never see this or any other doll like it as long as I lived.

I swallowed my pride and my tears and asked her to wake the doll so we could play some more and make her talk. She reluctantly obliged, picked up the doll from the grass, and made her say "Mama" again, but a few moments later, we were interrupted by the voice of the governess calling Haneczka in for her nap.

My heart stopped. I could not say a word. I didn't dare. Who was I to question the governess's authority? I only knew I hated her for interrupting our game, for depriving me of the long-awaited realization of my dream. Now the tears welled up in my eyes. I could no longer hold them back.

Haneczka gathered the doll into her arms, and we both advanced toward the house, where the governess instructed Haneczka to say good-bye to me and go to her room. The governess opened the door to the library and ushered me in. Both men were slouched over some papers on the large desk. At the sound of the opening door, their surprised gaze directed toward the door and they greeted us both. The governess explained that it was Haneczka's nap time. Mr. Horodynski was annoyed at the interruption, but the damage was already done. He knew better than to argue with the governess. It was known that she was very strict. Education and culture were an important part of the children's upbringing, and they employed the best money could buy. There was no contradicting a governess or a teacher.

The governess escorted me to the leather couch, and I climbed up and sat down. Father asked me to sit quietly and not disturb them. This was when I had the chance to examine the room closely.

I absorbed every detail of the decor, the art, the stuffed birds, and the animal heads hanging all around on the walls. I had certainly never been in such a room before or been surrounded by so many unusual, beautiful, and interesting objects.

The men soon finished their work, and Mr. Horodynski offered me a piece of candy from the large silver bowl on the desk. I slid down from the couch, helped myself to a candy, and sucked on it as my eyes roamed. It took probably about ten or fifteen minutes until the men finished their business. Father gathered the papers and returned them into his briefcase. The two men exchanged some words and shook hands, and we were ready to leave. At that point, I joined my father at the desk, curtsied, and said good-bye to Mr. Horodynski.

As we turned around to leave, I heard his voice behind me saying to my father, "Herszku" (that's how he called my father) are all your children so good looking and well behaved?" That was how he called my father. Father turned his head and smiled. Horodynski followed us out into the hallway. We said good-bye again and left the house. We walked back through the gravel path, in the direction of the iron gate surrounded by the heavy scent of blooming flowers.

As we stepped onto the road, Father turned to me and asked, "Did you enjoy yourself today?"

My mind, my thoughts, had not left the house yet. I was so overwhelmed and impressed by the stately mansion that I was speechless. I wanted that effect to remain with me all my life. I didn't want any other thought to enter my mind and disturb this picture of grandeur, riches, and style. Although I only saw a minute part of the big house, I measured everything else by what I saw. All I saw was the entrance foyer and the library, but my imagination ran wild. I could not truly visualize the rest of the house since I had never seen it or anything like it. Not until maybe forty years later, when I became a real estate broker and had access to many beautiful homes, could I truly compare, in my mind's eye, the Horodynski mansion. To this day, my favorite type of home is white stucco colonial with a red tile roof and white columns hugging the front entrance. I guess childhood impressions can last a lifetime.

Father was probably engrossed, as he often was, in his own thoughts, and he did not say another word to me all the way home. Entering our poor hovel (by comparison) must have sobered me up, because I ran to my mother and my first question was "Why aren't we rich like the Horodynskis? Why don't we have a beautiful big house like they do?" She looked at my father. He was silent.

Mother apparently had no answer and tried to steer the conversation in a different direction. Therefore, she asked, "What about the doll? Did you see the famous, talking big Parisian doll?"

Since I wanted so much to see that doll, Mother thought this would be the only object of my attention. The house had apparently such an overwhelming effect on me that the doll became secondary; this, nobody counted on. I used to see the roof of the house every time I passed it and had a notion that it might be big, but to witness its imposing majesty was something else altogether. Finally, Mother's eyes met mine, and she said, "One day you will also have a big and beautiful house." But this was not enough for me.

I wanted to know why we couldn't have a beautiful big house right now. If work made one rich, why weren't we rich? Father was always away from home, always working. The standard answer was "When you are older, you'll understand many more things and you'll understand this too." That answer did not satisfy my curiosity either, but I had no choice. The subject was closed. Father accused my mother of causing this tirade since it was her idea to send me along to Horodynski's house that day. A short argument ensued in Yiddish, which I did not understand. My parents must have attributed my complaints to childish dreams.

We all resumed our usual way of life, and I am sure that my parents forgot this event, but I did not. On Monday, I had quite a story to tell my friends. In the beginning, they didn't believe me because none of them or anyone they knew had ever even met Haneczka. She and her family were off-limits to us commoners. We were all in awe of them and only knew bits and pieces about their lives that got out through the help, but that was how things were in prewar Poland, and I'm sure in many other countries as well. The rich and the poor did not mix. Everyone knew his and her place.

Mr. Horodynski, though, had a fairly good relationship with his employees.

My Tonsil Saga

First Trip to Kraków

The following most memorable trip took place in the summer of 1937..

I continued to suffer from frequent colds and sore throats, and the local doctors were not able to help me. Mother finally took the famous military doctor's advice and contacted a renowned specialist in Kraków.

I don't recall his name, but I understood from my parents' conversations that he was a very capable pediatrician/surgeon who had helped many children. Mother decided to take me to Kraków for a consultation. It wasn't so simple to get an appointment due to his fame and busy schedule. The specialist was very much in demand. Mother asked my cousin Shulamit, who lived in Kraków, to use her clout and get me an appointment.

A few weeks later, we received a letter from my cousin informing us that we had an appointment. It would be in the summer, during my school vacation.

Mother and I took the train to Kraków. Until then, I had only gone to Rozwadów by train. This trip opened new vistas of unknown towns and villages on the way. It was a fascinating trip.

We arrived at dusk, and my cousin Shulamit and her little girl, Tamar, awaited us at the train station. The train station in Kraków was enormous and very ornate. There were several platforms and many tracks. Lots of people were going to and fro, carrying bags and luggage of every description.

It was overwhelming to witness this tremendous hustle and bustle around me. My eyes were everywhere as I tried to take in as much of this scene as possible. This was very exciting for me. Mother held my hand tightly and every so often had to pull me when I turned to look back at something and lagged behind. There was plenty to see.

The porters were busy, and we couldn't find one to help us with the luggage, so Mother had to carry our suitcase herself. A few minutes later, my cousin came running toward us, with Tamar in tow. This was a very happy meeting with hugs and kisses. After the initial exchange of greetings, Shulamit led us toward the street where horse-drawn carriages for hire were lined up. Shulamit hired a driver and gave him her address. The driver tied up our suitcase in the back, and we all got into the carriage that had an open top.

It was still light out, but the streetlights were on and some interior lights we on too. I felt like Alice in Wonderland. My eyes were wandering in every direction, trying to record the new and incredible sights around me, which were truly overwhelming. Five-, six-story apartment buildings and beautiful stores of every kind, and several cars and trucks passed us on the way.

People on the sidewalks rushed in every direction. My cousin inquired about the family, and Mother filled her in. She brought with her Tamar, who must have been three or four years old at that time, to entertain me while the women were talking about family matters, but I was very well entertained by the sights and sounds of the street and completely ignored her. I don't think I said one word to Tamar on the way to their home.

Their apartment was on the second floor of a multistory building on a beautiful, tree-lined street. It consisted of three or four rooms, and one of them had a door that opened to a balcony overlooking the street. This fascinated me. I could stand upstairs and watch the people down below.

I tried to take in and memorize as many of these new sights and sounds as possible so I could share my impressions with my friends, my brothers, and my nanny. My mother and I were given a separate private room just for the two of us. Wow, this was also a first for me. The trip and all the excitement of the day must have knocked me out, because Mother told me next morning that I fell asleep at the dinner table.

My doctor's appointment was the following morning. Mother, Shulamit, and I set out to see him.

This time, our means of transportation was the tram, another new experience. As we waited for the right one to arrive, several other trams passed in both directions. I had many questions regarding this new phenomenon. Cousin Shulamit was an able and willing educator. As our tram arrived and stopped in front of us, we took our seats and I looked out the window, observing all I could.

We alighted several stops later on a wide, busy street flanked by multiple-story gray buildings and my cousin announced that we have arrived at the correct address. We entered a cool small corridor, and again, Shulamit read a small tablet with the doctor's name affixed on a door. She rang the bell—another modern innovation for me. A moment later, a nurse in a white uniform opened the door and invited us to come in.

The waiting room was whitewashed. It had two tall windows facing the main street, which let the morning sun in. There were several chairs at the opposite wall and a small desk.

The nurse asked us to sit down and inquired which of the women was my mother. When my mother identified herself, the nurse asked her to bring a chair and sit at the desk in front of her.

She had many questions, which my mother ably answered. She glanced at the filled-out form and went to show it to the doctor in the adjacent room. A short while later, we were ushered into the doctor's office.

It was a small room, and it reeked of medicine and disinfectant. Though I was familiar with these odors, this was really oppressive. This room had white glass-enclosed cabinets full of gadgets, scissors, and other instruments still unfamiliar to me. The doctor was standing and reading my dossier.

The nurse told my mother to sit in an unusual big chair and hold me on her lap.

I had not seen the doctor's face yet and was afraid of him. I held back my tears and did as I was told.

I, This big specialist was supposed to know everything, heal me, and put me out of my misery forever. No more colds, no more sore throats and ear aches.

He finally turned around and greeted us. It was a kind face illuminated by a big smile. He made small talk with my mother then turned to me, asking all about my problems. I answered every question he asked.

He even complimented me on my knowledge of the subject and how well I spoke.

The doctor put a shiny round disk on his head, pulled up a swivel chair in front of us, and told my mother to hold my hands tightly. He told me to open my mouth as wide as I could and stick out my tongue. I knew this procedure by heart and dutifully followed orders. He gave me a big smile and told me to keep my mouth open and not move or talk. I had done this so many times before, so my fears began to wane.

I did not find anything unusual in this procedure. The examination took only a few minutes, and he said I could return to the waiting room while he talked to my mother.

I thought the doctor had performed a miracle and I would be well from now on. I joined Shulamit in the waiting room and happily told her that all was well and I would be fine from now on. She gave me a hug and kissed my forehead. I walked over to the window to watch the activities in the street. I was occupied with the outdoors until my mother came out of the doctor's office. She didn't look as happy as I was. She said we would have to do a few things the doctor ordered and in the end all would be fine. We were scheduled to see the doctor again in three days. I didn't mind at all and asked Mother if we could stay those three days with our relatives or if we had to go home and come back in three days to keep the appointment with the doctor.

My cousin announced that she would be happy to have us stay, and I was thrilled.

Because I behaved so well, I deserved a treat, so Shulamit would take Tamar and me to the park in the evening.

I got another treat, an ice cream cone, my favorite flavor: chocolate. I was thrilled.

The trolley ride home was just as fascinating, for this time, I sat on the opposite side and observed the other side of the street. When we got home, I was told to take a rest so I would have strength to enjoy myself in the amusement park in the evening. Apparently, all this excitement did tire me, and I slept while the women were busy in the kitchen, preparing the afternoon meal. I woke up when I heard Eliahu, Shulamit's husband, come home from his dentist office for the afternoon meal.

After we finished eating, Shulamit asked me to read to Tamar. I read slowly, but I could read most words.

We sat on the sofa, and I read to Tamar a children's book Shulamit gave me. It was a story about a girl lost in the woods, and it had many pretty pictures. After I finished reading, Mother and I took the trolley again and I was treated to the most popular tourist attraction in Kraków. We went to see the ancient kings' castle, the Wawel.

An uphill road led to an iron-gated entrance. On the way up there were many stalls displaying various tourist souvenirs. Mother bought me a green felt hat with a feather to match my outfit.

A photographer appeared out of nowhere, and we happily posed for him. He gave Mother his address and told her when she could pick up the pictures, and the address was right in the vicinity. Mother paid him in advance.

This was way before digital photography.

The tour of the Wawel was overwhelming—it was so vast and ornate. Mother told me the history of the kings who lived there and that some were buried there in crypts. At that time, I did not understand the significance of the castle.

I visited the Wawel again in 1989 and 2010. It's still standing there in all its glory for the world to see.

I treasured the photograph, taken in front of it, of me wearing my new green hat, but during the war, most of our pictures, including that one, got lost.

Another unforgettable gift Mother bought me on that memorable trip to Kraków was a *guralske* lamb fur coat. One day, she took me to the vast open-air market. There on one side close to a street stood, and still does, a fourteenth-century covered market, Sukiennice, which stood diagonally from the oldest church in Kraków, possibly in all of Poland. The church housed a wood-carved statue of the Virgin Mary by the artist Wit Stwosz (I hope the spelling is correct).

The Sukiennice was and is a very popular shopping arcade, where one can buy arts and crafts created by the local *gurale* (mountain people). They are very talented and created everything from embroidered sheepskin clothing to shoes, jewelry, carved wooden boxes, and many other objet d'art.

The stalls in the covered mall also offer amber jewelry, leather goods, wood-carved koo- koo clockcuc, and much more.

This beautiful, embroidered sheepskin coat has a history of its own.

After the tiring trip to the Wawel and the Sukiennice, I was tired both physically and emotionally and was told to take a rest. All these new and exciting experiences were truly overwhelming.

After dinner, we had a trip to the amusement park. The sun was setting when we boarded the trolley on the way to the amusement park.

It was a day of thrill, one after the other.

This ride was much longer. Streetlights and other illuminations totally changed the atmosphere. As usual, I made sure to sit near the window in order to absorb the scenery outside. The trolley traveled along a very wide avenue called Planty. These Plantys surrounded the old part of the city. This tree-lined avenue replaced a thick wall that was erected centuries ago to protect the city from attackers.

When we arrived at the amusement park, it was already dark. Here another enchanted surprise awaited me.

The large trees had illuminated tablets of every color hanging from large branches, advertising all kinds of stores and businesses. As Mother bought the tickets and we entered the park, the enchantment continued. Since I had never been to an amusement park before, Shulamit and Tamar graciously explained every attraction.

Tamar and I were put on several rides, while our Mothers sat on a bench and watched us enjoy the rides.

My excitement and joy were indescribable—I didn't want it to end.

When Shulamit came to fetch us, she announced that it was late and time to go home. Naturally, I didn't want to hear any such thing. Shulamit insisted, and when I got off, I noticed that my mother wasn't there. In response to my inquiry, Shulamit answered that Mother had to go take care of some things. Her answer put a damper on my excitement and joy. I looked around, but Mother was nowhere to be found.

Naturally, I was upset. We took the tram back home, and on the way I questioned Shulamit about my mother's sudden disappearance. When we got home, Mother wasn't there either. I began to cry, wanting my mother.

Shulamit tried her best to console me, but to no avail. I eventually cried myself to sleep.

When I woke up the next morning, I saw my father sitting on the edge of my bed, coffee cup in one hand, a cigarette in the other. When he saw that I had woken up, he put the coffee and cigarette on the night table and gave me a big hug. He also explained that Mother had to go home to take care of my little brothers. I was a big girl then and, on occasion, had to take care of myself. I was not thrilled to have my father as a substitute for Mother but had no choice.

He promised that we would have a great time together, but that never happened.

He was out all day, taking care of all kinds of businesses, but Shulamit and Tamar were very kind to me. Shulamit even took me to a café for an ice cream, just like a grown-up.

Two days later, Father disappeared at night and Mother reappeared in the morning. Now I understand that this changing of the guards must have been necessary.

The third day, the day of my mock tonsillectomy arrived. We had a doctor's appointment in the morning. I was awakened and told to dress. I was told that I could not have breakfast that morning because the doctor wanted to examine my throat very thoroughly for the last time and if I eat I might gag or vomit. I obeyed the order.

Mother, Shulamit, and I took a carriage to the doctor's office. The same nurse greeted us politely and ushered us into the doctor's office. The doctor was already there, waiting for us. He told Mother to sit on the same big chair and hold me on her lap, facing the doctor. We did as we were told.

This time, there were no smiles or pleasantries.

I began to shiver, and Mother sensed it. She did her very best to calm me. Then the nurse told my mother to hold my arms and hands at my sides. The doctor moved a white cart full of scary instruments toward us.

His smile vanished, and I was told to sit perfectly still, close my eyes, and open my mouth wide. I obeyed the orders but was petrified. The nurse stepped behind the big chair, pulled back my head at my forehead, and pressed it to my mother's breast.

Suddenly, I felt an excruciating, sharp pain in my throat. I was in shock but could not scream. Mother held me tight, and so did the nurse. A split second later, the sharp pain repeated itself on the other side of my throat.

The nurse let go of my head, and I was told to spit into the dish in front of my mouth. I opened my eyes and saw in that oblong dish two little bloody objects, and I was spitting more blood on them.

The nurse removed the dish and brought a clean one and handed me a cup of water to rinse my mouth but not to swallow any. Finally, my mother released my arms and I slid down her lap.

I was complimented by all for my exemplary behavior. The doctor told me that I was the best-behaved patient he had ever had. He also said that as of tomorrow, I could have all the ice cream I wanted. I was in pain and wanted to go home. I didn't even want to look at the doctor or nurse anymore.

I felt tricked, betrayed, humiliated, and in pain.

I could not talk or eat for several days. I was allowed to drink cold water and cold milk and lick ice cream. I liked the last one best.

After all this suffering and pain, I later found out that my tonsils were not removed, only partially cut.

Unfortunately, there was no relief to my suffering and illnesses.

That same evening, we took the overnight train to Zbydniów, and I didn't want to hear about Kraków and its wonders for a long time.

The sore throats, earaches, and colds continued to plague me.

Aunt Genia and Susan's Visit

Introduction to Bananas

Aunt Genia and her daughter Susan came from Paris to pay us a visit in Zbydniów just before the war. Susan and I were about the same age, though I think Susan was a bit younger. She spoke French and I spoke Polish, so communication between us was impossible. They stayed with my grandmother. We went to visit them several times, and they also came to see us in our home. Someone coming from the big city of Paris to Zbydniów in those days, and possibly today, felt like they were visiting another planet. They dressed differently, walked differently, and naturally, spoke differently. It was overwhelmingly fascinating.

When I first saw Susan—she was about my height—she was dressed in a gorgeous short pink dress. My mouth dropped, and my eyes almost popped out. The hem was finished with about an inch of white gathered lace, and the same was around the neck. I had certainly never seen anything so beautiful, not even in my dreams. She looked absolutely beautiful. My mother was very anxious to hear all about Paris. To her, Paris must have also been an unattainable dream. In Zbydniów, people could only dream about places like Paris. Susan and I were supposed to play together and stay out of the way while the two women were conversing, but, well, it was easier said than done. Susan was not only wearing a gorgeous dress, she also had the most beautiful big talking doll.

Haneczka Horodynski also had this type of doll, and when I saw this one, I was sure I would be able to play with it. After all, Susan was a cousin, not a stranger. Well, Susan was not obliging. She allowed me to see all the things the doll did when she pressed the buttons on her back, but I could not press any of these buttons myself. Teary-eyed, I went to my aunt and complained, and she, in turn, asked Susan in French to allow me to play with the doll. Susan refused. I was very upset and wanted to go home.

Mother was not ready to leave. My aunt walked over to the cupboard, took out a curved object of yellowish-green color, removed its outer layer, and handed it to me. I looked at her, not knowing what to do with it. "Eat," she said. It felt sort of slimy in my hand. I took a small bite, tasted it, and spit it out into my other hand, handing the rest of it to my mother.

At this point, I was angry at my aunt, thinking she was trying to poison me. With tears in my eyes, I retorted, "My mother cooks potatoes before she gives them to us to eat."

My aunt was insulted and angrily said to my mother, "A peasant stays a peasant. You can't teach them anything."

Now Mother was insulted, and they started arguing about how to bring up children. Well, Mother and I left in a huff, and the whole visit was a disaster. I later found out that the slimy, uncooked potato was a banana. My aunt and mother made up, but I never forgot the incident.

The Town of Rozwadów

The physical appearance of Rozwadów must have been similar to that of many other small towns in Poland. There was a square marketplace in the center of town, adorned with a water pump; otherwise, it was a vacant space. At the four corners of the market, four main streets of various widths and lengths had their beginnings, from which smaller, narrower ones extended in many directions.

The buildings surrounding the market were mostly attached to one another and were one, two, or three floors high. The municipal buildings concentrated close to the center. In front of each official building, there was a parking area designated for horses and wagons. We recognized them by the Polish flag displayed on each facade.

The roads were mostly cobblestone, but many side alleys were plain dirt roads that turned to mud after each rainfall or snow. The sidewalks around the market were slate or cement. Many were in disrepair at one time or another.

The houses were mainly of brick, stone, or concrete. The farther one ventured from the center, the more the scenery gradually changed. There were many wooden huts surrounded by fenced-in gardens to keep the livestock and foul in.

Rozwadów came alive with the addition of railroad tracks, and a new station was built at the end of the nineteenth century. This gave a tremendous boost to the development of commerce, industry, and travel. The railroad line connected the two big cities of Lvov and Krakow and made stops along the way bringing life and prosperity to those towns.

Rozwadów had Jews among its inhabitants as early as the beginning of the eighteenth century. The first synagogue was built around that time. The Jewish population increased rapidly toward the end of the nineteenth century.

Before the outbreak of WWII, there was even a Jewish mayor who doubled as judge, named Dov Bear Reich. I even recall a short visit to his home on a hot summer day. Father had some business to discuss with him and took me along. His name was mentioned in our home many times with respect and admiration.

Rozwadów had its share of turbulence, just as the rest of Poland did. Wars, riots, pogroms, uprisings, and other kinds of unrest were an integral part Rozwadów's history.

When the Ausro-Hungarian empire fell in 1918, Jews fled war zones in search of peace and safety.

Even though Rozwadów was a small town, education was of utmost importance. There was a Hebrew school for boys and separate one for girls (Bet Yaakov), several cheders (for younger boys), and a Hebrew library. There were sports clubs as well as Zionist organizations of different ideologies. It was a vibrant, important community of over two thousand at the beginning of the Second World War.

The town also boasted a long line of famous rabbis and scholars.

Rozwadów had a variety of business enterprises, factories, and shops. Many owned by Jews. Several years before the war, an ammunition factory was built adjacent to Rozwadów, and a town sprung around it. Soon, the new town was big enough to choose an appropriate name of Stalowa Wola, meaning "iron will." Eventually, it became big enough to swallow Rozwadów.

Today, most people know where Stalowa Wola is and have forgotten about Rozwadów.

Mother's Family

My dear mother, Naomi, was born in Pławo, a small village adjacent to Rozwadów. She was the youngest of eight children. Mother had three brothers and four sisters. The brothers were Chaim Wolf, Pincus, and Bernard. The sisters were Beila, Blima, Chana, Shifra, and my mother, Naomi. Their parents were Sarah and Zecharia Leib.

After Aunt Blima passed away at the ripe age of one hundred, we learned that their grandfather was a *dayan* (judge) in Kashau, Hungary. We had never heard or knew about this before. That must have been before WWI, when they lived in Hungary, which at that time was part of the Austro-Hungarian Empire. Aunt Blima had apparently instructed a nephew of her first husband to put this information on her tombstone.

My mother's sister Chana was already married since the 1920s and had two children, Yehuda and Dvorah. Her husband, Shea, was a tailor but could hardly eek out a living. My cousin Dvorah tells me that they had no money for rent, so after my grandfather Zecharia Leib passed away, Grandmother Sarah moved in with her eldest daughter, Beila, in Rozwadów and gave the house in Pławo to Aunt Chana and her family. When WWII broke out, they were expelled by the Germans and lived for a while in a refugee detention hall in Lvov, where they befriended a Russian man who talked them into going to Russia until the war ended, and so they did. Thanks to this man, they survived the war in the USSR and were spared the hardships of Siberia or other labor camps.

They returned to Poland when the war ended but did not return to their ancestral home after they learned of the horrors of the Nazi atrocities. As soon as the Jewish state was established, they made their way to Israel and remained there.

My aunt Chana and her husband had long passed, and so did their son Yehuda of a heart attack.

The only one still with us (as of this writing, 2015) and living in Israel is cousin Dvorah, who over the years had her share of tragedies and hardships. Cousin Dvora passed away in December of 2015 at the age of ninety-two.

Sister Shifra, the town beauty, was the tallest of them all. She had an alabaster skin, wide-set dark eyes, and high cheekbones framed by a mane of curly jet-black hair. She had a beautiful, broad smile that showed off her pearly white teeth. In other words, a striking presence.

Aunt Shifra was married to Shimon. He was shorter and bent over from sitting long hours at his sewing machine, and a cigarette in his lips completed the picture. Tailoring did not make him rich either. They brought up two very talented children.

One day, while in Rozwadów, I visited my aunt Shifra, and her daughter Zahava took me to a paper-bag factory where she worked part-time after school. She was already attending gymnasium (high school). The paper-bag factory was on the second floor of a building not very far from where they lived. We walked up the stairs and entered a large room where people, mostly young women, were standing around tables, folding and gluing the already-cut brown paper and making them into bags. The smell of the glue was very strong and unpleasant.

She allowed me to try my talent at paper-bag gluing, but I was not very successful. I stayed with my cousin a short while and told her that I had had enough and went back to my grandmother's house. I guess this work did not interest me much, and the smell of the glue was getting to me.

Zahava and Arie were teenagers at the outbreak of the war. They survived the war in the USSR and immigrated to Israel in 1946 or 1947. Zahavah continued her education in Israel and became a high school teacher. She married a hardworking, handsome David Zilbershtein. They brought up three talented and well-educated children, Moshe, Bilha (named after my aunt Beila), and Doron. As far as I know, they are all married now, are gainfully employed, and are raising the next generation. Zahava passed away in 2013 after a long bout with Alzheimer's disease. Her mother preceded her by many years and died of the same illness.

Uncle Shimon was the first to pass. The cause of his death must have been as expected, emphysema or lung cancer, after a lifetime of nonstop smoking.

Zahava's husband, David, is spending the remainder of his years in an assisted-living facility.

Zahava's handsome brother Arie, whom we also call Talmid Chacham, had some schooling during the war, but his thirst for knowledge was with him whether he attended a formal school or not. He was mainly self-taught. He speaks four languages and occupied high-ranking positions in several important companies.

Arie is married to Bela, a homemaker, and they also have three children, Chana, Oded, and Shulamit (named after our cousin Shulamit, who perished in the Holocaust).

Unfortunately, I don't know them well enough, so I have no details about their lives. I know they live in Israel and am sure they are well-educated and upstanding citizens. I am sure there are grandchildren too.

My cousin Arie is currently retired and devotes most of his time to studying the Holy Books and caring of the neighborhood synagogue.

Uncle Chaim Wolf was my mother's eldest brother, and he lived with his family in Rozwadów. He was not very tall and had a kind face, dark-brown eyes, and thick, somewhat bulbous nose, and short-cropped black beard framed his handsome face. He was always impeccably dressed in a dark three-piece suit. Outdoors, he usually wore a bowler hat, and his shoes always had a shine. He was soft-spoken, with a smile on his kind face.

Uncle Chaim Wolf was a self-educated scholar in Jewish as well as non-Jewish subjects. He was famous for his wisdom and knowledge of Jewish laws and scriptures. Many people, even some rabbis, would come to him, seeking advice on subjects of religion or law. He was what they called in Hebrew a Talmid Chacham (a scholar). He and his family lived in a two-story brick house in Rozwadów's market square.

The front window of their home displayed a bicycle or two, and in the back was a small repair shop where he would fix them. Above the entrance door hung a small sign in Polish stating the nature of the business. Their living quarters were on the second floor, but my cousin Dvorah challenged me on that, too, saying that their living quarters were mixed with the business. The store / repair shop was their source of income. None of us is certain if the house was rented or belonged to him.

Uncle Chaim Wolf was an active member of the Rozwadów Mizrachi, a Zionist religious organization, as well as other clubs and societies. The family took great pride in his knowledge and education. My aunt and uncle made sure that their children followed in his footsteps, so they went to university to obtain their secular education.

Cousin Shulamit, their eldest daughter, was a college graduate, something that was not very prevalent among religious Jewish families at that time. Both sons attended university at the outbreak of the war. My memory is very vague about his wife, Aunt Liftcha, as I didn't see her often.

Their sons, Moshe and Yehuda, were away at school, so I have no recollection of their looks.

Uncle Chaim Wolf had bad vibes about Hitler's rise to power and his anti-Jewish edicts. He had a school friend who had immigrated to Palestine in the -1930s. My uncle wrote him a long letter explaining the situation in Europe in the late 1930s and begged him for an affidavit for the family to immigrate to Palestine.

Unfortunately, the friend refused or could not fulfill my uncle's request. We still have a copy of that letter written in beautiful Hebrew. That friend might have saved the whole family.

Mother's eldest sister, Beila, was married to Itchale Kanarek. She was a short, slim woman. She spent most of her waking hours in the kitchen and must have been a good cook, because the aroma of her creations was very enticing and I liked eating what she prepared. The couple had no children.

Beila's husband, Uncle Itchale, had a delivery business; namely, he delivered beer and other soft drinks from the local brewery to stores and bars in the area.

After a day's work, whenever it ended, Uncle Itchale would come home, partake of the delicious meal my aunt had prepared, go out to their tiny porch in front of the house, and usually fall asleep while reading the newspaper.

After his rest, he would join the men in the synagogue for evening prayers. The synagogue was not only a house of prayer and learning but also a meeting place for men to exchange ideas, discuss politics, hear the latest gossip, and occasionally pick up some new business. Some would study a page of the Holy Books and, on occasion, pick up a stranger, a passerby, and bring him home for a meal. In other words, the synagogue in a small town in Poland was the pulse and the heart of its Jewish inhabitants.

Most of the Jews in these *shtetlach* (small towns) were religious, so it was natural that their lives were connected with the synagogue.

Uncle Itchale would usually return home from evening prayers with the evening paper under his arm. Weather permitting, he would sit in front of the house, on the tiny front porch, talk to some neighbors, sometimes join my aunt in the kitchen, or lose himself in the printed pages of the evening newspaper by the kerosene lamp. He would also inform my aunt of anything important that he might have read.

Wojtek, my uncle's helper, took care of the needs of the horse and the wagon and the merchandise. When his work was done, he would go inside to have his meals. He lived on the premises and, during the summer months, slept in the attic of the barn. Wojtek was a young man of about eighteen to twenty, with a short and stocky torso. His straight dark-blond hair was combed to one side. He had dark, shifty eyes, and I always felt that his glance followed me, accompanied by a smirk on his face.

At times, he tried to start a conversation with me, but I would run away. I was afraid of him.

A few years later, my premonitions came true. There was good reason to fear Wojtek.

He was the one who caused my grandmother's and Aunt Beila's demise.

The two women lived quietly in their home until the fall of 1942. When the Germans began transporting Jews to death camps, they went into hiding. A kind Christian neighbor hid them in his home for a while, until one day, this neighbor came home with the news of posters hung in the streets announcing that anyone hiding or aiding a Jew would be shot.

Naturally, he was afraid for his and his family's life. Everyone knew that the Gestapo was not joking, and he explained that he had no other choice but to ask them to leave. They understood his predicament but had no place to go. The situation in Rozwadów was as bad as everywhere else.

The man suggested they hide in the fields on the outskirts of town. It was September. Some of the crops had not been gathered yet and could shield them for a while, until another solution was found.

Though the idea sounded good, my aunt had to consider Grandmother's condition—she was undernourished, weak, and sick. My aunt Beila doubted if Grandmother could make it to the fields. And there were always German soldiers patrolling the streets. Aunt Beila refused to subject my grandmother to such an ordeal and decided instead to hide in the attic of the barn. The good neighbor agreed and offered them blankets and promised to deliver food whenever possible. They all agreed that it was the best choice under the circumstances.

But the hideaway was not of long duration.

The same Wojtek who had conveniently moved into my grandmother's house as temporary "caretaker" wanted to make sure that the rightful owners never returned. The idea of owning the house and the whole property was thus introduced to him.

He knew that my uncle Itchale was captured by the Germans, so there was a slim chance that he would ever return, and he wanted to make sure that the two women would not return either.

He looked for an opportunity to remove that obstacle too.

Food was scarce during the war, especially during winter months, so if one was seen buying extra food on the market, he or she was immediately suspected of hiding Jews.

The two women succeeded in hiding in that attic for quite some time.

Wojtek was uneasy, fearing that his old employers might return and claim the house. He wanted to make sure they were gone for good, preferably eliminated by the Germans. His wish was quite realistic.

A few nights later, he heard some noises in the yard. He went out to check what the cause of the disturbance was.

The good neighbor who delivered food to my aunt and grandmother saw Wojtek snooping around the yard while he was in the attic with his two wards. He was forced to wait long into the night until Wojtek went inside before he quietly and inconspicuously returned to his home. He warned my aunt that this would probably be the last time he would endanger his family's lives. They decided then and there to leave the safety of the barn and hide in the fields. They chose the following night for their escape.

Wojtek could not sleep while some mysterious things were going on right under his nose. He decided to stay up and find out. The night was cloudy and dark; Aunt Beila was thankful for that. She must have felt that God was protecting them.

As they slowly descended the ladder and walked out, Wojtek heard a faint squeak. He went out running with a pitchfork, ready to attack his victim. When he saw who it was, he dropped the pitchfork and ran to the Gestapo headquarters to tell them what was happening. Aunt Beila ran as quickly as she could, dragging my grandmother with all the strength she could muster. They made it to the wheat fields, but the Gestapo, with sniffing dogs, was in hot pursuit. The dogs picked up the scent and led the Germans directly to the spot

When they saw the two women sitting on the ground, trying to catch their breath, no questions were asked and no explanations were needed. The soldiers aimed their guns and shot them on the spot. Thus, Wojtek achieved his goal and became the owner of his former employers' home and everything in it.

The next day, he proudly told the story to all his neighbors, how successful he was in getting rid of the Jews. This account was related to my father by neighbors when he visited Rozwadów after the war.

My mother's older brother, Pincus, immigrated to America early in the twentieth century and settled in Brooklyn, New York. He married cousin Bertha, and they had three daughters, Anita, Leila, and Bernice. The only one I am still in touch with is Bernice, the youngest. Uncle Pincus also lived to a ripe old age.

The younger and most revered and generous brother, Bernard, had married a local beauty and moved to Frankfurt, Germany, in the early 1930s. Their only child, Ruth, was born in Frankfurt in 1931 or 1932. He opened a fabric store and did well for a time.

When Hitler made it impossible for Jews to live in Germany any longer, Uncle Bernard took his wife, Mala, and their daughter, Ruth, and fled Germany in 1938.

Uncle Pincus sent Bernard and his family an affidavit that enabled them to immigrate to the United States. On the way to America, they stopped in Rozwadów to see the family and say good-bye. I remember that visit, because he also came to see us in Zbydniów. He was a handsome tall, somewhat stocky man. He had a square face, small gray eyes, and thinning dark-brown hair. He was dressed like a lord. He came to Zbydniów alone, while his wife and daughter were visiting the other side of the family. He came by train early in the morning.

I remember Uncle Bernard donning my father's prayer shawl and phylacteries, standing in our bedroom and praying. He told my mother that while he was living in Germany, he strayed a little from his religious practices and did not pray every day. He said that this morning's prayer made him feel good.

Mother made him a lavish breakfast, which he consumed with pleasure. He said good-bye to me before I left for school and promised that we would see each other again.

The name America was familiar to me because two of my father's sisters were already living there and I heard the word mentioned many times, but it still sounded like a fantasy land far, far away.

A few days later, Uncle Bernard, Aunt Mala, and cousin Ruth said good-bye to the family and friends and continued their journey by train and ocean liner to the United States.

When they arrived in the United Sates, they first stayed with Uncle Pincus and his family in Brooklyn. After a short while, they rented an apartment and moved to Manhattan. Uncle Bernard brought with him quite a bit of merchandise from his store in Frankfurt. This gave him a start in his new business as a traveling salesman selling fabrics and ready-made women's clothes.

He continued in this line of work and ready-made women's clothes for many, many years.

Shortly after they arrived in the United States, the couple parted ways. The reason was never revealed to me. Subsequently, Uncle Bernard was introduced to a nice Jewish American woman by the name of Paula. I don't think Ruth ever forgave him for divorcing her mother.

Paula loved him very much and was very devoted to him. He continued to travel on business and help the family financially whenever he could. When I arrived in the United States, I saw him very often, whenever he came home from his business trip. I'll never forget my first baseball game ever. It must have been in the mid-1950s. It was the game when the famous Joe DiMaggio played and the legendary Marilyn Monroe kicked or threw the first ball. This was the only baseball game I ever went to see and will never forget it.

Uncle Bernard was a diabetic, like his sisters, but did not pay too much attention to his health. In January of 1960, he died of a heart attack in Mt. Sinai Hospital in New York.

Cousin Ruth had lived with her mother after the divorce. After her father passed away, they both moved to Miami Beach, Florida. We corresponded for quite some time, but I never found out where she really lived because she gave her address as a PO box.

Uncle Ichale, Beila's husband, survived the war in the Soviet Union. However, he also met an untimely tragic death.

My mother wrote very little of his life in Russia during the war. I only know that he was captured by the Germans at the very beginning of the invasion and attached to an army detail to dig trenches for the German Army. There were many Jews captured in those days, including my father, who were forced to do hard labor. One night, my uncle escaped into the woods and kept going until he found himself in the Russian-occupied zone of Eastern Poland. According to Mother, he lived in the town of Lviv until the Russians evacuated him together with other Jews to Siberia. Nobody in the family knew of his whereabouts.

He returned to Poland in 1946 together with the remnants of refugees. Upon his return, he learned of the crimes perpetrated by the Germans. He also realized that there was nothing to return to, as his wife and the rest of the family were murdered too.

When the State of Israel became a reality, he immigrated there. He settled in Jerusalem, the capital.

He experienced the same hardships as did all the other immigrants. Somehow, he gathered some money and opened a small fruit-and-vegetable store. Food was scarce in those days, so every food-store owner had to comb the farms and suppliers to get the merchandise. Since he was all alone, the task was overwhelming. So he looked for a partner in order to ease his burden. He found one, a close relative, a fairly young man who could lift crates or sacks whenever necessary. This was a great help. He was not a very old man yet, but after six years in the gulag during the war, even the strongest men were reduced to weak, sickly individuals. For a while, things went well between Uncle Itchiale and his young relative. He was glad to have a member of the family since he had none. He was quite content with what he had. A pious man by nature, he prayed daily and thanked God for his blessings.

However, this idyllic life did not last very long. One day, the two partners had a dispute regarding the business, and a loud and nasty argument ensued. The young man hit my uncle in the head with a stick. Neighbors arrived and separated the two. My uncle was taken to the hospital for treatment. He lost some blood and had several stitches on his forehead.

This part of the injury healed rather quickly, but the emotional part and the headaches persisted. His mind deteriorated, and he was eventually placed in an asylum and died soon after. He was buried in Acre, Israel. No known relatives were there during the burial rites.

The most beloved of my mother's sisters was Aunt Blima.

I first met her during the war, at the beginning of our expulsion. She was a tiny little woman, maybe five feet, maybe less, and was pious, was kind, and carried the biggest heart of all. When I met her, she and her husband, Heshl Koller, lived in Ulanów in a three-room apartment in the marketplace.

Uncle Heshl was literally tall, dark, and handsome. He was well educated in many subjects, spoke several languages, but was especially an expert in religious subjects. My aunt was very proud of being married to a Talmid Chacham (a scholar), which he really was.

They had also lived for a while in Frankfurt am Main, Germany, and returned home when Hitler made it difficult for Jews to live there.

Many years later, my uncle Srulek, who was born and lived in Ulanów until he married my aunt Mollie and joined her in the United States, and who knew Uncle Heshl, told me what an educated, well-mannered, and respected young man he was.

It was known that many young Jews who went abroad assimilated, changed their lifestyles, and even changed their names in order to blend in with the local population, but not my aunt Blima and uncle Heshl. While living in Germany, they absorbed additional knowledge and culture while remaining loyal to their own heritage until the day they died.

God did not bless them with children, so they loved everybody else's.

MOTHER

My dear beautiful mother, Naomi, was born in the village of Pławo, adjacent to Rozwadów. She was the youngest of eight children, three brothers and four sisters. Their parents (my grandparents) were Sarah and Zecharia Leib. The brothers were Chaim Wolf, Pincus, and Bernard, and the sisters were Beila, Blima, Chana, and Shifra. I think I have the chronology correct. At the outset of the war, all were married. All except Beila and Blima had children.

Mother was of medium height, about five feet three inches, and was slim, what they would call today a looker. She had a head of raven-black hair and had dark-brown eyes, slightly thick nose contained in squarish face, with an alabaster complexion. Then, she already knew that the sun has damaging affects on the skin, so she wore brimmed hats on sunny days. Mother knew how to sew, as all her sisters did, so she made sure that all her clothes were the latest fashion. When Mother was a teenager, after her father passed away, she and Grandmother moved in with Aunt Beila to Rozwadów. I was recently told by cousin Dvorah that Grandmother Sarah was well-to-do by the standards in those days and owned the house in Rozwadów as well as the one in Pławo.

Mother went to school in town and befriended many nice young people. New vistas opened up before her, and she thrived on city life. She acquired knowledge, sophistication, good taste, and many friends. I am not sure which schools she attended, probably a Jewish one, but she knew Polish well, quite a bit of German, and of course, Yiddish. She could read, write, and speak all three languages. She had a beautiful, untrained voice and loved to sing,

In Rozwadów, Mother also acquired a taste for the theater. Different Yiddish-speaking or Polish theater troupes used to come and entertain the public in small towns all over Poland.

Some of her married siblings also lived there, so she really felt at home.

As she was growing up many suitors tried to impress her and she was introduced to some of them and maybe dated a few, but she was not interested in any of them. Apparently she was waiting for the right one to come along. So when the matchmaker sang the praises of my father, she took the bait,,,. She was twenty-four and Father was thirty when they tied the knot in 1930.

She did not realize at that time that living in Zbydniów as a married woman would completely change her life, and it did.

She became a housewife with many responsibilities and a lot of work. She had to learn fast: how to garden, how to cook and bake, how to milk a cow and care for her, how to raise chickens, geese, ducks and everything else a country housewife needed to know.

She received some coaching from my aunt Reizl who lived next door. I was born a year later and when she became pregnant with my brother Israel, she demanded help. Father hired a young woman from a nearby village, who became our maid, nanny, housekeeper, later on my confidant, all rolled into one.

Expulsion

A few weeks after the German Army occupied Zbydniów, one of their officers came to inform us that they needed rooms for wounded soldiers and since this building was conveniently located and had a telephone and telegraph, it was very useful to them and we must vacate.

We did have an extra room, quite large, which we used as a summer kitchen, so Mother removed our belongings and relinquished the rooms to the Germans, but that arrangement was short-lived. There was a lot of activity around the house; German soldiers were coming and going, but they didn't bother us.

One day, a young German soldier, seeing me in the hallway, approached me and asked my name. I didn't understand what he was saying, so I turned around and ran to my mother. He followed me into the kitchen. Mother, knowing enough German, translated his words. I told him my name was Anna. "Oh, that's a pretty name," he said. "Sie sieht doch aus wie eine reine arien." She looks like a pure Aryan, he said to my mother. As a child, I had blond hair and hazel eyes. My hair color changed over the years, but the color of my eyes remained the same.

He took out a bar of chocolate and gave it to me. I thanked him in Polish and ran away. Mother was a little taken aback by his gesture.

The German Army marched in just before the High Holidays. My father, being a modern but pious Jew, went to pray in the neighboring village of Zaleszany, which was about three kilometers away. The village was centrally located, and several Jewish men, and on occasion their families as well, gathered at the home of the Elenbogen family to pray on some Sabbaths and holidays (when a quorum was required to conduct services). The Elenbogen home was larger than most, so they were able to accommodate a quorum and more if necessary.

Like in most of the surrounding villages, there was no synagogue in Zbydniów.

On Rosh Hashana holiday in 1939, my father went to Zaleszany alone to pray, and we stayed home. I do not know why Uncle Leibish did not accompany him; he was possibly hiding somewhere.

That afternoon, my father was the only one on the road on his way home from services. A German convoy was passing the village. Some soldiers must have recognized that he was a Jew and took advantage of the opportunity to hurt him. Two soldiers got off a jeep, grabbed my father, and beat him all over his body. They tore his prayer shawl, kicked him, and punched him in the face, all the while calling him varfluchte Jude. Damned Jew. When they were done with him, they dumped him on the road like a useless rag. Frightened and in pain, my father fell on the side of the road, unable to move.

The Germans left him there and continued on their way.

A short while later, a local farmer on a horse-drawn wagon was passing on his way home and noticed a body on the side of the road. He stopped to see who it was. Recognizing my father, he asked what had happened to him. He helped him up and dusted off his clothes. The farmer offered to take him home in the wagon, but Father declined, explaining that it was a holiday and riding was forbidden. The farmer let my father walk alongside and hold on to the wagon, and slowly they made their way home.

When Mother saw my father's sorry state, she screamed out loud—she almost fainted. We, the children, ran to him and cried when we saw his blood-covered face and hands. One of his sleeves was torn, and his clothes were disheveled and dirty. Mother helped him wash up and change his clothes. He went to bed hungry. He was not able to eat, as his mouth and nose were swollen and ached.

We were frightened, defenseless, and vulnerable. We did not know if this was an isolated incident perpetrated by a bunch of unruly German soldiers or a sign of things to come. After that incident, my father and the other Jewish men in the village went into hiding. I have no idea where.

During the first weeks of the German occupation, there was chaos. The Polish Army was retreating, the German Army advancing. The radio transmitted conflicting reports about the war, and there was great confusion. There was also great concern and fear in the Jewish community, and rightfully so.

Mother decided to go to Rozwadów to learn firsthand what was happening there, thinking that in the city they might have some protection from Polish authorities.

Grandmother Sarah was not feeling well in those days, and Mother was anxious to find out about her health.

Though we had access to a telephone, nobody else in the family did.

Another reason Mother went instead of my father was that they thought the Germans would not harm a woman.

Due to fear of the Germans, there was very little movement between towns and villages; people traveled only when absolutely necessary.

When Mother returned from Rozwadów, she was even more confused than before. No one knew what was going on and what the future held. The Germans placed notices all over town stating that the Jews must leave within twenty-four hours and go across the river San due east.

They also affixed posters in many prominent places proclaiming that any Christian hiding or aiding a Jew would be shot. There were not many Gentiles willing to help the Jews, and this order gave them the perfect excuse. There was no great love for the Jew in Poland, though after the war, we learned that there were many instances where Gentiles did help and saved some.

Jewish families, large and small, began gathering their belongings, getting ready for what they thought would be a temporary evacuation. Everyone thought that this exodus would be of short duration due to the war and the strategic position of the city, situated next to Stalowa Wola, which had military installations and a munitions factory.

The Jews were convinced that when the fighting in that area would end, and a border reestablished, everyone would be allowed to return to their homes. But Hitler had a different plan. Since we lived in a village, we had the honor of being personally notified by a German soldier.

The reason for the expulsion, we were told, was that the Jews were friends of the Soviets. This made them Communists and enemies of the Reich. The San River was supposed to become the new border between Germany and the Soviet Union when they divided Poland between them.

We were allowed to take what we could carry or load on a wagon but had to leave the furniture and everything else we could not carry. Phone lines in 1939 were a precious commodity. Since our building was one of three in the village that had a telephone, it was an important asset for the German Army.

Mother begged the German officer to allow us to stay. She told him she had three small children and had no place to go. He was quite gentlemanly and answered that he was only following orders that came directly from Berlin.

Father was still at the mill, working, unaware that in twenty-four hours, he would leave his office and home never to return. Mother telephoned him and told him the news. He knew that Rozwadów and surrounding villages had received the same evacuation orders, so he expected it to happen to us too, but when Mother called him, it really hit home.

The first thing he did was call his employer and longtime friend, Mr. Horodynski, who was stunned. He offered us his home. He told my father that we were welcome to move in with him and his family for a few days or weeks, until the whole thing had blown over. Father thanked him for his generous offer but could not accept it. Father answered that we, meaning our immediate family, were not the only ones being driven out.

There was also his sister and her family, his elderly mother, and his brother. Father believed that families should stay together, especially in such trying and uncertain times. Mr. Horodynski asked Father if there was anything he needed for the journey, like money or transportation. Father asked for a horse and wagon to get us to Rozwadów and asked his boss to find a replacement to manage the estate until he got back.

Mr. Horodynski was deeply moved by Father's concern and loyalty and said, "At a time like this, when you are being driven out of your home, you worry about my business? Go, and may your God protect you and your family. Whenever you return, the job is yours." Now Father was moved almost to tears. He went to Mr. Horodynski's home and gave him the ledgers and all instructions regarding the running of the business and all the keys. It was a difficult moment for both men.

They said their emotional good-byes, and Father walked home. When he arrived, Mother was in tears, trying to pack but not knowing what. She gathered all the valuables, jewelry, silver, crystal. She wrapped it all up in a neat bundle and sent Father to bring it to a Gentile neighbor, a good friend, for safekeeping.

That was Father's idea. Since we didn't know where we were going and how long we would be away, Father decided that those valuables would be safer with the neighbor.

Mother did not want to leave her jewelry. She thought the neighbors might take it. After all, it was tempting, as she had some valuable pieces. She said to Father, "What if our money runs out? Let's take the jewelry. We'll be able to sell it to buy necessities."

Father got angry and accused her of thinking about herself and her jewelry at a time like this. "After all, we'll be away for a few days or a week at most," he said. The jewelry went together with the rest of the valuables, never to be seen again. The only thing my mother kept was her wedding band, engagement ring, and watch. Father kept his pocket watch.

Mother insisted on taking some winter clothing and the heavy down quilts. She had a lovely black fur cape that she loved and decided to take it. When Father objected, she hid it among the pillows and quilts so he wouldn't see it. It was October, and nights were getting colder. About a year or two later, those quilts literally saved us from freezing to death.

The maid/nanny we had at that time was a seventeen-year-old girl. She was very nice and very loyal. Mother said that she was abused by her father, who was a drunk, and that was why she went into domestic service, to stay away from him. She didn't want to return home and wanted very much to come with us, but Mother explained that only Jews had to leave, not Christians. The girl cried bitter tears when the time came to say good-bye. We all loved her very much and also cried when she left. It was an emotional, tearful good-bye.

The next morning, Mr. Horodynski sent a horse-drawn wagon and coachman with instructions to take us wherever we wanted to go. The sky was dark, and the promise of rain was in the air. Father and the coachman began loading our belongings onto the wagon. Mother insisted on taking some kitchen utensils as she claimed that with small children, one must always be prepared for every eventuality. Children do not understand why they have to be hungry or thirsty. My father was annoyed, as he liked to travel light.

Later, we were all thankful for Mother's foresight and sense of responsibility.

My aunt Reizl and her family also loaded their belongings onto the wagon. We picked up my grandmother Leah and uncle Leibish on the way to Rozwadów.

My aunt Reizl criticized my mother for loading so many things onto the wagon. There was not much room left for the people to ride. Eventually, only the children and Grandmother were riding, and the others followed on foot. The distance to Rozwadów was about eight kilometers. Since my cousins were older, they were asked occasionally to relinquish their seats so that the adults could ride for a while and rest their feet. When the coachman saw how much was being loaded and how many people were coming, he realized that one horse would never make the eight-kilometer trip with such a heavy load. He went to Horodynski and asked for an additional horse. The two horses were very effective.

When the fateful moment came to leave our home, the scene was very sad, to say the least.

Mother's eyes were already red from the tears she had shed since the previous night. We said good-bye to the postmaster, with whom we also left the keys to our apartment. Father asked him to keep an eye on what we had left behind. The postmaster promised to do his very best. Father called his boss, certainly not knowing that he would speak to the man for the very last time. He thanked him for his concern and the transportation and gave him additional instructions regarding the running of the estate. Father's loyalty to his employer was beyond reproach.

As we approached Rozwadów, we saw other Jewish families on foot and in wagons moving in the direction of the San River. My mother insisted we go first to see her family and check whether they were also leaving.

My father was anxious about his sister Hannah and other relatives who also lived in Rozwadów. He directed the coachman to my grandmother Sarah's house, where we got off, and then Father continued to my aunt Hannah's house to find out what they were doing.

The town was in pandemonium. German soldiers were everywhere. People with question marks on their sad faces, some with tears in their eyes, were moving in all directions.

Grandmother Sarah was in bed and very happy to see us. I remember her wrinkled face and smiling lips vividly. She always wore a kerchief on her head. Mother called it a *shtern teechl*. It was a small kerchief with embroidery or other ornaments on the forehead. Grandmother Sarah always smiled and spoke softly, possibly because of weakness. She was a sick woman—it might have been her heart.

My brothers and I stayed with her, while Mother talked to Aunt Bailah in the kitchen. A while later, Mother came in with some warm tea and cookies for us.

The rain was heavy at times, and Mother worried about us getting wet and possibly sick. She was also worried about our belongings getting wet on the wagon outside.

Eventually, Father returned with the wagon, our bundles already wet. He announced that we must hurry and get to the other side of the river to reach Ulanów before dark. The reason they chose Ulanów was that it was the closest town and my mother's sister Blima lived there. She would be happy to put us up for the night.

The bridge over the river San, which was sizeable and strong, had been bombed by the Germans a few days earlier and was partially destroyed. The Germans were aiming to destroy as many roads and bridges as they could in order to prevent the Polish Army's escape.

It was just the beginning of the rainy season, so luckily, the river was still shallow. Some people were able to cross it on foot where water in some areas was about knee-deep. German soldiers blasted orders through loudspeakers, urging the people to move faster. We were told that we would have to be out of the area by nightfall.

Some people already knew that the Germans meant business and that they delivered on their promises. When they issued an order, they expected it to be carried out.

Panic-stricken people desperately tried to save their lives. Father told us that his sister Hannah and her family were also leaving town. She was hitching a ride with my aunt Reizl.

It was then that Mother announced that her sister Beila was staying put in order to take care of their ailing mother. Grandmother protested, arguing that the Germans would be kind to her because she was old and sickly and even spoke some German. After all, they were nice, educated people. She also had very good neighbors who would surely help her if needed be. My father tried to explain that in war, kindness and education have no meaning. The other reason for my aunt wanting to stay behind was that her husband, Itchale, was apprehended by the Germans a day earlier together with some other men. They were taken to clear roads, dig trenches, and perform other manual labor. My aunt decided to wait for him at home so that when he returned, they would all leave together. They owned a horse and wagon, so Grandmother would be comfortable in case they would have to travel a distance.

My uncle Chaim Wolf Birnbaum had managed to persuade a good friend, a Christian, to hide him and his wife for a few days until he was able to notify his children about the situation in Rozwadów. They all had a "good" plan and a "good" excuse for not leaving their home and coming with us.

It was time to say good-bye. Tears were flowing abundantly, and there were promises to keep in touch as often as possible. Our destination for the time being was Ulanów, another small town on the other side of the San River. My aunt Blima, mother's sister, lived there so we were going to stay with her until the situation became clearer.

A steady October rain was falling, and it was cold. Mother bundled us up. I was wearing my new sheepskin coat that Mother had bought for me that summer in Kraków. Mother was a strong believer in dressing us warmly in cold weather. Father wanted to leave Rozwadów as soon as possible so that we could arrive in Ulanów before dark. Ulanów was several miles away. The unpaved, muddy roads and driving rain hindered everyone's movements. The roads were crowded with wagons, carts, and people. This slowed our trip considerably, and when we reached the riverbank on the Rozwadów side, we witnessed true chaos. The wooden bridge over the San River, which was bombed by the Germans, was partially repaired, but it was weak and many hesitated to cross. Our coachman said he knew a shallow area of the river where we could cross, and so we did, and many others followed us. There were several German soldiers at the foot of the bridge, directing traffic; they were urging the crowds to move faster. They were not too keen on getting soaking wet while watching masses of Jews on the run. Some enterprising Gentile fishermen with boats offered their services for a handsome fee and took many evacuees across the river. Not everyone had a horse and a wagon, so the boats were a welcome means of transportation, which speeded things up.

The driver we had now was not Horodynski's employee. Mr. Horodynski's driver delivered us to Rozwadów, and Father sent him back home. At that time, we were not sure of our destination, and Father hired a different driver to take us to Ulanów. As soon as we reached the other bank, the driver hastily unloaded our belongings and piled them up under a tree. Mother was in shock. He made us get off the wagon, turned around, and said that he was going back across the river to bring other families. He was paid in advance to take us to Ulanów, but my father failed to supply an address, so he figured he would unload us on the other bank and go back for more Jews. He saw a good opportunity to make extra money and wanted to take advantage of the situation. Father argued that he paid him for door-to-door service and he would not settle for anything else. The driver reluctantly reloaded our bundles on the wagon and took us to my aunt Blima's house, which was a short distance away.

We could hear the German soldiers yelling at the people, urging them to move faster. We even heard occasional gunfire but did not know if it was in the air or aimed at someone. It was getting dark, and it was difficult to see what the situation was on the other side of the river.

My aunt Blima, being the angel that she was, welcomed us to her four-room apartment with an equal amount of joy and sadness. The other family members went to stay with other relatives in town. My aunt told us that Ulanów was full of Russian soldiers but they did not bother anyone. They did urge the townspeople to stay indoors for safety reasons.

We were soaked to the bone, and so were all our belongings. We saw some of the Jews being evicted and their homes occupied by the German Army, but we were not aware of a mass expulsion.

The first order of the day was to strip us of our wet clothing and feed us. My aunt did not expect us, and there was no dinner awaiting us. But there was hot tea and cake to warm us and fill our bellies.

My brothers and I were placed in a large bed under a fluffy down quilt to warm our bodies.

Mother dried some clothes by hanging them on chairs around a wood-burning stove. It did not take long, and we were dressed in dry, warm pajamas. The warm fabric felt good against our cold bodies.

I overheard some of the discussion my parents were having with my aunt and uncle. Though it was in Yiddish, I understood a few words. Together they tried to find a solution to our predicament.

I did not hear the whole conversation because, just like my brothers, I soon fell asleep in the warmth of the down quilt. The next morning, I woke up to the wonderful aroma of freshly baked bread and other delicacies permeating the small apartment.

At first, it was frightening to look around at the unfamiliar objects in the room. Noticing my brothers still asleep, I recalled the previous day and the reason for being there. The room was chilly, and a driving rain was still beating on the windowpane.

I looked for something to wear, but none of my clothes were in sight. I heard voices in the next room, one of which was my mother's. I did not want to call her so as not to wake my brothers.

I wanted some individual attention. I wanted her all to myself.

I looked around and noticed a large sweater hanging on a chair. I climbed down from the high bed, wrapped the sweater around me, and went barefoot to the kitchen, where the voices were coming from. Mother was sitting at the kitchen table, peeling potatoes. My aunt Blima was at the stove. Upon seeing me enter the room, Mother noticed my bare feet. She jumped up from the chair and scooped me up into her arms.

I was immediately scolded for walking barefoot. Mother never allowed us to walk barefoot except in the summer. Mother's theory was that cold feet were an invitation to a runny nose. There must be something to this theory, because to this day, when my feet are cold, I get a chill and often a cold.

I felt safe in my mother's arms. She sat me down at the table and went to fetch socks and shoes for me. My aunt came over, kissed me on the forehead, and asked what I would like for breakfast. She was a strong advocate of good nutrition. I was somewhat bashful and did not answer. I also did not know what I could ask for. "Let me surprise you," she said. "I'm sure you will like it." Mother returned with my shoes and a pair of dry socks and handed them to me. She said that I had plenty of time. It was raining, and we were not going anywhere.

I asked where Father was, and she answered that he went to visit some relatives. Aunt Blima was making French toast out of leftover challah. The challah was dipped in eggs and fried in butter, and the wonderful aroma was making me even hungrier. After all, I had not eaten since the previous afternoon, except for the tea and cookies upon arriving at my aunt's home. Before I was served this delectable breakfast, I was told to wash up and recite my morning prayers. I already knew my prayers by heart, so it didn't take long. My aunt Blima asked me to recite them aloud so she could hear too.

She wanted to make sure I did not miss a word. She complimented me when I finished and said that she would teach me some new ones.

My aunt was a deeply religious person and knew all the prayers by heart. She memorized not only the daily prayers but also the long chapters for all the holidays. She also put to memory many passages from the Bible and other holy writings.

I must have devoured the food in an instant. Aunt Blima smiled with satisfaction and asked if I wanted more. I nodded as she put a glass of milk in front of me and proceeded to make more delicious French toast.

While she was preparing the food for my brothers, she was questioning me about school—what I learned in cheder, who my friends were. Were any of them Jewish? I did not know my aunt Blima very well then. She and her husband, Heshl, had lived in Frankfurt, Germany, for many years. Their business was textiles, as was Uncle Bernard's (my mother's youngest brother). When Hitler came to power, life for Jews in Germany became difficult. Uncle Bernard, with his wife, Mala, and daughter, Ruth, immigrated to America in 1938, and Aunt Blima and her husband returned to their home in Ulanów, Poland. They were not blessed with children. That was the reason she adored everybody else's.

My brother David's crying interrupted our tranquil conversation. Mother left the kitchen and, a short while later, returned with both boys. David was in her arms, and Israel was close by, holding on to her skirt. They also felt uneasy in these unfamiliar surroundings. My brothers were served breakfast (after washing up and reciting morning prayers) and ate it ravenously. My aunt Blima always found a way to make people pray and always fed everybody. We finally all got dressed, but there was nothing for us to do.

I went to explore the apartment. I walked into a room that resembled a dry goods store that doubled as a dining room and a library.

My uncle Heshl was sitting behind a counter, looking over some large books. He was a tall, slim, very elegant-looking man. His black beard and side curls framed his handsome, pale face, and his eyes were a shiny black. He was wearing a black hat, and his clothes were black too, except for the collar of his white shirt.

Upon hearing the door open, he raised his head, turned to the door, and greeted me with a smile. He began to speak to me in Yiddish, but when he saw that I didn't react, he realized that I didn't understand, so he switched to Polish. His words were measured and spoken slowly and precisely. I was later told that my uncle Heshl Koller was a highly educated man; he was fluent in at least four languages, a known Bible scholar, and very pious. My aunt was very proud of his accomplishments. It was a great honor, and still is, for a Jewish woman to marry a bible scholar.

It kept raining on and off. Stormy, windy days kept us close to home. Though my aunt's apartment was small, she made every effort to make us comfortable.

We, the children, received special attention. Our hosts were very happy to have us around and catered to us hand and foot. My uncle was a great storyteller, and he exercised his craft with us. Every evening at bedtime, he would tell us a story. They were primarily stories from the Bible, but he knew how to embellish them and made them sound very interesting. Even I, the insomniac, was anxious to go to bed just to hear his stories.

My uncle spoke Polish beautifully and occasionally would throw in a rarely used word just to test our knowledge and check if we were paying attention. Naturally, David was too young to understand, but he aimed this exercise at my brother Israel and me.

My mother and father used to tell us bedtime stories too, but none were as fascinating as Uncle Heshl's.

During the day, weather permitting, Mother would take us for a walk in town. My aunt and uncle lived in the center of town, in the market square. Ulanów did not look much different from Rozwadów, so it looked somewhat familiar.

The entrance door and window of my aunt's home faced the market square. This fact alone made it a fascinating place to be. On market days, usually Mondays and Thursdays, there was a lot of activity outside. Wagons of all shapes and sizes laden with wares of every description passed in front of our window. All kinds of merchandise—sacks of flour, grain, autumn fruits, vegetables, large cans of milk and milk products—were on the way to their stalls. Market days were good for my uncle's business too, because, if the peasants sold their merchandise, there was a chance they might come in and buy something from him.

On one such day, Mother decided to go to the market to shop. We wanted to come along, but that was out of the question due to the inclement weather and amount of activity in the area that could be dangerous for us. We were told to stay home, but we were allowed to stay in the "store" and look out the window. Uncle brought over a small bench, and all three of us sat at the window and watched with fascination the activities outside.

I think it was more interesting than going to the market itself.

There were wagons and pedestrians going to and fro. Peasant women wore colorful shawls and skirts. We had never seen so many people, animals, or wagons at one time in Zbydniów.

Uncle Heshl was our babysitter, and we liked that because he was willing and able to answer any questions we asked. He was a very patient man and, as I mentioned, very well educated.

I am sure he enjoyed being with us too.

Our observations were occasionally interrupted by the bell at the entrance door, and a customer would come in. When that happened, we knew to sit quietly and just observe. Aunt Blima stayed home, too, just in case we became unruly and Uncle could not manage us. She kept busy in the kitchen. When Mother returned several hours later and asked Uncle if we behaved, he gave her the rundown and offered to repeat the job whenever she would allow him. He said that because we behaved so well, we would each get a bar of chocolate after dinner. We were very happy and ran over to kiss him but stopped short because of his ticklish beard. He understood our predicament, and we each got a hug and a kiss on the head.

My father was busy going from relative to acquaintance to gather information about the war and tried to decide what to do next. We knew we could not remain in Ulanów indefinitely and could not remain in my aunt's house much longer. We certainly could not return home either.

My uncle Srulek, who also lived in Ulanów and knew them well, told me about them fifty years later. He told me that my uncle Heshl was a well-to-do man, a known Talmud scholar who was much respected by the community.

It is known that many Jews who went abroad assimilated, changed their lifestyles, and even changed their names in order to blend in with the local population, but not my aunt Blima and uncle Heshl.

While abroad in Frankfurt, Germany, they absorbed additional culture, knowledge, and sophistication but remained loyal to their heritage and religion to the day they died.

One day, Uncle Heshl invited me to come into his room, the room I had mentioned earlier. I think it warrants a description.

At first glance, I saw a wall of bookshelves filled with books of all sizes. There were also shelves on the opposite wall, but those contained bolts of fabric. In the middle of the room stood a large oblong dining room table of highly polished wood, surrounded by chairs. My uncle walked over to the table and sat down. He invited me to sit next to him. I obliged, somewhat reluctantly.

He asked me if I knew any Hebrew, if I could read and write. I told him that during the recent summer, I attended a cheder in Rozwadów and learned how to read a little, but not to write. He took a book off the shelf, opened it, and asked me to demonstrate my ability. I read a few lines. When I finished, he smiled with satisfaction and praised my accomplishment. I asked permission to walk over to the window. He nodded, and I approached the window slowly and looked out.

The rain had subsided.

There were puddles everywhere, and horse-drawn carriages were spraying passersby.

It was a gray, cold morning. The street looked very busy. I was told that a home on a main street facing the market was considered a prestigious address then.

I remained at the window for quite some time, fascinated by the hustle and bustle in the street. People of all ages and sizes, dressed in different garb, were constantly on the move. Some were on bicycles, some on horseback, and some in carriages, but most were pedestrians. A lot was going on outdoors in Ulanów. A complete opposite of Zbydniów.

My uncle returned to his studies. It was quiet in the room. All the commotion was outdoors. A while later, my aunt came in with a hot glass of tea and placed it on the table in front of her husband, then she came over to me and asked how I liked it there. Naturally, I answered that I did. "Then maybe you will stay with us for a while?" she asked.

"Can the rest of the family stay too?" I asked back.

She smiled broadly and answered in the affirmative.

We stayed about two or three weeks. During that time, many things happened.

The occupiers changed several times. Occasionally we heard gunfire at night and sometimes even during the day. It was Russians against Germans, Germans against Russians, but there was no Polish Army in sight. One day, when we were under Russian occupation, we received an order to evacuate within twenty-four hours. The Russians and Germans had decided to make the San River the border between the two entities and evacuate the population, primarily the Jews, as far as possible from the frontier. It was supposed to be a safety measure. The first people ordered to leave were nonresidents, and that meant us.

At this time, I would like to turn my attention to my brother David. This was when I first saw how this poor child had suffered.

One afternoon, as I walked into my aunt's kitchen, I witnessed something horrible and heartbreaking concerning my youngest brother, David. I had never seen this before, because Mother probably did not want us to see or to know. She must have thought we would not understand. This angelic four-year-old child suffered from a most severe case of hemorrhoids. He went on the potty, and when he finished, Mother put him on her lap facedown and pushed a bloody red blob back into his rectum. The bowel, which was protruding from his rectum, was about two to three inches long, all covered with blood, and Mother pushed it back into him with a ball of cotton. The child was red in the face, tears of pain rolling down his cheeks, but he did not utter a sound. I assume he was treated by a doctor, but it was possible that in 1930s, medicine had no immediate cure for such an ailment. I will venture to say that his condition might have been neglected. Mother probably tried her own cure at first, which did not work. I also assume that fiber, liquids, and diet were not explored as a remedy.

Now, as we were embarking on an uncertain journey to an unknown destination, it was not the proper time for healing such an ailment. I remember, a few months later, when Mother was away visiting our relatives in Rozwadów, David still suffered from the same condition, and I was the one who pushed the bleeding blob back into his rectum. The poor child suffered in silence. I don't know when or if this condition was ever cured or corrected.

Today, as I recall with horror the suffering of my dear brother, my heart breaks for the child, and tears are rolling down my cheeks. David was a very handsome boy and a very obedient child.

I have only one picture of him from before the war. It's a photograph of all three of us with Mother, taken shortly before the war and sent to Uncle Pincus, who lived in Brooklyn. (I found it in his album, and he gladly gave it to me.) David was the most beautiful child among us. God took him very early in life. David was seven years old when he passed away in Siberia.

After two or three weeks of uncertainty in my aunt Blima's house and the town occupiers changing almost every night, we were told again to move along. The Russians ordered all the Jews who were not residents of the town to get out and go farther east.

The decision was made for us, so my father did not have to speculate what to do next. He hired a coachman and wagon with two horses, and on a cloudy, dreary late-October morning, we set out on the next leg of our journey.

My father's sister Reizl and her family, my grandmother Leah, and Uncle Leibish followed us in another wagon, and we all continued for parts unknown eastward.

We heard that the Germans were confiscating Jewish property and burning homes, synagogues, and Holy Books. Even if we could go back, it was not a very pleasant atmosphere to go back to. So we decided to go in the opposite direction, as we were ordered. Another tearful good-bye ensued.

Nobody could foretell when or if we would see one another again.

As a matter of fact, we never saw Uncle Heshl again. And we did not see my aunt Blima until after the war.

A few days later, all the resident Jews in Ulanów were ordered to go east, among them my aunt Blima and uncle Heshl. I don't know how it happened, but they also wound up in Siberia. (After their release from Siberia, they settled in Bukhara, Uzbekistan. Her handsome and learned husband died of typhoid in Bukhara in the early 1940s.)

There was a long procession of horse-drawn wagons on the muddy road going in the easterly direction. About midday, it began to rain, and we were getting wet again.

Mother tried her best to protect us from the cold rain, but there was no use. After a while, we were all soaked to the bone. My relatives traveled along with us in another wagon. The wheels of the wagon were sinking in the mud, and the horses struggled to pull their burden. My parents and the coachman got off the wagon to lighten the horse's burden. They walked along the wagon knee-deep in mud. We passed small villages one after another. Suddenly, we heard the noises of truck engines coming from a side road. It was the German Army. We were under the impression that the area was occupied by the Russians, but probably not everywhere. One truck passed us and went to the front of the procession.

The Germans yelled "Halt," meaning "stop." Everyone obeyed the order. The Germans ordered all the men to stand on the side of the road in a single line.

There was one old man with a white beard on a wagon in front of us. They made him get off the wagon and stand in line with all the others. A younger man, probably his son, who was traveling with him begged the German soldier to spare the old man, but to no avail. No one knew yet what was going on and why all the men were separated. My mother, being the brave soul that she was, approached one of the German soldiers and asked him why they were doing that.

She spoke some German. He was surprised to hear his native tongue and answered rather politely that the men were needed to help dig trenches and help repair a bombed-out bridge. The German soldiers were too tired and too important to do such manual work. This was work for Jews and other lowlifes. Mother immediately began begging him to release our father. She pointed out that she had three small children; she was just thrown out of her home and did not know where she was going.

Her pleas fell on deaf ears. He pushed her away and gave the order for the men to march and follow his jeep. The men were surrounded by other soldiers with pointed rifles.

About eighteen or twenty men were taken away by the German soldiers and led away on a narrow muddy road. The terrain was flat, and we passed through empty fields, from which the harvest had been recently collected. Our eyes followed the group for a while, but they soon disappeared from view due to the heavy fog.

The whole wagon train stopped, and the helpless people discussed their options, though in reality, they had none. Women and children cried, including my mother and the three of us.

No one knew what to do. There was nobody to turn to for help. It was cold, and the driving rain did not let up. We, as well as all our belongings, were soaked through. Mother decided to take us to the next village, where we would wait for Father. Mother relieved the coachman from his duty and told him to go back home, as there was nothing for him to do. He would have to hitch a ride to get back to Ulanów. The horse and wagon were ours, so at least we had transportation.

When we encountered the Russian Army farther down the road, they also advised us to go east. The Russians said that the new border between Germany and Russia would be along the San River, and it was not advisable for civilians, especially Jews, to remain close to the border. They were right. I may have mentioned that our relatives on my father's side traveled with us in a separate wagon.

All of our adult male relatives were taken away by the Germans, together with my father. Only women and children remained.

The villages in Poland were in close proximity, so we arrived at the outskirts of one pretty soon. Mother knocked on the door of the first house and asked if they could put us up for a night, but they had no room as they already had people staying with them. She repeated this action several times and finally found a family willing to take us in. The village huts were small and unable to accommodate too many guests, but many families eventually found refuge from the harsh elements. It was getting dark already. We were hungry, wet, and cold. The warmth of the burning hearth inside the hut and the smell of the evening meal on the stove were very welcoming, no matter how cramped the quarters were.

We unloaded our belongings, and everything was soaking wet. Mother begged the lady of the house to allow us to warm up near the stove and boil some water for tea. Mother used her own utensils because of kashrut. She bought some milk from the woman and made some porridge and tea for us.

We ate in great haste as we were starved. Though we were usually fussy eaters, that night we were glad to have anything. The proprietor brought in a large bundle of dry straw from the barn, spread it on the floor near the hearth, and made a bed for us. We fell asleep instantly. Mother asked him to tend to the horse too, which he did.

Mother removed some of our wet clothes in order to dry them overnight. The only way to do that was to spread the clothes on top of the brick oven, which stayed warm for many hours after the last spark went out. I had worn my beautiful first fur coat, which mother had bought for me in Kraków in the famous Sukiennice market. This famous market was erected around the thirteenth century. The outside was yellowish stucco with arches on all sides. It might have been the first shopping mall in history. (It is still standing in the middle of a tremendous squire in the middle of Kraków. It still serves the same purpose for which it was built.)

These fur coats were created by the mountain people called Gurale in the Tatra Mountains in Southern Poland. These were sheep shearlings, beautifully hand-embroidered with colored thread. It was the first time I had worn the coat. The rain soaked it through and through. Mother wanted to dry it overnight so I could wear it the next day. She meant well. Not knowing that the oven was still too hot and the heat too intense, it burned a big hole in the middle of the back of the coat, and the rest of it was stiff as a board.

Next morning, when she removed the coat from the oven together with the rest of our clothes, she froze. When I saw my beloved coat in this sad condition, I cried uncontrollably, and I'm crying in my heart to this day. The loss of a material item has never affected me since as did the loss of this fur coat. I remember every detail of this chapter in the life of the coat. I had to wear it since I had no other warm outer clothing. The leather was stiff as a board. It irritated me and made movement difficult and clumsy. Even in this terrible condition, the coat was a blessing. Mother had covered the hole by sewing a fabric patch on the inside. It kept me warm the next winter in Siberia. Though I grew and it became too small, its warmth still enveloped me. My brother Israel wore it the following winter.

How I loved my beautiful first fur coat! In retrospect, I think that coat began my love affair with fur.

After we were dressed and fed, Mother asked the woman if we could stay another night. Mother told her that my father was taken by the Germans, that he would return soon, we would continue our journey, and she would be handsomely rewarded. No one knew where those men were taken or when they would return, but my mother, the optimist, always had faith in the Almighty. The woman agreed to let us stay.

The next day, the weather improved somewhat and it was only drizzling slightly, but it was still cold and foggy. Mother would not let us go out for fear of getting sick. She reassured us that we would be safe with the woman and that she wanted to go out and find our relatives, as we had no idea where they spent the night. Mother was hoping they might know the whereabouts of our father and the other men.

Mother was gone a long time. At first, we huddled quietly in a corner of the room, but after a while, my brother Israel (nicknamed Ninius) became restless and wanted to go find Mother.

I scolded him and made him sit in his spot on the floor, and he began to cry. And so did my younger brother David (Dudush). I had my hands full and didn't know what to do. I had no experience as a babysitter. At home it was the nanny who kept us quiet when Mother was away. The lady of the house was busy with her domestic chores, but when she heard the boys cry, she came over to find out why. I told her that they wanted our mother. She had been gone a long time, and we did not know where she was. We were afraid she might not come back. We told the woman that our father was taken from us the day before, and now Mother was gone too.

She reassured us that Mother would come back soon and everything would be all right. She gave us each a slice of bread, which we devoured in an instant. We were all hungry and thus upset and irritable. It must have been late in the afternoon when Mother returned with a bundle on her arm.

She bought milk, potatoes, apples, and some other foodstuff. We were thrilled to see her. She reassured us that everything was going to be okay. We wanted to know if she had any news about Father. Though she had no positive answer, she said with a reassuring tone in her voice, "God protects those who believe in him. God will protect your father, and he will come when the time is right."

"When will that time be?" I asked.

"When God decides it is right, and only He knows when," she replied.

We had to be satisfied with that answer and had to accept it. Mother was always a strong believer in God and His powers.

Mother asked the lady of the house if we had behaved properly. She answered in the affirmative. I guess she did not want to add to our misery, as she figured we had enough trouble. Mother got permission to use the stove, and she began preparing our meal from the staples she had bought. By the time our food was ready, it had started getting dark outside. The drizzle finally stopped, but it was still windy and cold. A freshly cooked, hot meal, no matter how primitive, was very welcome. We all sat at the table, enjoying every morsel. Our feast consisted of potatoes with onions fried in butter and a glass of milk. Mother was glad we ate so willingly and without a fuss. I am sure she knew that we were hungry and would eat anything. Mother joined us too. It was her first and only meal that day.

The woman watched us from the corner of her eye while standing at the stove.

Father must have joined us during the night. I saw him first thing in the morning when I woke up, just as he was finishing his morning prayers. Mother wrapped me in her coat, took me by the hand, and asked me to be quiet so as not to wake my brothers. I asked a thousand questions about Father's whereabouts. We were whispering in the corner while Mother helped me dress. My shoes were still damp, but I had no others.

The lady of the house walked in with a heavy basket on her arm. Upon noticing my father wrapped in his prayer shawl, she stopped in her tracks with an expression of fright on her face and crossed herself. Though local countryfolk knew Jews in the area, they might have never seen one at morning prayer. Superstition was quite common among the masses. Seeing a man wrapped in a white prayer shawl for the first time could easily frighten anyone. She probably imagined a ghost. Mother saw the expression on the woman's face and rushed to explain what Father was doing. The poor woman took a deep breath, crossed herself again, and entered the room. She put the basket down on the heavy wooden table and began removing its contents. She offered my mother some cheese and eggs. Mother thanked her and took out money to pay for them, but the woman wouldn't hear of it. She said it was for the children.

"You have such beautiful young children. Take good care of them. With the war raging and all those Germans and Russians here, who knows what kind of hardships they will endure."

Mother was moved to tears. She said later to Father that the woman probably had no children of her own. She was about thirty-five or forty, and there were no children in the house.

By this time, Father was already removing his prayer shawl and phylacteries, folding them and returning them to their sack. My brothers were waking up, calling Mother, and she was busy tending to them.

I approached my father again with questions. He was pensive and obviously preoccupied with a million thoughts.

To satisfy my curiosity, he only said to me that the Germans made him dig ditches and, early this morning, they released him and he came here to be with us.

There was a kettle of boiling water on the stove, and Mother proceeded to make coffee. This was my father's drink of choice in the morning and many times during the day. His day began with coffee and a cigarette; he continued drinking coffee throughout the day, accompanied by a cigarette, until he went to sleep. The only day he drank tea was on Saturdays (when religion forbids smoking) and on cold winter nights.

I assume that he associated coffee with smoking. When he could not smoke, he switched to tea. He loved his tea in a glass and held it in both hands to keep them warm.

Mother made us hard-boiled eggs (Father liked very soft, almost-raw eggs). The bread was fresh and very tasty, and we all ate with great appetites. When we finished, Mother cleaned whatever utensils she used and packed them away. I was curious to know how father knew where to find us. Mother then proceeded to tell me that when the Germans took our father away, he told her to go to the next village and wait for him there, which was exactly what we did. "But how did he know which house we were in?" I asked.

"He asked in a few houses until he found the right one," said Mother.

Now that my curiosity had been satisfied, I calmed down. Father went out to get the horse and wagon ready for the next leg of our journey to the unknown. He bought a dry bundle of straw from the farmer and spread it on the bottom of the wagon, which was still damp from the rain. He also bought fodder for the horse. We loaded our belongings onto the wagon. Mother went to pay the woman. At first, she refused to take the money, claiming that we had a long and uncertain journey ahead of us and the money would come in handy. Mother insisted, and the woman accepted the payment. Mother gave her extra money to repay for her kindness. These were poor farmers, and Mother would never take advantage of them. After all, we still had money that we brought with us from home.

We started moving again and learned later that the other relatives had left the day before and went to a little town called Nemerow.

The wind had subsided somewhat, but the sky was gray, with gathering dark clouds behind us. I was very uncomfortable in my burned-out, stiff coat and moved around, trying different positions to ease my discomfort, but there was no relief. I kept quiet, knowing very well that I would only bring on my father's wrath if I continued to complain.

There were more important things to worry about than my discomfort.

When the Germans took the men, they also confiscated horses from those who had two. They also took one of ours. Father was not sure if one horse would be able to make the long journey, and we had no idea at that time how far we would have to travel. If he would not need one, he could always sell it. But the one horse seemed to be pulling the wagon with quite a bit of force. The roads were covered with mud, which at times came up to the horse's knees, but Father fed him well in the morning and urged him gently. The horse did his job well.

The rest of the journey to Janów, a small town near Lwow, is obscure.

I know we traveled that entire day until we reached Janów. The balance of the journey must have been uneventful, because I do not remember anything significant about it. Names like Cieszanów and Lubaczów do have a familiar ring, so it's possible that we passed those towns.

I know that my father was taken by the Germans on the outskirts of Tarnogród.

Janów

Why we settled in Janów, I have no idea. Maybe my parents knew someone there?

It was either the end of October or the beginning of November 1939 when we arrived in Janów, a small nondescript town in Eastern Poland (now it's Ukraine) about twenty or thirty kilometers from the large city of Lwow, called Lemberg in Jewish.

The local population was primarily Ukrainian, interspersed with Polish, Jewish, Russian, and German. This part of Poland used to belong to the Ukraine, as it does today, since the Ukraine regained its independence from Russia in the 1990s.

The official language was Ukrainian. It is a mixture of Polish and Russian.

In Janów, we rented a two-room apartment on a small narrow street in the vicinity of the market square. It was actually half of a house. The other half was occupied by its owner. One of the two rooms served as a combination of the kitchen, dining room, and living room, and the other was the bedroom—the same as in Zbydniów. There was no running water or indoor plumbing. For me, this was no surprise, as that was how we lived at home too.

I recall it to be a cute little one-story house with whitewashed walls and a pitched gray roof. Mother was very creative and immediately found some white lace for bedroom curtains and eyelet for the kitchen.

She always strived to make our surroundings pleasant, to make our house a home. She had no sewing machine since she had left hers at home, but she sewed the curtains by hand and they were beautiful. Mother used to have a saying, "A clean table, a stove for cooking, and curtains on the window turned a house into a home." There was a water pump about two hundred yards from the house, and many times I was sent to fetch a pail of water.

The apartment was sparsely furnished. Firstly, we were convinced that these were temporary quarters, and secondly, we wanted to save the money for other necessities , and right in the middle of the kitchen stood an oblong wooden table with benches on each side, just like in Zbydniów. The kitchen had a wood-burning stove against one wall and a long bench under one window.

The bedroom naturally contained beds. My parents' bed had a headboard; ours did not. Our bed was wide, so all three of us could sleep comfortably. The mattress was filled with straw, and on occasion, when we found lumps, none of us wanted to sleep on that spot. We would argue whose turn it was to sleep on the lump until Mother would come in, remove the sheet, and straighten out the lump so we could go to sleep. Father's responsibility, as usual, was to find a way to earn a living. Since we had the horse and wagon, he decided to put them to good use. He had previous experience with lumber, having done business and managing the woodcutting mill for Mr. Horodynski. He soon embarked on a career of buying and selling firewood. We did not become millionaires, but it put my father back in action and gave him dignity, and we were fed and clothed. Father would often travel to the big city of Lvov. There he met many acquaintances from our area and even some of Mother's relatives. All were in the same predicament.

Lvov was a city with tall buildings, indoor plumbing, and running water. I will never forget my introduction to real indoor plumbing. We were visiting some friends, and I had the urge to go to the bathroom. Father asked where it was and led me to the toilet. Since I was used to an outhouse with plenty of daylight seeping through the window and other openings, I found this one different. It was rather small, with a very high ceiling. Since it was the first time I witnessed and used this type of facility, Father made sure I knew how to use it. The most interesting part of it was the chain I was told to pull, and water came gushing down and washed down the toilet bowl. I had many questions for my father about this contraption but had to save them for later after we left their home. Father didn't want me to embarrass him or me.

There were wide, paved, and cobblestone tree-lined streets, a tram, buses, and a big modern central railroad station. There was even a university in Lvov.

Janów, as I mentioned, was a small town by comparison, an unpretentious town with mainly narrow streets except for the main cobblestone road, which went from end to end, cutting through the market square.

Winter was approaching fast. My parents had no idea how long we would remain in Janów, so Mother decided to enroll my brother Israel and me in school. I was enrolled in the second grade of the Ukrainian public school. My brother Israel started first grade. It was not very hard to adjust to the new language because there were many similarities between Polish and Ukrainian. The difficulty was in the alphabet. The Ukrainians used the Cyrillic alphabet. It did not take us too long to master the new alphabet, though. Our biggest problem was social. Though there were other Jewish children in the school, we were new pupils—total strangers. The Jewish children reluctantly took to us, but they did not bother us. The problem was mainly the boys, the Christian and German ones. They would taunt us, call us derogatory names, and sometimes throw rocks at us.

When it happened the first time, I came home crying and told Mother about it. The next day, she went with us to the principal and complained. She thought it would be like in Zbydniów. The principal listened to my mother's complaint and then said with a smirk on his face, "Why are you surprised at the children's behavior? You are strangers here, and you are Jews. This is a normal reaction of children."

Mother was stunned, but after a moment, she found her tongue and said to the man, "Yes, we are Jews. Does that mean we cannot attend your school? I thought this is a public school that all children have a right to attend. Is there a new law that I don't know about? If yes, please tell me about it, and I'll know what to do."

The principal rose slowly from behind his desk as if to say "Your time is up" and said, this time looking at me, "Don't worry, child, they will stop after a while. Children say many things but don't always mean what they say. I'll have a talk with their teacher."

We left his office. Mother was furious, but there was not much she could do. She took us both to class and promised to come and pick us up at the end of the day. She picked us up from school a few times, at which time boys were quiet and went their own way. But she could not always come to pick us up, and when she didn't, the boys did bother us. After a while, I made some Jewish friends in my class, and we walked home together. This apparently helped in some way and kept the anti-Semites at bay.

It was not all smooth sailing, but it became more bearable. We also got used to it, I guess, and maybe they got used to the idea that we, the Jews, were there and they would have to tolerate us. Once in a while, a bully would flex his muscles and try to beat up one of the Jewish children, but we learned to fight them off. The scariest time was when Mother left us alone for six weeks to visit her family on the German side. I felt very insecure and vulnerable. Father was never home during the day, and he made us understand that we would either learn to fight back or learn to live with it. He could not stay home to fight our battles.

He told us that his job was to make a living so we could eat and have a roof over our heads.

Gypsy Forecast

Time passed quickly. The school year was over at the end of June, and this brought an end to the indignities and occasional violence we had to endure. This did not eliminate the neighborhood kids, however, but I learned to bribe them with candy and cookies, so for the most part, they didn't bother us.

It was a warm summer day in June or July of 1940. The windows were open, letting a breeze flutter the sheer kitchen curtains. Mother was busy at the stove. I heard footsteps and ran to the window to see who was coming. The window was facing the narrow path along the house leading to the entrance to our apartment. In those days, there was very little fear of strangers, but my curiosity prompted me to go and see who was coming to see us in the middle of the day. Before I got to the window, a tall figure covered the whole window frame, casting a shadow in the room. The sight of this stranger frightened me, and I ran to Mother, seeking shelter.

He bent over, and the upper half of his body was inside the kitchen. As he turned his head, he spotted my mother and, in an accented Polish, asked for money, a handout. Mother was just as startled as I was. She instantly recognized the face and accent and knew he was a Gypsy. It was their custom to perform in the streets, engage in fortune-telling, or just ask anyone for a handout. Mother was agitated and told him to go find a job and not bother people.

When he realized that Mother refused and he would have to leave empty-handed, he offered the services of a fortune-teller. He was a strikingly handsome man, young, tall, and slim, with curly jet-black hair and piercing black eyes to match. Half his head was covered with a printed red kerchief tied on one side. He was wearing an embroidered multicolored vest over what must have once been a white shirt with billowing sleeves. The top buttons were open to reveal his hairy, masculine chest. He had a gold loop earring in one ear.

I was too young then to understand how much power and masculinity a man like this exuded. I could see my mother was taken aback. His most striking feature was his piercing black eyes. Mother was afraid he might do us harm, so she reluctantly agreed to the fortune-telling.

My brothers were taking a nap, so only Mother and I were in the kitchen.

I had seen Gypsies many times before as they passed through our village in caravans, menacing the population, trying to extort whatever they could. They had a reputation as very skillful thieves. They used to play violins, accordions, and other musical instruments and entertained the population with their lively song and dance. At the end of each performance, they would pass a hat around, asking for money. Before mother and I recovered from the shock, the handsome man disappeared into thin air, and almost instantly, there was a knock on the door. A young Gypsy woman let herself in. Mother didn't even know the door was open or have a chance to lock it. The young woman almost danced in, swaying her hips, rustling her billowing skirts as she swayed.

Her attire was the traditional Gypsy dress, very colorful and very becoming. Her skin was olive, her face framed in a mane of curly black hair that accentuated her delicate features. Her slim waist made the layered skirts appear so much bigger. Her eyes were everywhere. Mother asked her to sit at the table. Mother was somewhat shaken with the speed at which everything was happening.

The young woman was assessing the surroundings. The physical appearance of a home usually reflected the financial status of a client. My mother had an eye for beauty, but this young beauty took her breath away. Mother grabbed a dish towel, wiped her hands, and sat down on the opposite bench, facing the woman. This gorgeous creature introduced herself as Tonia. I was clinging to my mother, somewhat afraid, not knowing what to expect. There were rumors that

Gypsies stole young children and took them to faraway places. She asked my name and complimented me on my looks and good behavior. Tonia pulled out a deck of cards from her waist. They had a slight odor of perspiration, as did Tonia. The two women bargained a little about the fee, but this was quickly resolved and I was asked to lock the door so no intruder would disturb. Mother offered the woman a cold drink, which she gulped down in an instant. The Gypsy started shuffling the old deck of cards and began asking Mother some personal questions.

In response, Mother said, "You are the fortune-teller. You tell me. You're supposed to know."

The young woman smiled, revealing two rows of pearly white teeth. She shuffled the cards several times and began laying them on the table in diagonal rows.

I stood next to my mother, mesmerized.

Tonia began by stating that this was our temporary home. We had come from somewhere else and would not remain here too long. We had left our home and possessions behind, never to return or recover them.

Mother gave me a quizzical look but said nothing. I was saddened as I took the Gypsy's words to heart.

After a moment of reflection, Mother said to her, "You're talking nonsense."

"This is what the cards say, not I," the young woman retorted. Tonia realized that she had a skeptic sitting in front of her. She was somewhat irritated but continued. "You will stay here a short while only. From here you will travel very far. It will be a long and unpleasant journey." She gave my mother a stern look, gathered the cards, and asked if she should continue. Her Polish was poor and heavily accented. At times, I had a problem understanding her.

By now Mother was interested to hear the rest of the story.

"Do you want to hear everything?" Tania asked again. "No matter what the cards will say?"

Mother agreed. She felt uneasy but curious to hear what the Gypsy had to say. Mother knew that some Gypsies were known to foretell the future quite accurately, but some also were masters in fabricating stories.

Before Mother allowed her to continue, she wanted to test the young woman to see if she really knew anything about fortune-telling or was just telling us a lot of nonsense. Mother asked her how many people were in our family. Tonia, without hesitation, announced, "You have a husband and two boys." Father was not home, and the boys were sleeping in the next room. This put a shiver through my mother's body as she grabbed my hand and squeezed it. This was scary. Mother was silent as Tonia reshuffled the cards again and began telling us that this was our temporary home. We came from another place and would not remain there very long. We were going to a foreign country, and it would be a long journey.

Mother and I were very eager to learn what the woman had to tell us. Mother did not interrupt anymore. I was mesmerized. "I see many tears," Tonia said. "You will lose loved ones." She raised her eyes at Mother silently, questioning if she should go on. Mother was silent, and the fortune-teller continued. "You are not very rich now," she said, probably judging by our surroundings, "but you will be much poorer still."

Mother began to stir. She was visibly sad and irritated. "How do you know all that?" she inquired of Tonia.

"My cards tell me, and they don't lie!" the Gypsy retorted. "Shall I stop here?" she asked.

"No, continue," Mother answered slowly. By now she was frightened, but her curiosity won.

"You will live through very tough times, very tough times," Tonia repeated periodically. "You will long to return to your birthplace, to your home, but you will not be unable to. I am sorry to tell you, but you will never return to your birthplace. You will probably never see the family you left behind as well."

I could see Mother's eyes well up with tears. She remanded the Gypsy for telling such outrageous lies. Tonia took offense, gathered the cards, stood up, and was ready to leave. Mother caught her sleeve and made her sit down again. "I warned you," Tonia said. "I asked you in advance if you want to hear the truth, and you agreed. The cards do not lie. All I do is read them. Pay me now, and I will leave," she announced.

Mother, and of course I, wanted to hear the rest of what she had to say. Mother offered her some tea or water, but Tonia refused, stating that she didn't like being interrupted in the middle of a reading.

She took a deep breath, reshuffled the cards, and began to lay them out on the table. Her movements were rigid and nervous, her voice slow, and her words measured.

"As I said," she continued, "you will travel very far, but you will not remain there forever. After some years, you will return to Poland or another country, but you will not remain there either. You will continue traveling until you settle in a small faraway country that does not even exist now, and there you will remain."

Mother smiled and said, "You see, you're talking nonsense! How can I live in a country that does not exist?"

The young woman stood up abruptly, collected her cards, and stretched out her hand, demanding payment.

"Why are you leaving?" Mother asked. "Are you finished?"

But Tonia was silent. She just stood there with an outstretched hand and angry eyes riveted on Mother. Mother realized that this was the end of the reading. Mother reached into her apron pocket and took out some bills. She must have given Tonia more than agreed upon, because there was a faint smile on her face as she took the money, turned to the door, and disappeared.

Mother sat on the bench for a long moment, deep in thought and visibly shaken. She then turned to me and said, "Don't believe a word this woman had said. Gypsies have a habit of lying for dramatic effect."

"But she did know about our family," I said. "She answered your questions correctly."

Mother tried to convince me that the Gypsy's fortune-telling was rubbish and that I should not even think about it. But the more Mother tried to convince me and invalidate the whole event, the more it intrigued me.

Mother returned to her chores and I to my thoughts. She reminded me not to whisper a word about this to my father or anyone else. He would be very upset with Mother for believing Gypsy stories.

I was not sure I would be able to keep such a secret. But I did, until now.

MOTHER'S JOURNEY BACK HOME

Translated from Mother's Journal

I have to backtrack a little in order to tell about Mother's trip back home. It was toward the end of December 1939. We lived in Janów.

One evening, two men came to visit. They were from Rozwadów, one of them a distant cousin of my husband. They told us that they are planning to cross the border into German-occupied Poland to see their relatives who had stayed behind. There was hardly any communication between the German and Soviet sides of Poland, and people were worried and anxious about their next of kin.

The two men told us that several people were interested in joining and forming a group. They had heard of guides who knew the area well and, for a good remuneration, would take us across the border. It was only a question of money, and all of them were ready to share in the expense. The more people in the group, the less it would cost per person. In reality, it was not that simple. All my husband's immediate relatives, except his eldest brother, Chaim Layzer, and children, living in Bojanów, had left their homes and were on the Soviet side. His married daughter, Genia, from Ulanów, joined the exodus to the east.

My sister Beila, our mother (Sara), and brother Chaim Wolf, with his children, had remained on the German side. My mother was frail due to a heart condition, which was the main reason my sister Beila stayed behind.

I wanted very much to see my next of kin and, if possible, bring back some our belongings we had left behind.

My husband could not leave his business at that time of year; he was in the firewood business, and this was the month of December, the height of the heating season. He was the breadwinner and could not afford to take time off. Nobody could foretell how long this escapade would last.

My husband suggested that I join the group since the Germans would probably not bother a woman.

Before we left Zbydniów, I had hidden some of our winter clothes in the attic. Since we were driven out of our home in such a hurry, we hardly had time to take anything with us. It was October when we left, and winter was still a month or two away. Who knew that we would be away so long? We had also hidden other valuables—silver, china, and more—which I wanted to retrieve. In wartime, one needs a safety net. Gold, silver, foreign currency, or jewelry were easy to hide and transport; thus, they were the right vehicles. These valuables could be sold or exchanged for food and/or other necessities.

Though my heart ached for leaving my children alone, the anxiety to see my mother and other members of the family won, and I consented to go. My husband reassured me that he would take good care of the children and, if necessary, would seek help from some relatives who lived in town.

The group decided to leave two days later, which was toward the end of December. They also speculated that the Christian population would be preoccupied with preparations for Christmas and New Year and would not pay us attention.

We left Janów by train. First, we went to Lvov, and there we changed trains to the border town of Sieniawa. It was twenty-eight kilometers from Lvov to the current border. At that time, the Germans still allowed Jews to travel from place to place. They searched Jews and confiscated all the valuables if they found any.

We were caught getting off the train in Sieniawa and searched. I, the other woman in our group, and several men were let go, but two of our comrades were severely beaten and left in the street. The Germans were angry that the search did not produce any booty, so they picked two sacrificial lambs and beat them in every part of their bodies. When the attackers finished with the two men, one was barely alive, lying on the sidewalk, and the other was doubled over in excruciating pain. During this ordeal, another man from our group tried to intervene, but he was pushed away with such force that he stumbled, fell, and severely hurt his arm. We were helpless before the enemy.

When this horrible ordeal was over and the perpetrators left empty-handed, we revived our friend, applied ice to the wounds on his face, and cleaned them with snow. His left eye was swollen and black-and-blue, but he could see. All this went on in plain view of some townspeople who had gathered to watch the spectacle. We asked some people if there was a doctor in town so he could dress the injured man's wounds. One of the townspeople answered that yes, there was a doctor but that he did not treat Jews.

These were our Ukrainian "friends." Several of our men dispersed to find some means of transportation, namely a horse and wagon.

Our destination was Ulanów, on the San River, which was some forty kilometers away. All my cotravelers had false German ID cards except me. Such documents were very costly, and I did not have that kind of money and time was too short to obtain one. I knew it was risky to travel without an ID card, but I took the chance. I was afraid and was already sorry that I decided to go and left my husband and children behind.

Eventually we found a footman with a horse and carriage who was willing to take us to Ulanów, a few hours' ride. Of course, we had to pay him in advance. When we arrived in town, we all went in different directions, each one in search of his family.

Ulanów was the starting point of our separate destinations. We were all to meet at a designated time and place back in Ulanów five days later and, from that starting point, begin our return trip. We wished one another luck and went on our way.

My sister Blima, who fled the Germans and now lived in Lvov, on the Soviet side, had a friendly neighbor. I decided to visit her, hoping she might help me and put me up for the night. As I knocked on her door, she opened it and I entered her home. She looked at me, frightened. She knew me well. I used to visit my sister often, and we had spent two weeks in my sister's home only a few months earlier.

The good neighbor's anxiety was justified. The Christian population was warned by the Germans not to harbor or give aid to Jews under penalty of death. We knew nothing of these edicts or warnings; therefore, I was taken aback at the look on her face. I assured her that I had no intention of staying or hiding in her home, that I would only like to borrow a large kerchief and a milk bucket, which I would return a few days later. She looked at me quizzically and went to fetch the two items. She returned from the adjacent room carrying the kerchief and a small bucket.

I thanked her and promised to return them as soon as possible. I clearly saw her hands shaking. She gave me some friendly advice. "Make sure they do not see you or catch you, for if they do, it will be your end and mine." I removed my wool shawl from my head, tied it around my neck under my coat, and put the kerchief on my head peasant-style. I looked out the window to see if there was anyone in the street who could recognize me. The street was deserted due to the bitter cold. I turned my head to look at the windows of my sister's apartment, but they were covered with shutters. I swiftly left, heading for the bridge. As I approached it, two German guards stopped me. One raised his hand, yelling "Halt," meaning "stop."

I did. One of them asked me in German, "Do you have ID papers?" I answered him in Polish that I was going to my aunt to get some milk and that she lived in the nearby village across the river.

I was shivering with fear and cold. The wind picked up somewhat, and I saw that the soldiers were shivering too. One of them yelled back at me, "Ich frage dich ob du papire hast, du Polnisher shwein!" I'm asking you if you have papers, you Polish pig. I repeated the previous sentence. He apparently did not understand me. Frustrated, he called his buddy and asked him what to do with me. The other one said, "Don't you see she is stupid? She's no spy! Let her go." They whispered something to each other, and then the first one said, "Go to hell, you stupid Polish pig!" He waved his hand and yelled, "Go!"

I crossed the bridge, and about two hundred yards, in a side alley, I met my friends, who were waiting for me. They didn't know what took me so long. They thought the worst and were glad to see me.

We began our twelve-kilometer walk to the town of Nisko. In Nisko, we found bread and some other food items we could buy. I also bought candles. It was Friday, and I was hoping and praying to see my mother and sister before the Sabbath. We never walked all together so as not to draw attention to our group. At times we walked in twos, but mostly each one walked alone, but not far from one another so that we could see one another. We were lucky to catch a train in Nisko and, in the afternoon, arrived in Rozwadów.

I arrived at my sister's home and knocked on the back door. I had no idea who would answer. When my sister Beila opened the door and saw me, she almost cried out with joy, but life conditions make people think very fast. She opened her mouth and eyes wide and instantly covered her mouth with her hand. Tears of joy rushed to our eyes as we embraced in the doorway. She quickly let go of me, pulled me inside, and shut the door. We hugged and kissed for a long time. Then my mother's voice came from the kitchen. She must have heard the commotion and wanted to know what was happening. I was anxious to see her, having no idea that this would be the last time I would ever see my mother. Beila stopped me. It would be a shock for her to see me, as we hadn't seen each other for several months. No mail was getting through, so she didn't know where we were and if we were alive. Beila went into the kitchen to prepare her for my visit. Mother was a sick, frail old lady, and we did not want to scare her. After a few minutes, Beila came out and took me into the kitchen. I think it would be superfluous to describe our meeting. It had been very wise of me to buy food in Nisko; my mother and sister went hungry many days. They had nothing more to sell or exchange for food. My brother Chaim Wolf occasionally sent over something at night. He and his family were in hiding.

Occasionally, the mute neighbor across the street would bring them something to eat.

It was most generous of him to share. After all, it was wartime, wintertime, and food was scarce. In addition, the Germans pillaged villages and stores, confiscating the food they found in order to feed their army.

My mother, my sister, and I spent a bittersweet Sabbath together, telling one another about our difficult lives. We cried a lot and occasionally laughed too. We knew, though, that this special reunion would end, so we tried to cram in as much conversation, hugs, and kisses as we could. I did not want to leave them in this horrible state, but I had no choice.

I promised that when spring came—the war would probably be over by then—we would return home and everything would go back to normal, and if the Germans would still be in Poland, we would send for them and they would come to live with us in Ukraine or wherever we might be. By that time, Itchale, Beila's husband, might be back from wherever he was. We were hoping and praying that the Germans did not kill him. A day of rest in a warm home and a decent meal invigorated me. I woke up early Sunday morning, ready to face the world. I did not know what lay ahead and what my plans would accomplish. I went about executing them at great risk. A light snow fell at night, covering everything with a white blanket. The temperature fell too. The air was crisp and freezing. My woolen shawl came in very handy. I bundled up, said good-bye to my mother and sister, and walked briskly to the railroad station. I took the first train to Zbydniów. I was truly lucky because there were no German guards on the train, or maybe just in the car I was in. My face was covered except for my eyes, and thus, the three men and the woman in the railcar did not know who I was. I recognized one of the men, a resident of Rozwadów, but he did not recognize me. Every time fear came to my mind, which was quite often, I pictured myself dead and my children orphans. All my prayers were concentrated on my children. I always asked God for their welfare.

The railroad station in Zbydniów was near Horodynski's estate, a five- to ten-minute walk.

I went directly to the nearby flour mill and woodcutting plant that my husband had managed before the war. I wanted to see if they were in operation. I could see from afar that there were men and vehicles in the area. This was a good sign. I did not go near the buildings for fear of being recognized. Instead, I headed directly for Horodynski's palatial home.

I had been there only once or twice before. No one visited the mansion unless invited. Noblemen and plain folk did not mix. That was understood.

The gate was not locked, so I let myself in and proceeded on the gravel path to the house. Oh yes, it was a beautiful house. Winter was not a very complimenting season. All around, including the house, was covered by a thin white blanket of fresh snow.

The striking color of this estate in wintertime was the red tile roof, but now it was also almost all covered with snow. I walked swiftly, the snow and gravel making a crunching noise under my boots. My heartbeat was taking up speed.

I noticed smoke coming out of the chimney, a sign that someone was home, but then, some of the help was always home.

I was hoping and praying that the master of the house would be in residence. It was Christmas and New Year season, and they were usually away, either abroad or visiting family. I could not see his car or any of his carriages. They must have been sheltered in the back, away from the main house, in the garage and carriage house. There were no signs of wheels on the fresh snow either. It was Sunday and still early in the morning.

I walked up the few steps of the portico and rang the bell. A maid opened the door and was surprised to see a woman this early. She did not know who I was. I asked if the master was home. "And who are you?" she asked.

"Tell him Heshl's wife is here."

She hesitated a moment, but my gaze was firm. She went into the library, which was on the right side of the front hallway. In her haste, she left the door open, so I let myself into the large vestibule and quietly closed the door behind me. The home was heated, and I instantly felt the warmth on my face. I heard the maid announce me to her master. A moment of silence, then I heard a muffled sound of shuffling feet on the wooden floor.

It was early in the morning, so Mr. Horodynski was not fully dressed; he was in his housecoat as he rushed out to greet me. He was thoroughly surprised and very happy to see me. He took me by the hand and walked me into the library. He ordered the maid to bring a hot breakfast for me and coffee for him, then he sat me down on the leather sofa and he sat next to me.

I took off my warm shawl, and he helped me with my coat. The room was warmed by a roaring fire in the fireplace. I walked over it to warm my hands. "Tell me, tell me," he demanded anxiously, "where are you? How are you? Is Hershekl all right? And the children?" He wanted to know everything, and I proceeded to tell him all about us. He was amazed at my courage to undertake such a dangerous journey.

A few minutes later, breakfast arrived on a silver tray.

The aroma of the fresh-brewed coffee immediately entered my nostrils and remained there long after I finished it. The maid, not knowing that I was Jewish and observed kashruth (Jewish dietary laws), loaded the tray with fried eggs, bacon, fresh-baked rolls, butter, a steaming carafe of coffee, and a small pitcher of boiled milk.

I was hungry, and my body was still cold from the walk from the railway station to the estate. I welcomed the hospitality and ravenously consumed the fresh rolls with butter and the hot coffee.

The squire knew why I didn't eat the rest of the food. He waited until I finished eating and then began questioning me about my journey.

He asked how I had crossed the border, made it alive, and reached his home. I knew he was a friend and could be trusted, so I told him about the first part of my adventure. He listened attentively, as though memorizing every word I was saying. Once in a while, he moaned and expressed words of sympathy as I described our lives and my trip. He felt genuinely sorry for us. He tried to console me and promised to return my husband to his previous job and stature just as soon as the war was over and we returned home. He promised that he would have better appreciation for my husband's work and that the rewards would be greater than in the past. We talked for a long time, sometimes reminiscing about the past, but the main topic was the present.

He told me that their lives were also not a bed of roses. They had to watch their every step and every word. He wanted to send his wife and young daughter to Paris to stay with their relatives, but he was not permitted. Two of his sons were there still studying at the Sorbonne.

He had a very rich aunt from an aristocratic family who lived in Lvov. Since Janów was close to Lvov and my husband frequented that city on business, Mr. Horodynski asked if I would be willing to take a letter to her. I gladly agreed. Apparently, he did not know that this aunt was among the first casualties of the Soviet regime. She was among the first ones to be deported to Siberia. Her transgression was her wealth. I certainly did not want to be the bearer of bad news, so I gladly agreed to take the letter to her, hoping that some next of kin might still be living at that address.

Mr. Horodynski owed my husband ten thousand zloty (Polish money). He said he would have gladly given it to me but he did not keep that much money at home. He said he would give me five thousand and that in the letter he had asked his aunt to give us the balance. I knew then and there that we would never see the other five thousand. Nonetheless, I was thankful for what I got. He wrote a short note to his aunt, put it in an envelope, and sealed and addressed it. I took his letter and hid it in my bosom.

He opened the drawer of the desk, took out a key, and proceeded across the beautiful room to the opposite wall. There he reached behind a book in the bookcase, pushed a button, and a whole shelf moved to the right. He turned a knob, and after several turns, it gave way, revealing another small door. He used the small key to open it.

I was amazed that he was doing all this in my presence. He knew from experience that my husband was trustworthy, so I guess he trusted me too. I was sitting on the sofa right across the safe and saw stacks of papers and a small box, which might have been filled with jewels. He pulled out an envelope containing the money. He counted out five thousand zloty and gave it to me. He also gave me the envelope, and I placed the money into it. I put the envelope in my bosom too. Of course I turned around so as not to expose myself.

"You must have a pretty *zaftig* bosom since you can fit quite a bundle in there." He knew some Yiddish words. We both laughed aloud. He returned to the safe, locked it, returned the key to its place in the drawer, and rang for the maid. As she walked in a few minutes later, she took the silver tray, and while she was doing that, he asked her to get a basket and fill it with foodstuff, anything she could find except meat products, and bring it in. She looked at me disdainfully, beginning to understand. The bacon on the tray was untouched, a basket of food but no meat. That might have told her I was Jewish. She took the tray and left the room. About fifteen minutes later, the maid returned with a basket filled with food.

Mr. Horodynski took it from her and handed it to me. "Take this to your family. I share with you what I have." I was truly touched and thanked him with tears in my eyes. I stretched out my hand to shake his, but he gave me a long bear hug. I then bundled up and left the room. We both had tears in our eyes as we said good-bye.

I had completely thawed out in Mr. Horodynski's welcoming home. I felt good and dreaded the elements outside. The basket was rather heavy, but I lifted it with joy. He escorted me to the door. As he opened it, a gust of cold wind greeted us. I tied my shawl tighter around my head and neck and went down the gravel path to the gate. I was so absorbed in our conversation that I failed to ask about his wife and children. He openly felt sorry for my family and me. He was a staunch Polish patriot and did not cooperate with the enemy. Mr. Horodynski, his wife, and their daughter and several other members of the family (fourteen in all) were executed in 1943, the morning after a relative's wedding took place at the mansion. We learned after the war that two of his sons had joined the Polish partisans and one died in battle. Only one son remained alive, and we heard that he became a journalist and was living in Warsaw. He never returned to his home.

I was happier about the food than the money. I knew my mother and sister were almost starving, and now I was able to help. As I approached the gate, I heard a noise behind me, and my heart stopped. I heard my name called, and I turned around. To my amazement, I recognized the chauffeur in Horodynski's black Ford asking me to stop. He stopped the car, came around and opened the door, and asked me to get in the car. Now I was truly astonished, but he reassured me that he was doing this on his employer's orders.

Mr. Horodynski, seeing me with the heavy basket, decided that it would be safer and easier for me to travel in his car than by train. He ordered the chauffeur to bring me safely to my mother's home in Rozwadów. The Germans were in need of supplies, as they had to feed their army, so they confiscated foodstuff from the farmers and warehouses in the occupied lands. Food was rationed to the local population, and a black market was created out of necessity. People who had money or valuables could obtain certain items on the black market. Mr. Horodynski was one of them.

The chauffer let me off on the outskirts of town so as not to raise suspicion. It was a short walk to my mother's house. The full basket weighed heavily in my arms, but I walked as fast as I could, my face almost fully covered so no one would recognize me. It was dangerous for Jews to walk in the streets without a permit. Thankfully, I reached my destination without being detected. It was Sunday and freezing, so most people were either in church or home with their families; very few people were outdoors. I went to the back of the house and knocked on the kitchen door. My sister looked out the window fearfully. She recognized me instantly, and with a broad smile, she opened the door for me. Once I was inside, she closed it behind me and rushed to relieve me of my burden. We walked into the kitchen, with her bombarding me with questions. I removed my heavy clothes and proceeded to recount the day's activities. Mother heard the commotion and joined us in the kitchen. They were so happy with the food I brought that they began making long-term plans for it. They proceeded to calculate that for the two of them, the supplies should last up to two weeks. They did not count on my staying much longer, and I told them that I couldn't. Their only fear was for me and my safety on the way back. There were stories circulating that the Germans entered private homes at will and took whatever food they could find. If they did not find what they were looking for, they would beat people, accusing them of hiding food from them.

My day's accomplishments were considered a miracle by my family. They could not hide the joy and thanked me for the sustenance I brought. My sister said it was like Purim and Simchat Torah put together (these are the two most joyous holidays on the Jewish calendar). They prayed to God that nothing should disturb their happiness.

That evening, we feasted on some of the abundant gifts.

We could not be extravagant. We had to think about tomorrow. Today, looking back at those wartime hardships, it is difficult for me to understand how much courage and audacity I was able to master in times of need.

The next morning, I took the train to Zbydniów again. This time I went directly to the house we had lived in.

The house belonged to Mr. Horodynski. Though the Germans told us that they wanted to occupy it, they apparently changed their mind and instead occupied the elementary school, which was much larger.

The house was vacant, and I had a key to our apartment, but there was no need. The doors were open. The apartment was empty except for some debris here and there. The entrance was in the back through the yard. I found the ladder and climbed up to the attic. The access to the attic was from the hallway. There, covered with straw, I found the five-gallon bottles of *vishniak* (cherry brandy) I had made in the summer. I made them every year during the cherry season. Our Passover dishes were intact, waiting to be taken down for the next Passover holiday. This never happened. I sat down and cried. Yes, the things I left were in place, but we were far away and could not use them.

I dried my eyes, collected my thoughts, and returned to the present. I went down the ladder and put it back in place. From there I went to visit some of our former neighbors. They were very surprised to see me. Before we left for the unknown, we left much of our belongings with them for safekeeping. They were kind and honest people and returned most of them.

They knew that the situation for Jews was bad; they had pity on me and returned our property. Moreover, almost everyone gave me some food. I returned several times to my village, and every time I was able to buy some provisions to bring back with me to share with my family.

My brother Chaim Wolf and his wife were being hidden in a nearby village by a kind Christian family. I could not see them, for it would have been dangerous for them as well as for me. I wanted to share some of the food with them but was advised by my sister not to endanger anybody's life. She reassured me that she would make every effort to send some with a Christian neighbor. My sister had very kind, loyal neighbors.

I was away from my husband and children for quite some time already, and it was time to return. I missed them terribly and was worried about their well-being. After all, my children were still so young; they had never been without their mother for so long. I had to return to Ulanów to meet my friends, as we had agreed before we parted.

I remembered that the main bridge was guarded by German soldiers, so I decided to cross the river by boat. Luckily, the river was not totally frozen, though the edges were covered with a very thin strip of ice.

I said a heart-wrenching good-bye to my mother and sister, not knowing this would be the last time we would see one another. Tears flowed freely, and our hearts ached terribly.

My sister helped me pack as many things as we could fit into the makeshift backpack we created, mainly warm clothes for my children and some food for me for the trip. I certainly did not know where or when I could get food again. Stores were closed because there was nothing to sell. I also knew that my journey back to Janów would take several days, provided all went according to plan.

I walked to the river San and looked for a boat. After a short while, I saw a small fisherman's boat and approached it, figuring that there would be an owner in the vicinity. I was right, because within minutes, two men appeared and asked me what I wanted. I told them that I needed a ride to the other side. We quickly agreed on a price, and within minutes, we were on our way. The river was not very wide and not deep either. They were strong men and handled the ores expertly.

One of the men looked at me with suspicious eyes then turned to his partner and whispered, thinking I would not hear, "She is a Jewess. We can throw her into the river and take her possessions. She must have money too."

His partner returned an angry look and retorted, "She is as human as you and me. She has enough trouble as is, having to hide from the Germans. Leave her alone. Her possessions will not make you rich."

The other man was visibly disappointed but continued to steer the boat. A few minutes later, we reached the opposite shore. They made sure it was away from the town and from the bridge, where it would be safer.

I raised my eyes to the heavens, thanking the Almighty for saving my life once again. One of the men helped me step onshore and even helped me with my backpack. I thanked them both, paid what I owed, and was on my way. I returned to my sister Blima's house safely. I returned the pail and kerchief to the kind neighbor and spent the night in my sister's apartment. I should say, I cried the night there. Though my sister was gone and the apartment empty, the neighbor had a key and let me in. I found some wood next to the tile-heating oven, made a fire, and slept on the bare floor. Though my sister Blima had left behind all her furniture, someone had helped himself to them. The experiences of the past few days weighed heavily on my heart.

This was the first opportunity I had not to be observed, so I could release my emotions. I was tired from carrying the heavy backpack for several kilometers and a basket filled with food, which my sister insisted I take for the road.

I could not fall asleep until dawn despite my fatigue. My thoughts wandered between the tragic situation of my family under the Germans and my dear children, whom I had left behind on the Russian side. All this time, there was no communication between us. I missed them terribly, and I was sure they missed me. I did not know how they were faring and if they were taken care of. Were they warm? Were they fed?

I had never been away from my children for so long. It was more than two weeks already since I had left home.

The following day, I ventured out in search of a familiar face and met a Jewish woman, all alone, who also wanted to cross the border to the Russian side. Her family was on the other side, and she was left alone under the Germans.

We found a man who owned a horse and wagon and was familiar with the territory. He knew where it was possible to cross the border without being detected by German guards. We paid him handsomely in advance. There were not too many people who were willing to risk their lives even for money. We were to leave the following morning at 3:00 a.m.

It was the month of January, a freezing, windy, snowy night. It was ideal weather for crossing the border, for the snow covered our tracks almost instantly. We met the man at the designated spot, on a narrow street almost on the outskirts of town. He told us to climb in the wagon and lie down. He covered us with a blanket and then with straw so no one could see us. The man climbed up in the front seat and was driving while we lay close to each other in order to keep warm. We could hardly breathe, but the straw and the blanket helped keep us warm. The wagon was actually a sleigh. It was impossible to travel in a wagon with wheels in this kind of weather. This man was supposed to take us to a town called Surochów, where it was easier to cross the border. We were to cross the border through the forest on the outskirts of Surochów to the Russian side.

We traveled the whole day, lying under the straw, and were supposed to make the crossing at night under the cover of darkness. He stopped only once on the way so we could relieve ourselves behind some bushes. Our meal that day was a cheese sandwich, which we were smart enough to take.

The deal also included another guide, a friend of his who was supposed to take us safely through the woods to a town, Sieniawa. I was already counting the hours when I would see my children, but fate had delivered another blow and our reunion had to be postponed. It was a dark, cloudy night. The wind was howling, and the snowdrifts were four to five feet high. What we embarked upon was a Herculean undertaking. We both carried heavy loads and sank in the snow up to our waist with each step we took.

Today, I marvel at our guts, strength, and endurance. Despite the bitter cold, we were hot and perspiring from the superhuman exertion. Our new guide turned out to be a traitor. Yes, he guided us through the woods to the other side of the border. He had told us that he was taking us to the railway station, but instead, he delivered us straight to the Soviet Border Police.

We walked a considerable distance where the second guide was waiting for us.

We approached a two-story building with hope in our hearts that we had made it safely across and would soon be reunited with our families, but this was not to be, at least not for a while. Our journey took a serious setback. Our Ukrainian guide approached a Soviet guard and told him that we tried to cross the border to the German side and he caught us in the act and was delivering us to the authorities. The guard pointed his rifle at us and ordered us to enter the building.

The Ukrainian guide disappeared into thin air. It's possible that the Soviets paid him to do what he had just done with us.

I felt as though a knife pierced my heart. Instead of the railway station, we found ourselves at the headquarters of the Soviet Border Police. As we entered the building, we heard noises and undistinguishable voices, male and female. The voices were coming from two different directions.

The policeman pointed his rifle to a door on the right and motioned for us to walk in, but before we entered, they took our names and the purpose of our visit in Sieniawa. We entered a vast room filled with women talking, crying, laughing, or just sitting on the floor, guarding their possessions and staring into space. Some were standing in groups, talking or arguing. A wave of heat engulfed me as I entered. The odors enveloped me from all sides, mostly of sweat and unwashed bodies. There might have been about thirty or forty women in that hall.

The two of us tried to find an empty spot and unload our burdens. My companion spotted an unoccupied small area near a window, so we hastily made our way toward it. I removed my backpack and put the basket down on the floor.

I was surprised that the policeman didn't search our belongings, but that would come later. We could have very well been smugglers. I guess they figured that no one could hide anything from the Soviet police. Every so often, a policeman would come in and call out a name or two. As the people answered the call, they were told to gather their belongings and follow him. Some returned after a while, but many did not. Those who returned to the room told us that the police searched them thoroughly and interrogated them. They were probably looking for spies, smugglers, or other criminals. Everyone was under suspicion. I thought to myself, *How can they suspect me of any wrongdoing, a mother who risked her life in order to bring some warm clothes for her children?*

I decided that, if questioned, I would tell them the truth; they must believe me. They would not separate a mother from her children. I was too naive at that time to know what they were capable of.

My turn came the following morning. I was called into the commandant's office at about 10:00 a.m. I got up and gathered my belongings. I must have looked very clumsy, carrying my bundles, including my coat and heavy wool shawl. The big room where we slept that night was very hot and smelled of sweat and disinfectant.

I crossed the hallway and caught a whiff of fresh, cold air before I entered the commandant's room. He was sitting behind a large desk, looking at some papers. He was a stocky, strong man, about forty-five to fifty years old. He looked quite handsome in his uniform. He might have been a captain by rank. I'm really not familiar with military or police ranks. After a moment, he looked up from the page and asked absentmindedly, "And what did you smuggle this time?"

I noticed that his desk and the nearby table were laden with valuables. There was money, foreign banknotes, jewelry, watches, and other items thrown there haphazardly. The floor was full of saccharine tablets and other pills unknown to me. The place was a mess.

I looked him straight in the eye and said in the best Ukrainian language I knew, "I am no smuggler. I am an honest person. I went to the other side to see my sick mother and retrieve some warm clothes from my home for my dear children. I am a poor woman and cannot afford to buy new winter clothes for them. I had left many of my belongings with neighbors when we were evicted by the Germans. Please look into my sack and see for yourself."

He listened to me attentively and made an effort to understand. I did not speak Russian, but I knew a little Ukrainian, which was closely related to Russian. He gave me a questioning look and yelled out, "Marusia!"

The door opened on the other side of the room, and a young woman of about twenty-five walked in. She was also in uniform. She walked straight and tall toward his desk, saluted, and said matter-of-factly, "Da Tovarishch, Kapitan."

He did not answer but only pointed to me. She knew exactly what he meant. The young woman pointed to the door from whence she came and helped me with my things, and I followed.

Marusia closed the door behind us and put my backpack on the table. It was a small empty room except for the one table. A framed picture of Stalin hung on the opposite wall. I failed to mention that the room in which the captain sat also had the same picture of Stalin on the wall. The young soldier proceeded to search my backpack, then the basket, and then she asked me to undress. I was shocked and refused in the beginning, but none of my objections helped. I soon realized that the more I objected, the more suspicion I would arouse. I stripped to my undergarments. She went through every piece of my clothing but did not find anything suspicious. She ordered me to get dressed and take my belongings. I repacked my things, and she escorted me back into the captain's care.

Seeing that messy room again, I came upon an idea. I turned to the captain and said, "Sir, I see that you are a very busy man and the young lady is too. Why don't I clean this room for you, and any other if you like, or give me any other work? I can't just sit there in that big, unventilated room and do nothing all day."

I could see that he was genuinely surprised. He smiled and said, "You know, that's a great idea. Why don't you do that?"

I placed my belongings in the far corner of the room and asked for a broom. The young woman went out and soon returned with a broom and dustpan. She handed them to me, and I began sweeping the wooden floor and picking up the things that were thrown all over.

While I was cleaning up, other people were called in for questioning and searches. The commandant was not as attentive and gentle with everyone as he was with me. Those who hid valuables and didn't disclose them got the raw end of the stick. All their belongings were confiscated, and the people were loaded onto a train that we later learned had taken them to Siberia.

I took my time sweeping the floor and sorting the booty. This room was much more interesting to be in than the stuffy one with lots of people in it. After I finished sweeping, I was told to light the fire in the oven. The room was large, cold, and empty, with only one or two people at a time being searched.

I was told to bring some firewood from the cellar. The officer gave me the key to the cellar door and a flashlight. I went down the dark stairs, lighting my way with the flashlight.

As I opened the cellar door, I looked for the wood and could not help but notice stacks and stacks of boxes, suitcases, and bags of every size that must have been filled with confiscated goods. There were also quite a few expensive furs lying on top of some boxes. It was very clear to me where all those things came from and where they were going.

These Soviet soldiers were not much different from the Germans.

This made me realize that worldly possessions are only temporary and fate decides when we part with them. The true valuables are health and family. I contemplated for a moment then quickly returned to reality. I found the firewood, filled my arms with it, and ascended the stairs. I started the fire in the tile oven, and ten minutes later, the warmth filled the room. The commandant was visibly pleased. He called me to his desk and handed me two large bars of chocolate and said, "Here, take these to your children. How many do you have?"

"Three," I answered with glee.

He poked around the desk and found another bar and gave it to me too. Then he said, "You will be freed shortly. I like people like you. In Russia, we appreciate people who want to work."

My face lit up in a broad smile as I thanked him for his kindness.

A policeman escorted me back to my place. The big room became more crowded each day. There was hardly room for a person to lie down and sleep. My imprisonment lasted six days, and every morning a policeman came to take me to the commandant's office. I already knew what I had to do and gladly performed the task. Every morning the room was laden with all kinds of goods, from clothing to pills, jewelry, and everything in between. My job was also to sort the items and put them in separate boxes.

On the sixth night, at about 10:00 p.m., one of the guards opened the door, placed a small table in the door opening, deposited a large ledger on it, and called out the name of a thirteen-year-old girl. Somehow, she became separated from her parents during the expulsion and only now illegally crossed the border to rejoin her family and was caught by the Russians. Her parents came to claim her a few days earlier, bribed the commandant, and secured her release. Another couple was called, and a while later, I heard my name. As I approached the policeman's desk, he said to me, "Beri veshci i uber-aysia." Take your things and go. Hearing these words caused my hands to shake. I quickly gathered my belongings, put on my coat and shawl, and ran out the door. They locked the door behind me. I could hear the yelling, moaning, and begging of the inmates, but the door remained locked. The policeman left, and only the regular guards remained guarding the entrance.

Later, we heard that some of the people who remained there were sent to labor camps in Siberia. My companion was released two days later.

My travel pass in my pocket, I opened the front door, and a freezing gust of wind almost knocked me over.

The fresh air, which I longed for six days, woke me up, invigorated me, and put a smile on my face.

It was 11:00 p.m. I was in a strange town, not knowing where to go and what to do. The guard who came to release me came over and said that across the street, there was a coachman with a pair of horses and sled. He was taking another couple to the train station and he might have room for me too.

I thanked him and walked out quickly into the blinding snowstorm. The street was deserted and white, but a moment later, I was able to discern the sleigh. I ran to the driver as fast as I could. He was my salvation. I asked him, with tears in my eyes, to give me a ride to the train station, which was quite a distance away. I didn't ask him how much money he wanted. I didn't have any Russian money, but I had Polish money, which I got from Horodynski.

Due to sheer luck, the Russians did not find the money on me. The price was irrelevant. My main objective was to get to the train. The coachman helped me up into the sleigh. The couple, my copassengers, was already there, anxious to leave. I climbed up and sat next to them.

They had a large fur blanket, and they covered me with it too.

The road was very slippery, and the blinding snow made it very difficult for the horses to pull the sleigh. We were stopped on the way by border police. They thought we just crossed the border illegally. We showed them our documents, and they let us go. We were also accosted by some robbers, but this time, the coachman saved us. He told them that we were in the Russian prison and they had taken everything from us. Luckily, they believed him and we continued on the treacherous way to the train station.

We arrived to the railway station at dawn and had no idea when there would be a train to Lvov. The coachman must have been an angel sent from heaven. He was helpful and considerate in every way. Instead of payment, I gave him a pair of fur gloves that I had bought for my husband. He accepted it with thanks. He jumped off the sleigh and went to ask about the train to Lvov.

The station was deserted, but he noticed a man with a lantern walking toward us. When asked, the man pointed to a slowly moving train coming in our direction.

The coachman yelled out, "Get off and catch your train!"

The three of us scrambled out of the sleigh, grabbed our bundles, and ran toward the train. The reason the train did not come to a full stop was that they didn't see any people on the platform, so the engineer thought there were no passengers to pick up. The train was late because of the snowstorm, and the engineer did not want to waste any more time.

The couple traveled light, so they caught up with the train and got on, but I was laden with my backpack and basket and it was hard for me to run fast. The coachman saw my predicament and ran after me, grabbed my knapsack, grabbed me by the hand, and ran with me. A man on the train saw us. He stepped out on the lower step, caught my hand, and pulled me toward him. My foot landed on the step with him. Another man came to my aid; he caught the knapsack from the coachman, and both of them pulled me inside. As I finally stepped into the railcar, I burst out, crying uncontrollably. They were tears of relief. Only then did I realize that I was free to go home and that I would soon be reunited with my children and my husband. I also realized that I could have been killed under the wheels of the train.

The other passengers did not bother me; they let me sit and cry. They figured I needed it. When I calmed down, I also realized that I had no ticket and began to worry. What would happen to me? Would the conductor have pity, sell me a ticket, and let me reach my destination? Or would he make me get off the train at the next stop?

I had been lucky so far that I thought God would not forsake me now that I was nearing the end of my journey.

I cried until I had no more tears left. The people around me were quiet, allowing me to release my emotions and eventually calm down. I really needed that. Ever since I left home almost six weeks earlier, I constantly lived in fear, which followed me everywhere. The guilt of leaving my children and not knowing if I would ever see them again haunted me. The knowledge of leaving my mother, sister, and other dear ones without knowing what their fate would be added to my misery. The difficulty of travel in the harsh winter weather and the last stint with the Russians at the border all took a toll on my nerves and emotions. I needed a good cry.

As I was calming down, I wiped my face and, for the first time, noticed my cotravelers. There were two men and a woman in the compartment. The woman was sitting next to me. She turned her face to me and asked in a hushed, kind voice, "Can we help you in any way?" I understood that they were traveling together. "We are going to Lvov. Are you going there too?"

"Yes," I answered, "but I don't have a ticket. Before I worry about a ticket, though, allow me to thank the men from the bottom of my heart for saving my life. You have no idea what a *mitzvah*, a good deed, you have performed. You just saved a mother of three children. May God repay you in kind."

One of the men said, "Let's wait for the conductor, and we'll explain how you got on the train and that you had no time to buy a ticket. He will understand. If he insists that you must have a ticket, we will lend you the money."

My eyes filled up with tears again upon hearing those kind words. From the way I looked, they must have realized that I was not rich. We spoke for a while, then it became quiet and I fell asleep. I was exhausted. I woke up due to a commotion outside the door. There was some kind of argument in progress. A few moments later, the conductor walked in, asking for tickets. The kind man sitting across me took out his wallet and paid for my ticket. I was grateful but, at the same time, terribly embarrassed. I demanded to know how I could repay him. I didn't want to pull out the roll of banknotes I still carried in my bosom in front of my companions. Stories of robberies and murders were abundant. People killed for much less.

After a short inquiry, I learned that he lived in Lvov, several blocks away from my sister's. I wrote down his address and promised to return the money as soon as possible. My three sisters, who had also been ousted from their homes, were currently living in Lvov in a makeshift refugee shelter. It was a crowded place, and many families lived in those cramped quarters. There were thousands of refugees everywhere expelled by the Germans living in Lvov and surrounding towns and villages. Lvov was a big city. Many people had high hopes of finding more permanent accommodations and the possibility of employment. Though everyone thought this war would be of short duration, they still needed housing and food.

We arrived in Lvov Friday afternoon. There was no train going to Janów that day due to the snowstorm. We were told that we were lucky we made it to Lvov because many trains were stuck in the middle of nowhere due to high snowdrifts.

I walked to where my sister was staying, which was about half a kilometer from the station. It turned out to be a large hall in a previously Polish government building. I had difficulty finding my relatives in this vast, steamy sea of people. Some people already knew one another because they had already been in this place several weeks. Upon my inquiry, an elderly man pointed me in the right direction.

I had to step over people, suitcases, makeshift beds, and other items until I finally found my relatives. They were all in one place. They were shocked to see me.

They knew I was away. They knew about the trip I undertook but had no idea that I had made it back. There was a very emotional reunion. We hugged and kissed and stayed up late into the night as I recounted my story.

They had many questions, and I tried to answer them as best as I could. We all agreed that we had to save our mother, sister, brother Chaim Wolf, and his family but had no idea how to do it. Nobody knew the whereabouts of Itchale, my sister Beila's husband.

I did not forget the kindly gentleman who paid my fare. I finally took out the money from my bosom, removed a few banknotes, counted the amount I owed, and asked my sister to deliver the money to him on Sunday at the given address.

The next train for Janów was scheduled to depart Saturday at midnight, but due to the inclement weather and snowdrifts, it left Sunday at 4:00 a.m. I had notified my husband on Friday by sending a telegram that I would take the midnight train Saturday night to Janów. He came to the train station shortly after twelve (the train ride was about twenty minutes). He had no idea that the train would be delayed. There was no one at the station to ask. Apparently, the attendant was notified that the midnight train was canceled, so he must have gone home instead of waiting in the freezing little hut.

There were a few other people waiting for the train to arrive. They also didn't know that the midnight train was canceled. It was freezing, and the wind was howling, which made the temperature drop even more. By the time we arrived in Janów, it was 4:30 a.m. My husband was frozen stiff and beside himself with worry. When the train finally stopped at the station, it was still dark, but the snow made everything much brighter. As we came to a full stop, I saw my husband's bent figure searching the passing train cars. He must have also recognized me at the window and ran toward the railcar I was in. I hurried down the steps and, a moment later, felt his arms around me. We both stood there for a long while, crying hysterically. We finally separated, and he took my backpack and we walked home.

The streets were deserted. It was about a twenty-minute walk to our apartment. My first questions naturally were about the children. Were they well? How did they look? Did they eat well? Did they miss their mother?

He tried to answer my questions as best as he could. Of course he told me only the good things.

He wanted to know how my trip went, but I said this would have to wait. First, I wanted to know about the children. When we entered the apartment, the children were asleep, but I couldn't control myself any longer. I ran to them, kissed them, and hugged them and cried again, but these were tears of joy.

They woke up instantly, and upon seeing me, they clung to me, climbed all over me, kissed me, and hugged me. They laughed and jumped for joy. Being without a mother's care took a toll on them. They looked gaunt; they had lost weight, and I could see that they had suffered. My eldest daughter, who was eight and a half years old at that time, was the caregiver. She took care of her two younger brothers, herself, and the apartment. She carried water from the pump every day, helped with some food preparation, though food was scarce already, and was in charge of all domestic chores. My husband went out every day to deliver wood to his customers. This was the heating season and his opportunity to make a living.

Their guardian angel during my absence was Reyzia, a close relative of my husband. She had my children in her home almost daily.

My daughter would take some raw foodstuff to Reyzia, who would cook it and feed my children. I am sure that this kindly woman added things of her own that she gave to my children so that they would not be slighted or go hungry. There was a food shortage on the Russian side, too. It was winter, and it was wartime—two good reasons for scarcity of food. The war between Germany and Russia was yet to come. Some food items were rationed already.

I later found out that there were days when my children went to sleep hungry during my absence.

As my hands thawed out, I began unpacking my things and began distributing all the goodies I had brought for them. When I showed them the chocolate, they jumped for joy. They had not tasted this sweet in a long time. The chocolate, I told them, was compliments of a kind Russian commandant.

Questions began pouring out of them as well as my husband. They wanted to know everything about my trip. There was no communication between us for almost four weeks, so there was a lot of catching up to do.

For the first time in several weeks, I felt a release of tension in my entire body.

Mother Back in Janów

Translated from Mother's Memoir

Our lives took their "normal" course, and I was very happy to be back with my family. My two older children went back to school, and they were very happy with the warm clothes I had brought back with me.

There was no word from any of my relatives who had stayed behind under the German occupation.

The winter of 1939–1940 was harsh, and we were looking forward to spring and some warmth.

In the spring, the Soviet authorities began to register the refugees who had fled the German-occupied territories. Most settled in the eastern part of Poland, which was occupied by the Soviet Army in 1939. The border was not yet sealed, and some refugees, like my sister Chana and her family, continued their flight into Soviet Russia.

The registrants had to fill out a questionnaire. The questions included name, address, ages of all members in the family, religious affiliation, occupation, and place of birth. The last question read as follows: "Do you want to remain here under the Soviet rule, or do you prefer to return home?"

Naturally, most, if not all, opted to return home. Nobody suspected that the answer to that question would determine their fate for the next five to six years.

Many thought it was a nice gesture on the part of the Russians to give us a choice and that they would send us all back home if we so desired. The registrants who chose to remain were notified a month later to come back to Lvov and receive Soviet ID cards. The others were told nothing. The registration took several months, and there were thousands of families who were displaced by the Germans. Everyone was waiting for the war to end and to return home, and now they saw an opportunity.

The children were thriving under my care, and we were awaiting the end of the inclement weather. With the arrival of spring came preparations for the upcoming Passover holiday.

It was a quiet time before the storm. Passover had passed, and the school year came to an end. It was the month of July or August.

Friday, as usual, I was busy preparing meals for the Sabbath. Spring and summer brought an abundance of fresh produce. The prices were reasonable, and I prepared a tasty, nourishing Friday-night dinner and also food for the Sabbath.

I worked hard that day, and the heat added to my fatigue.

After we finished our Friday-night meal, the children went to sleep and I followed soon after. My husband stayed up to read the newspaper.

He was an avid newspaper reader all his life and loved to discuss politics whenever the opportunity presented itself. Occasionally he would tell me stories he had read in the paper since I had little time for that luxury.

He could have been a very good political leader had he had the education and the right environment to apply his knowledge.

I do not know when he joined me in bed. I must have been fast asleep when I heard a loud knock on the front door. I grabbed my shawl and ran to the door.

I demanded to know who it was at such a late hour. In passing, I glanced at the kitchen clock, which stood on the counter, and saw that it was after 2:00 a.m.

It was the landlady. I recognized her voice. She said that two Russian soldiers were looking for us. What would Russian soldiers want of us? My mind raced back to Sieniawa, where I was arrested at the border crossing a few months earlier. I had been released and sent home; they could not have changed their minds and sent for me now!

Then I thought that maybe my husband had done something wrong. As I opened the door, I saw them standing right behind our landlady, with rifles on their shoulders. "This must be a mistake," I said. They called out my name and asked me to identify myself.

I did not know what was happening. I asked them to wait and went to wake my husband.

What crime could he have committed, I thought to myself, *that the Russian Army was looking for him in the middle of the night?* I repeated my suspicion to my husband. I was talking nonsense, he retorted angrily and attempted to go back to sleep. "There are two Russian soldiers at the door, looking for you, me, and the children. Maybe I didn't understand them. Why don't you go and talk to them?" I said.

There were stories circulating that in Russia, government officials often came in the middle of the night to arrest people. They were known to arrest whole families and send them to Siberia without any prior notice.

Knowing he did not do anything wrong, my husband was not in a hurry to get up.

He also figured it must be a mistake. Whoever it was out there was probably looking for someone else. I finally went to the door again to find out what this was all about.

They called our last name again, asking in a civil tone to open the door. No pleas or refusals helped. They said they had orders from the authorities and were sent to carry them out.

I finally opened the door, and the two Russian soldiers, with rifles, stepped into the kitchen. "Don't be afraid. You will not be harmed in any way," one of them said. "Wake up your children, have them dressed, take as many belongings as will fit in the wagon waiting for you outside, and you will come with us."

I listened in disbelief, not knowing what to say or do. I still was not sure I understood what they wanted of us.

My husband finally joined me in the kitchen. Apparently, the commotion disturbed him and he could not go back to sleep. He began questioning the soldiers, just like I did, not understanding what this was all about. The soldiers were very patient and polite. They explained again that they received orders an hour earlier to take us to the train station before daybreak. They did not know why. They could not answer most of our questions. They either didn't have the answers or were ordered to be silent.

Since childhood, I was taught to turn to prayer when in fear or in doubt. God will have the answers. He is omnipotent and knows everything. And so I began to pray.

I asked God to protect my children from harm, to have mercy on my husband and me, to forgive us of our transgressions. At that time, I had no idea what was in store for us, but I asked God in advance—prayer can never hurt. Tears streamed freely from my eyes while I murmured my prayers. Even my husband had tears in his eyes and was visibly shaken. This strong, seasoned man had succumbed to shock and helplessness. One of the soldiers tried to console us, but he had a time limit in which he had to deliver us to the train station, so he asked us again gently and quietly to calm down; after all, we were not going to jail or to be shot.

He told us to let the children sleep until we were packed and ready to leave. "Where are we going?" I asked again and again. He did not and most likely could not answer.

"Why do the children have to go too? Maybe they can stay with the landlady or with a relative until we return?" No, we were told, the whole family must go.

My hands shaking, my heart beating like a drum, tears flowing from my eyes, I began gathering our belongings. I asked the soldier, "What should I take? How long will we be gone?"

He said, "Take what you can."

We didn't have much; it had only been eight or ten months since the Germans had expelled us.

We had only the bare necessities. It was July, possibly the beginning of August 1940, the middle of the summer. Though I didn't know where we were going and when or if we would return, I did make sure to take my down quilts and pillows. My husband was angry with me for doing that; he argued that it was the middle of the summer and asked what I needed the quilts for. We could leave them with the landlady as she was a kind and honest woman—she would not mind keeping them for us—or leave them in the apartment, to which we would surely soon return. After all, our rent was paid till the end of the month.

But I insisted on taking them since we had no return date. Yes, it was burdensome—they were bulky and took up a lot of space—but I was not going without my down quilts. Actually, they were my most prized possessions as they were part of my trousseau, which I myself made only a few years earlier.

Little did I know that a few months later, these very quilts would save our lives.

I gathered all I could, stuffed them into sacks, made bundles out of sheets, and gathered my kitchen utensils into a wooden box, and by 4:00 a.m., I was ready to get the children prepared for the trip to the unknown.

I woke my daughter, Anna, first. She was the eldest, a little more than nine years old. Though still a child and small for her age, she had a very mature and practical mind.

I knew that I had to deal with her first because she never did anything unless she understood what she was doing and why. I knew that I would have to explain what was happening, but I myself did not know what that was. Even as a child, Anna was a light sleeper, and I was surprised that the commotion in the adjacent room didn't wake her. With tears welling up in my eyes again, I approached the bed where all three children were sleeping and touched her shoulder. She was up in an instant, eyes wide-open, asking why I had woken her.

"It's the Sabbath! Why can't I sleep a little longer?" she asked.

I tried to put into words the reason I had to wake her so early. I said that we all had to rise and get ready to leave. She began bombarding me with questions, as usual, but I had no answers for her. Anna began getting dressed, reluctantly, while I woke the boys and began dressing David, the youngest. The middle one, Israel, covered his head with the blanket and tried to go back to sleep.

One of the soldiers came in and urged me to hurry up. They had a duty to perform, and they had to gather many other families, he said. Dawn's early light began to seep in through the window, making things more visible. We could not light any lights for religious reasons, so the landlady, knowing this, lit a candle in the kitchen.

We were ready to leave at about 5:30 a.m. I took a long, sad look at the empty walls and sparse furniture, not knowing if I would ever see them again, not knowing where I was going. The soldiers helped us load our belongings onto the wagon.

One of them picked up my little son David and placed him on top of the bundles. As he lifted him, he said to the child, "You will be a brave soldier in the USSR." This was the first time we heard the word USSR as a destination.

My husband began questioning the soldiers again, but they both clammed up and would not converse with us. As soon as the wagon was loaded, we were ordered to move. I asked one of the soldiers what would happen to our furniture. Although we did not have much, those meager possessions were all we had, and we were not happy to leave them behind. We took what we thought we might need for a short trip—our beddings, clothing, pots, pans, and the food that I had prepared for the Sabbath.

In the age of no refrigeration, one did not buy for future use, but I was a great believer in taking food along wherever I went. In those days, one never knew when and where the next meal would come from. I went back to take a last look at the apartment, handed the key to the landlady, and asked her to keep an eye on our possessions until we returned. I said good-bye to her and left with tears in my eyes.

The children sat in the wagon while my husband and I walked alongside. After about fifteen minutes, we noticed the direction in which we were heading. The soldiers were leading us toward the railway station. There was an ache at the pit of my stomach when I realized that this journey would not be a short one. As we neared the train station, we noticed other wagons loaded with bundles and people in tow. Some walked, carrying the loads on their backs. All were going in the same direction.

Each family was accompanied by one or two Russian soldiers with rifles. We began to realize that we were not singled out for this pleasure trip. As it turned out, there were many thousands like us. It was said that close to one million Polish citizens, mostly Jews, were sent to Siberia by Stalin on that single night, but the exact number was never verified.

On the Way to Siberia

Some Segments Translated from Mother's Diary

We arrived at the train station, where we witnessed the hustle and bustle of the masses. Many were already loaded onto freight cars; others were waiting to be assigned to one. The soldiers helped us unload our belongings on the platform, turned the horse and wagon around, and went to fetch more victims. The sad look in their eyes spoke volumes, but we had no idea at that time what that meant.

My husband told me to stay put with the children as he walked away in search of relatives or acquaintances in the crowd. He walked along the train tracks and soon returned with my nephew Victor.

It turned out that my husband's whole family who had lived in Nemierow, Ukraine, were also taken that same night by Soviet soldiers and brought to the Janów train station. This must have been one of the central stations where they brought people from surrounding areas and loaded them onto cattle cars.

In Janów, the freight cars were connected and the train became one long caravan.

Of course we wanted to be together with the family. Victor approached a man who seemed to be in charge of the operation and asked if the family could stay together. Permission was granted, and we began loading our belongings onto the train car that our relatives already occupied. Our family did not fill up the whole freight car, so they loaded as many people in each wagon as they could. About sixty to seventy passengers were loaded onto each freight car.

After a short while, strangers began to fill the balance of the empty space in our cattle car.

Every family occupied an area big enough to spread a blanket on the lightly swept wooden floor, enough for each person to lie down and sleep at night.

The sun was shining, and the day turned out to be a warm one, but the freight car was cool inside. There must have been thousands of people milling around in a daze at the train platform.

People were going from wagon to wagon, calling out names of relatives in the hope of finding one. Everyone was caught by surprise, and no one knew where he was going or why. Private phone communication in those days was almost nonexistent, so notifying a next of kin or anyone else was impossible. The train cars were being loaded one by one and connected to one another. It was a very long train. Once, as we traveled, we counted the number of wagons attached to the two locomotives. We counted up to forty, but there must have been more. As we traveled, we saw other such long trains heading in the same easterly direction.

As all the freight cars filled up, there were still people on the platform. They were told to wait for the next train, which was supposed to pull in as soon as this one left. Many religious Jews refused to board the train on the Sabbath. They were allowed to wait on the platform. We had no idea when or if they left.

Seeing the way some of the soldiers handled the people was a sign that this would not be a pleasure trip.

Our train was finally filled to capacity, and in the early afternoon, a loud whistle tore through the air and we were ordered to board immediately and close the doors, and a few minutes later, the train began to move.

The locomotives moved slowly at first, then faster and faster. We were soon out of town, traveling in an easterly direction, and in the countryside.

Our freight car was crowded and stuffy. Each family tried to find a comfortable spot where there were none. There were no sanitary facilities whatsoever. There was the floor, the roof, the walls, and two small windows high up on each side. The windows had iron bars and dirty glass in them.

There were bundles, suitcases, and people all over the place.

Someone opened a door a few centimeters wide in order to let some air in and to see a sliver of the countryside.

At first, we saw names of towns and villages in Polish and Ukrainian.

The locomotive blew the whistle each time we were approaching a crossing or passing a village or a town.

The train did not slow down or stop until the next day, around noon.

We stopped at the end of a platform of a nondescript small town with a Russian name. A loudspeaker blared, announcing that we were stopping in order to get food. We were told to pick two to three men from each railcar and bring a pail and a sack. My husband, Victor, and another man volunteered, and (curious) Anna tagged along.

A large group of representatives followed two soldiers with rifles to an old gray building that turned out to be a kitchen. They were told to line up to receive food courtesy of the Soviet government. Since this was the first time, the people behaved admirably. Soon the behavior changed.

The delegation returned with a sackful of loaves of bread and two pails of horrible-tasting soup. The bread was freshly baked and tasted good. We knew that the soup, which looked like diluted, greasy grits, could not be kosher, so very few people ate it.

Those who did eat it informed us that we did not miss much.

The same or similar scenario was our daily experience.

The villages we passed looked poorer and shabbier than the ones we were used to in Poland.

Oftentimes, when we stopped at a regular station, the inhabitants of the towns and villages would bring some foodstuff to the train and try to exchange it for other items. Salt and sugar were in great demand.

We could not use many of the items they offered, like live chickens, potatoes, and any other raw provisions requiring cooking.

On occasion, the train would stop for several hours. If we were notified of a longer stay, many people would start bonfires and try to cook. It was not an easy task to find wood for a fire in the vicinity of a train station, but some enterprising individuals succeeded in doing just that. After a while, we learned that wood was also a commodity, so we began collecting wood wherever we could find it and stored it for possible use at a future stop or exchange.

A "home-cooked" meal, no matter what the ingredient, was a feast. One thing we had plenty of was hot water. Every train station had an outside faucet with abundant *kipiatok*—hot water. That was a great help.

About three weeks into our journey, we saw fewer towns and villages. The landscape had changed considerably. The area was sparsely populated. We were passing mostly forests, meadows, and clearings.

The farther we traveled, the taller the trees and thicker the forests.

People were raising eyebrows.

The first couple of weeks, there were many soldiers accompanying our train, but when we reached the thick forest region, there were fewer soldiers visible.

Nobody was able to explain that either. Another unexplainable phenomenon was that each morning, we noticed that the train became shorter and shorter.

After a whole month on the road, the train stopped at its final destination, on the outskirts of a small town by the name of Cherepanovo, totally surrounded by pine trees and an occasional birch tree.

At the last stop, there were only four freight cars connected to one locomotive. Where the others went, nobody knew.

We Have Arrived!

The adults surmised that some train cars must have been disconnected during the night and sent to other destinations. As the locomotive screeched to a halt, we saw a long wooden structure and a concrete platform in front of us.

The megaphone blared, and we were told to remain inside the freight cars until given an order to disembark. After we had waited about an hour, the loudspeaker announced that we were to leave the train cars with all our belongings, find a place under the large tin roof, and await further instructions.

We all gathered our meager belongings and started leaving our makeshift home for the past month. The railway station was a long bluish-gray wooden one-story structure with tall double windows and shutters. There were several railroad tracks and train signals next to each track. A lot of cut-up trees thrown about haphazardly covered the floor under the tin roof. The surrounding thick pine forest completed the picture of the train station in Cherepanovo. We had no idea where we were on the map.

Beyond the structure was a large clearing. We were told to deposit our belongings on that clearing and wait for further instructions.

The scent of the pine trees was intoxicating. It was keenly felt and appreciated after four weeks in closed quarters with dozens of people and minimal hygienic facilities.

The empty clearing quickly filled up. The clearing was too small to accommodate that many people. There were questions on everybody's mind, and people began speculating and trying to guess what was in store for us next.

This must have been a station for transporting lumber out of the area. There was no sign of life as far as we could see. We could not learn anything about anything due to the language barrier and the fact that the authorities were not forthcoming with information. The stationmaster seemed to be in charge of our group. He must have also been in the dark and was awaiting orders from above.

After all the train cars were emptied, an announcement came over the loudspeaker saying that the women and children under the age of eight could move for the night into the wooden shed at the end of the clearing. The shed consisted of three walls and a tin roof. The floor was constructed of wooden boards covered with lots of debris, probably left by the previous transport. We carried our bundles to the shed, but Mother would not put them down until it was clean enough.

She sent Father to find a broom so that she could sweep the boards. Father soon returned with a makeshift broom, and Mother started cleaning. She accomplished her objective while other people waited patiently for the "broom" so they could do the same.

It was about noon, and the sun was warm. Mothers and their children began flocking to the shelter. The roof of the shed was a welcome protection from the noon sun. (A few months later, the sun would be a welcome friend.) People were dragging the few meager belongings they were able to gather in haste in the middle of the night four weeks earlier. People looked bewildered. The inquisitive look in everyone's eyes was saying, "What next? Where to?"

As time progressed, some tried to speculate about our future, but of course, no one knew or could even guess what awaited us. The shed could not contain the throng of mothers and children gathered there. The ones left out had to be content to move into the forest for shelter or remain on the grass in the clearing. Many settled on the lumber that was scattered everywhere. We all thought that the next train would come soon, pick us up, and deliver us to the proper destination. Who would have imagined that we would spend a whole week under the open sky in that faraway wilderness?

Toward evening, a horse-drawn wagon arrived laden with steaming large kettles, similar to large milk cans, which contained a corn soup with some potatoes swimming in it. The closest description I can give the taste of that soup would be rotten potatoes. Two additional wagons brought wooden boxes filled with bread. We quickly realized that this was our dinner and we would most likely stay the night. As expected, the pushing and shoving began. Everyone was hungry and wanted to be the first to receive this fabulous feast. Little did we know that this would be one of the better meals we would receive in the foreseeable future. Observant Jews did not touch the soup. They made do with the bread they received.

Mothers asked for milk for their small children but were told that there was none that day, but maybe the next day there would be. They said that a request for milk would be forwarded to the authorities after they received an exact count of the children under the age of ten.

The last four weeks of the journey taught us some hardships and some patience, but as time progressed, patience wore thin. Some people tried to question the drivers. They endeavored to extract some information about our location, the surrounding area, the geography, the topography, the population, but all they got in return were an empty stare and silence. Apparently, they were instructed not to talk to us.

At that time, we didn't know that all the atrocities perpetrated against the Soviet population were conducted in this and similar areas in utmost secrecy.

Mothers cried quietly and loudly, lamenting over their fate, feeling helpless, unable to feed their children. Children also cried for their own reasons.

The sun was setting, and people were becoming nervous. The fear of the unknown overtook many of them.

We were dumped in the middle of a thick forest, not a house or sign of life in sight, except for the trainmaster. There was the name Cherepanovo written in Russian on the train station, but to us it meant nothing. A day earlier, we had stopped at a large city called Novosibirsk, but we didn't know what part of Russia that was. One thing we did know was that we were on the road for a month and now we were dumped in a deep forest with no end. That was all we saw for the past several days, thick forests dotted with an occasional small village or farm.

Mother kept sending my father to the station to try to find out what we were to do next. Where would we sleep? How long would we be in this godforsaken wilderness? Many other questions kept cropping up, but there were no answers. At one point, when Mother asked the question "Where will we sleep?" Father answered angrily, "Where everyone else will sleep." Naturally, he was nervous, anxious, and bewildered, just like everyone else.

At twilight, suddenly, the megaphone blasted and announced that mothers with small children would be allowed to sleep inside the train station. Moments later, a long line formed at the entrance. Only my brother David was admitted with my mother. This luxurious "hotel" was only for the little ones and their mothers.

The crying of children of all ages separated from their mothers pierced the air intermittently. The building was not large enough to accommodate all of them.

Pushing and shoving, screaming, and arguing began. The Russian overseer intervened. He admitted the last woman and her child and locked the door, leaving many screaming and arguing women outside. My brother Ninius (Israel) and I were crying too. We wanted to be with our mother and David. Father did his best to calm us down. He promised that the next night, one of us would sleep inside and David would stay outside. He tried to explain the situation and showed us that many other children had also remained outside.

The remainder of women and children dispersed to their respective places, and we also returned to the wooden shack to join the rest of the family. My aunt Reizl took over. She found our quilts, spread one on the wooden boards, and told us to go to sleep. Israel and I stayed up long into the night. We huddled together, afraid of the noises coming from the forest. This was our first experience with nature at night.

Father did not stay to watch us. He went to mingle with the people in search of information. Occasionally, my aunt looked in on us to check if we were sleeping, and we made her believe that we were. We were too scared and quiet; we didn't want to cause any trouble.

Occasional outcries pierced the stillness of the warm summer night. Sometimes it was laughter, sometimes cries of children, or maybe loud voices of an argument. Those were friendly disturbances. The unfamiliar ones, like howling wolves or laughing hyenas, put fear in our hearts. It must have been very late when human voices were heard no more and we finally fell asleep. Everyone must have been exhausted and succumbed to blessed sleep. After all, we had a very long, eventful day. No one knew what tomorrow had in store.

During the four weeks on the road, many people took sick with varied ailments.

A day or two after we arrived in Cherepanovo, I began vomiting and having diarrhea. Mother suspected it was from the awful soup we were fed on arrival. She went to the trainmaster to seek help. She asked to see a doctor.

All he did in return was stare at her in silence. She was frustrated and helpless.

She sent Father to inquire among the people if there was a doctor or any other help. He came back with two pills, one of which Mother crushed between two spoons, dissolved it in a little water, and made me drink.

I always hated medicine and do to this day. Being a sickly child, I had my share of all kinds of medicine.

No wonder I hate it.

I think my illness was diagnosed as dysentery. That was the word I heard repeated. I was also kept away from my brothers and other members of the family. I spent most of the time on my makeshift bed, except when I had to relieve myself, which was quite often. I had to drink a lot of water and tea. There was not much to eat, but I could not hold it down anyway. Usually, my father accompanied me to the forest, which was an obstacle course. There was one outhouse for several hundred people, and the lines were endless. I as well as many others could not wait, so the vast forest became the outhouse.

A doctor arrived on the third day, and he examined me as well as many other patients. I was really diagnosed with dysentery. The following day, medicines arrived with the afternoon food wagon.

My illness lasted more than a week. I lost weight and was very weak that I could hardly stand up. Other children were running around, playing games, but I could not join them.

The days were sunny and warm, the night cool and pleasant. It was the end of August.

The adults spent the days getting to know one another, reminiscing about the past, contemplating the future.

Nobody dared to predict it.

On the seventh day, the loudspeaker blasted an announcement. "Our new quarters are being readied, and the first group will leave Cherepanovo the following day." First there was a hush, then applause.

No more information was given. We learned very quickly that there was no use asking—we would get no answers. The authorities would inform us when they were ready, and we would obey their orders.

People began packing their belongings, getting ready for the next phase of our journey. Mystery still prevailed because nobody knew who would be leaving or where to.

Next morning, two officials arrived with the bread wagon. One carried a bag resembling a briefcase, and a short while later, an announcement was heard: All those traveling with close relatives and wishing to remain together should make a list of names and ages and submit to the authorities, but it was not guaranteed. Each head of the family should come forward and line up in front of the station with all the documents in their possession for verification. Again, there was pushing and shoving. Some people must have thought that behind the door lay the road to salvation, and everyone wanted to get there first.

An announcement declared that everything would be done in alphabetical order. Only then did calm return.

The officials confiscated all previous documents that people submitted and issued new Soviet ID cards. We were told that only these were valid and this was all we needed.

About one hour after the registration, four open trucks arrived. These were the first mechanized vehicles we had seen in Cherepanovo. Soon after, the announcer called the names of families who were to board them.

People began dragging their children and bundles and loading them on the first truck.

We never saw most of these people again. Who knew how many survived or returned to their homes.

The registration ended, and two trucks were loaded and gone. Now it was our turn. All the members of my family who left Janów five weeks earlier were loaded on the third truck. All nineteen of us plus cousin Genia, her husband (Itchi), and their two young children. There were also other families whom we had not met before.

Not one of my mother's family was with us, and we knew nothing of their whereabouts until the war ended.

We all sat on our luggage. I was sitting close to my father, and next to him sat Itchi Kofman, Genia's husband.

When all were aboard, the truck began to move on a narrow, uneven dirt road, first slowly, but soon it picked up speed and we were forced to sit so as not to fall over or be hit by tree branches that were quite low.

Surrounding us were tall pine trees of every size and height, creating a roof over our heads. On occasion, we were able to see a sliver of a cloudless blue sky.

At first, everybody was quiet, but soon some people began to talk. At one point, Itchi said to my father, "It looks to me like we are here for good. We will never get out of this place."

After a short pause, my father answered him with one word: "Bituchn." Have faith. He said, "You must never lose hope."

I remember these words as though they were spoken yesterday.

"Karczma" the house I was born and lived until expulsion in 1939 The condition in 1988

Karczma renovated inside and out in 2010

My elementary school still looks the same

Horodynski mansion in 2010 fully restored

Summer fun at river San

Zbydniow train station

Maternal grandmother, Sarah   Maternal grandfather, Zecharia Leib

paternal grandmother, Leah seated in center
behind her: uncle Leibish and aunt Cha-Golda
year unknown

Cousin Dvora (in red) age 92 with my sister Sarah

Cousins Zahavah, Arie and Ruth 1953

Aunts Shifra, Chana and baby Yehuda circa 1923

Uncles Chaim Wolf and Itchale Kanarek (center row)

Cousins Shulamit with husband Eliahu
and daughter Tamar perished in death camp

R to L aunt Regina Genia and friend in Paris mid 1920's

Aunt Gisel and daughter Susan after the war

A street in Rozwadow in 2010

Grandmother Sarah's house in Rozwadow

The house we bought and never lived in Rozwadow

Aunt Blima 1948/1949

Aunt Reizl after the war

Uncle Leibish Passport picture 1949

My benefactors in the US
aunt Molly and uncle Srulek

Uncle Pincus with wife Bertha in 1961

Cousins Victor and Aaron on motorcycle In USSR

My brother Israel with Victor 1945

Cousins L to R Esther, Rachel, Israel before the war

L to R cousin Zipora, myself, aunt Adela
holding daughter Leah 1946

With our tenants in Dzambul
L to R (seated) my brother Israel,
baby sister Leah, (I forgot her name)
back row: myself, Deborah, Helen

With my sisters in 1947

Wartime picture of my mother

Father saying goodbye to his son

Photo for a budding singing career

On the job as a realtor

My mother in 1990

Tying the knot with Herman in 1955

My children Daphne and Zev

Recent photo with my sisters Sarah and Leah

Last time I saw cousin Rachel (seated) (was Nov. 2015) Standing behind her: cousin Leah, Rachel's daughter Leah. myself and my sister Sarah

SIBERIA

It took several hours to deliver us to our final destination. All we saw that entire trip were trees.

Before departure, we were given a loaf of bread per family and a few slices of salty cheese. We were urged to fill bottles or any other vessels with water, which everyone did. The water was a blessing.

When the truck finally stopped at a clearing, we were told to disembark and remove all our belongings.

The clearing was surrounded by several log barracks of different sizes. What surrounded us and the barracks was forest, forest, forest.

The *nachalnik* (overseer) appeared out of nowhere, carrying a rifle on his shoulder.

When we saw the rifle, we understood that this was serious business. Escape was the furthest from our mind.

When the driver handed him the list of inmates, he glanced at it and began shouting orders, not realizing that he had a bunch of foreigners in front of him who, for the most part, did not speak Russian.

With the help of his arms and fingers pointing, we soon began to realize that this was the last stop and would be our home. Of course, nobody had any idea for how long.

Every family was assigned one room or two, depending on the size of the family. Each room, which was the size of about six by ten feet, housed four to five persons. Larger families received larger accommodations, if available, or two rooms. Our relatives, who were fourteen in all, asked to stay together and received a separate large room.

Everyone was instructed to settle in their new "homes" and get a good night's sleep, and all males and females above the age of sixteen were to be up at 6:00 a.m. at the same place (at the clearing) for work instructions and assignment.

If anyone did not have a watch or alarm clock, the loudspeaker would help.

The sun was setting when all the people moved into their assigned quarters.

The first thing the men did was gather for evening prayer, while the others unpacked and began to settle down.

Each room was equipped with iron-framed beds, straw-filled mattresses, a small table, and four stools. There were large nails in the walls, so we understood that this must be a closet. Mother got busy unpacking our linen and made up the one large bed. She gave each of us a slice of bread for our dinner and told us to go to sleep.

All this she did while tears were falling from her face.

Some people had a wood-burning stove in their room; other families had one stove for three rooms.

Next morning, everyone reported at the clearing as ordered.

It was a twelve-hour workday, dawn to dusk, six days a week. As the days grew shorter, the workdays were adjusted accordingly.

Men were given a three-foot stick with a sharp metal gadget resembling a bent teaspoon attached to one end. With this tool they were taught to cut straight-up one-meter grooves on the trees. From the upright main groove they cut branches left and right. At the bottom of the upright groove, a clay pot was attached, which was the receptacle for the sap flowing through these grooves.

The women's job was to collect the sap from each cup, pour it into a pail, and when the pail was full, carry the twenty- to thirty-kilogram pails to a central shack, empty it into barrels, and return for more.

Both men and women had to do the amount of work, called norma, each day that they were assigned.

The nachalnik watched and supervised every worker. He also spent the whole day in the forest, rain or shine. The workers were warned and told that the ones who did not fulfill their norma would not receive their daily bread. There was a famous Communist expression in the USSR: "Kto nie rabotayet to nie yest." The one who does not work does not eat.

Though we arrived in Siberia in late August, we hardly noticed the passing of the fall season. We were too preoccupied with the new country, new place, new language, new environment, new laws—in other words, a completely new way of life. So the fall season passed us by.

Everything was new and different, including the weather and the seasons. Fall came and went unnoticed.

The Siberian forest surrounding us was vast and made up mainly of tall evergreen pine trees. The few birch and other trees growing in the area were hardly noticeable.

People were more preoccupied with survival than with nature. We did still notice a few of the blueberries and mushrooms, though the season was over.

Most of the ground in the forest was covered with moss, and that did not change much, except now it was covered with a white blanket of snow.

The snow began falling in October and continued intermittently through March. None of it melted all winter long. By the time winter was in full force, there was about six to eight feet of the white stuff on the ground. The white blanket stretched through the woods as far as the eye could see and beyond. It covered the rooftops of the barracks and everything else in sight.

Strong winds that blew quite often redistributed the white blanket from time to time. On a sunny day, the reflection of the white crystals blinded us with its brilliance and sparkle.

It was a pretty sight to behold, a real winter wonderland, but at the same time, it was a dangerous, threatening, and occasionally deadly environment. The temperature stayed between negative twenty to negative forty degrees Celsius from November to March.

The adults, aged sixteen and older, had to work no matter the weather. Several men had frostbitten toes, fingers, and even noses. Some men were given shovels to dig passages from the barracks into the woods. We came from Poland, where the winters were severe too and quite a bit of snow covered the ground every year, but no one was ready for the Siberian winter.

It was much longer and much more treacherous. Though we were in the southern part of the Siberian wilderness, the climate was very similar. My brothers and I, as well as other children, stayed in bed, under the warm covers, for most of the day. Mother literally saved our lives by insisting on taking our down quilts when we left home. On occasional evenings, when Father was not too tired after a day's work, he would tell us stories from the Bible or from his past.

And the snow, the crisp, light, freezing white crystals of fluff, can be beautiful and enjoyable, but they are also capable of devastation. The days were very short, and there was not much for us to do or play with.

We could not go outdoors. Very few of us had enough warm clothing or boots. Only the working population received special winter clothing from the state: boots made of pressed wool called pimy, which were very warm but not waterproof. The special jackets they received were quilted and filled with wool.

We were also afraid of getting sick. The adults told us that in the winter, the bears were asleep but wolves, hyenas, and other hungry animals looked for food and could catch children and eat them. That certainly prevented us from going outside the barracks.

Few children, if any, had toys and were not always willing to share. Our favorite game became catch, where we would run up and down the long corridor. That kept us warm and occupied us for a while.

Most of the adults were out working, so the noise we made didn't bother too much. The entire area surrounding the barracks was covered with at least six feet of snow. The windows of the rooms were low, so after a day or two of snowfall, it covered the windows and obstructed the light of day. When that happened, the men had to shovel the snow away. This was an added task after a day's work.

The only way to walk outdoors was on skis. But only workers received them. Trying to walk on top of the snow was impossible, as in certain areas it was higher than a person.

Mother didn't allow us to go out for fear of getting sick. Now we know that even microbes cannot survive in this Arctic climate. The constant problem, especially in winter, was the lack of food. When one has little to do to occupy the mind, food becomes a constant preoccupation.

There were no sanitary facilities to speak of. The outhouse, situated near the river, was not always accessible. We had a potty and used it in the room. Our parents emptied it when they came home from work.

I will let you use your imagination. The people in the barracks designated an area for waste disposal so that the surrounding areas could remain fairly clean. In the spring, when the snow melted, it was washed down into the river.

During those harsh winter months, my mother, as well as some other women, worked indoors, weaving baskets and other artifacts made of reeds. The baskets were sent to a central station, and what the authorities did with them, nobody knew. The men had to go out into the woods to cut down trees and do other types of outdoor work. Woodcutting was a daily necessity so that the stoves and ovens could be active day and night. Many logs were sent down the river in the spring. The men's job was also to prepare the trees for spring awakening, when the sap began to flow again. Every man received a pair of skis, the only means of transportation during the winter months. Young people mastered the art of skiing easily, but with the older men, it was another story. They tried to help one another the best they could. They would walk in the skis on top of the snow. No one dared to go anywhere without them or alone. One could fall into the snow and remain buried and dead until the snow melted in the spring.

One of my cousins was a wise guy and dared the elements. He walked out onto the snow without skis, about twenty-five yards into the forest. The snow gave in under him, and he disappeared. Luckily, people heard his screams and dug him out. He never tried that stunt again.

Once, my mother sent me to another barrack to deliver some finished baskets and bring back raw materials.

I was dressed from head to toe. Only my eyes were visible, and I felt heavy and clumsy. I didn't want to wear the skis as they were adult skis belonging to my mother, so they were too big and too heavy.

I welcomed the opportunity to go outdoors; I had not been out in weeks. When I finally reached the outdoors, a strong gust of wind hit me with such a force that it knocked me over. Luckily, Mother was right behind me and helped me secure the skis to my feet. At this point, Mother was sorry that she had asked me to go and wanted to abort my errand, but I insisted on going and completing the job. I was eager to breathe some fresh air and see something else besides the inside of the barrack.

The other barrack, my destination, was not very far away, about eight hundred to one thousand feet. It was across the river, though, and I had to cross the narrow wooden bridge accessible through a narrow path that lay over it.

I had to wear the heavy skis in order to remain on top of the snow. Dragging the skis and the heavy baskets made this assignment a very difficult one. I was very happy to have my Guralsky, my fur coat, somewhat short, even though it had a burned hole on the back, which Mother did her best to cover.

I completed my errand. Mother was happy I could do it, and I was proud of my accomplishment.

It is known that the Siberian winter is long and unforgiving. The little stream flowing nearby had crystal clear water under a foot of ice, which was used for all our needs. We also collected clean white snow in pails, which we melted on top of the stove and used for washing, laundry, etc.

After a while, we had to go out pretty far to find clean snow because some unscrupulous people emptied their garbage pails, potties, and the like pretty close to the barracks.

As I said earlier, sanitary facilities were almost nonexistent.

In April, nature began to wake from its frozen slumber. There was still plenty of snow on the ground, and the earth was frozen and hard as a rock. The clearings began to show signs of the long-awaited spring. The earth was still frozen, and the farmers had to wait sometimes until May to plow and plant again. We were all anxious to see what Siberian spring was like.

During the first few days, he taught the workers how to do their job. Soon after he was in the forest every day, rifle in hand, mostly on horseback, checking if and how the work was being executed. No doubt he was responsible to his superiors for the workers under his watch and their production.

My father, being a religious man, tried to find a way so that he would not have to work on the Sabbath. When he mastered the job well enough, he would work twice as fast on Friday and try to double the output so that he could rest the next day and still produce what was expected of him. One such Friday, he was watched by the overseer from behind a tree. The nachalnik, seeing how fast my father was running from tree to tree, decided to double his norma. After watching my father for a while, he decided to confront him and tell him that from that day forward, he had to do double the amount of work. Father tried to explain why he was doing this, but the nachalnik refused to understand or simply could not. Religion was forbidden in the USSR, so this could not be an excuse. Moreover, it was illegal to practice any religion. That week, my father received half the amount of bread. We all shared our bread with him. After some time, the nachalnik realized that he could not punish my father for too long. He even developed a respect for my father and liked to converse with him in the forest when nobody was around.

The work was very hard for both men and women. They used to come home from the woods with aching backs and feet and calluses on their palms, but the next day, they faced more of the same.

This hard labor continued until the first snow fell and the sap froze in the trees. The authorities were prepared for the winter weather and devised different kinds of hard work for the inmates.

I just remembered an incident that took place not long after we had arrived. It might have been late September or October when we celebrated (if you can call it that) the holiday of Sukkoth or Tabernacles.

The weather had cooled off considerably. By that time, the natchalnik was familiar with his flock and knew almost everyone by name. The names were hard for him to pronounce, so he gave them Russian names.

Every morning during roll call, he called out everyone's name and then counted the heads just to make sure no one was missing.

One such morning during Sukkoth, the nachalnik noticed that my father was absent from his place in the lineup. He walked over to my mother and asked where Father was. She just shrugged. He asked her again, and she said that she didn't know.

This was suspicious, so he decided to investigate on his own. It was already about 6:15 a.m., and he realized that he was losing time and the people were standing idly instead of working.

He ordered everyone to remain in their places and quickly went into our barrack and forcefully opened the door to our room.

My brothers and I were still in bed, but when we heard the door open, we picked up our heads from under the covers. My first reaction was fear. It was not the natchalnik's habit to barge into people's rooms even though he had every right to.

I had no idea that Father was still home. We usually woke up when our parents had gone off to work. There was no reason for us to rise early. There was no school or anything else to do. If we slept late, we would have breakfast later, so we were less hungry during the day. Mother always prepared our daily food and left it on the small table.

There is a special prayer on Succoth (Feast of Tabernacles) called Hoshanot where we ask God to save us and deliver us from strife and evil. My father had a beautiful voice and certainly knew his prayers by heart. Apparently, he got carried away and was engrossed in this very appropriate prayer for the time. He was enveloped in his prayer shawl and had no idea of the nachalnik's presence. As the nachalnik put one foot inside the room and saw my father enveloped in his white prayer shawl, asking God for salvation in a loud outcry, the overseer turned white as a sheet, withdrew as fast as he came in, and closed the door behind him.

Shivering with cold and fear, I jumped off the bed, tiptoed over to my father, tapped him on his arm, and told him what had just transpired. Only then did he realize that he was so engrossed in the prayer and completely forgot about reality and going to work. He certainly did not hear the nachalnik's arrival or departure.

He quickly removed his prayer shawl and phylacteries; he didn't even fold them or put them back in the special sack. He grabbed his *stomieska*, his work tool, and ran out. He was sure that the overseer would punish him severely for this transgression.

In the meantime, the nachalnik ran out, sent all the workers into the woods to their respective jobs, and waited for my father at the end of the clearing. When Father walked out and saw that everybody was gone, true fear gripped him. He didn't know what to expect. As he entered the forest at his usual quick pace, the nachalnik came out from behind a bush. He approached Father and demanded to know what he was doing earlier. He asked Father if he was a ghost or if he did some kind of black magic. Father smiled and tried to explain in his broken Russian that he was simply praying to God, something he did every day of his life.

"And what does God tell you?" the man asked.

"He tells me to have patience," Father answered.

The nachalnik commanded my father to stop praying because all religions were forbidden in the USSR. He would forgive him this one time because he was a newcomer and unfamiliar with the laws of the Soviet Union. There would be no more praying here, the nachalnik stated firmly. Father promised to stop praying but had no intention of doing so. During evening prayers, Father told his praying comrades what had happened that morning. There was always someone on the lookout to make sure that the natchalnik was not in the area. Nobody wanted a run-in with the law.

My Brother David

It was August 1942 when my family suffered its first terrible loss.

My youngest brother, David, was not even seven years old when he died. David took sick. He was running a high fever and was complaining of a sore throat. Since my mother had to go to work, I was the one who took care of my two younger brothers. I was told to give David lots to drink, but his throat hurt a lot and he refused. Since I myself often suffered from sore throats, I understood his pain and sympathized with him. We were about thirty-five kilometers from the nearest town, where there was a doctor and a hospital. The name of the town was Suzun. We were prisoners and were not allowed to leave the camp except to go to work in the woods or by written permission from the commandant. We had no means of transportation. We asked everybody in the camp if they had any medicine that could help my brother, but no one had any.

When by the third day there was no improvement, Mother became frantic and ran to the commandant for help. She related the grave state David was in. The commandant came to check if she was telling the truth. When he saw how the poor child was suffering, he took pity. The commandant had two children of his own. He allowed my parents to use the horse and buggy that brought the daily bread to transport David to the hospital in Suzun. He also told my parents to stop in Cherepanovo, where there might be a doctor. This meant that there would be no bread delivery the next day or possibly two days. The nachalnik assigned several men who would walk the three or four kilometers to the next *uchastok* (barrack cluster) and carry the bread on their backs. He himself had a horse but apparently was not allowed to part with it. In the event someone decided to flee, he could pursue the fugitive on horseback. Today, this may sound funny. Who in his right mind would run into the forest, a forest with no end?

We stayed up all night with my brother crying. Mother applied cold-water compresses to his forehead, but David was still burning with fever. In the morning, the commandant had all the necessary papers ready for my parents.

The wagon finally arrived at about noon. The bread was quickly unloaded. The driver was apprised of the situation and given his orders, and in no time at all, my parents and David were off to seek help. They reached Cherepanovo and found a doctor, who diagnosed David's illness as diphtheria, but he had no medicine for it. They continued their journey to Suzun with the hope of finding help there. Alas, it was too late to save my brother. It was 1942, and the war with the Germans was on. Any medicine manufactured at that time was sent to the front, and very little reached Siberia, especially for people like us.

There were other priorities, like KGB officials and their families.

My dear brother had his young life ended in my mother's arms that very day on the way back from Suzun.

It was the thirtieth of August 1942 (Hebrew date, seventeenth of Elul). My beautiful seven-year-young brother, David, was buried in the forest, in an unmarked grave somewhere in the wilderness of Siberia.

When my parents returned empty-handed, one look at their faces and their red and swollen eyes told us of the horror and their immense pain.

My mother was hysterical—no one could console her. The beds were stripped to the bare boards. My parents sat *shivah* (the seven days of mourning) on the floor. The Jewish custom had to be explained to the commandant so that my parents could receive special dispensation and would not have to go to work those seven days and they received their daily portion of bread.

It was summer, and the forest was abundant with all kinds of berries and mushrooms. I went to the forest daily to pick what I could find. Mother taught me to differentiate between poisonous and edible mushrooms. In the evening, when the people came back from work, they did what they could to help with food preparation and to console my parents. They brought us food. Nobody had much of anything, but people were kind and shared with us what they had.

Mother refused to eat or drink, but neighbors and relatives forced her to put some food in her stomach. They pointed out that she must remain a healthy mother for her two remaining children.

We observed the extended mourning period for eleven months, during which my father did not shave and recited the Kaddish (prayer for the dead). I don't think my parents ever got over the death of my brother. They camouflaged their feelings most of the time, but they never got over the terrible loss.

I was about five years old when David was born. I remember his birth to this day.

In those days, especially in a small village, a woman did not go to a hospital to give birth. Every town and village had a midwife who delivered the babies. I've heard now that midwifes are in vogue again.

I cannot recall my mother walking around with a belly. (I would not have known what it was, anyway, and she would not have told me. In those days, children were not told much.) But I do remember David's birth.

I did not know what was going on. I just saw a lot of commotion and realized that something was about to happen.

I think it was June or July. The weather was balmy, and the windows were open to let the fresh, warm air in. I do not know the exact date David was born, which I should, because my dear mother made sure that everybody's birthday was celebrated in some special way.

My maternal grandmother, Sarah, was supposed to have come from Rozwadów, but she did not. I was looking forward to her visit, as I loved her dearly. She was a pious, kind, loving person.

Apparently, my mother went into labor sooner than expected and Grandmother Sarah did not arrive in time. Mother was in pain. She called in my aunt Reizl, who lived next door.

My aunt apprised the situation immediately and sent Halina (our maid) to fetch the midwife and told her to put a big pot of water on the stove before she left. I offered to accompany Halina, and she accepted. My aunt stayed with my mother. I tried to find out what all the haste was about, what a midwife was, why she was needed in such a hurry, if Mother was going to be all right, why she was sick and in pain.

All I got from Halina was a mysterious look and reassurance that Mother would be all right and that I would have a big surprise. Her answers only heightened my curiosity.

The midwife lived not too far away (the whole village was not that big). As we approached the hut, Halina knocked rapidly on the door and entered without waiting for an answer. A stocky woman was standing at the stove.

At the sound of the opening door and our entrance, she turned to us and smiled. "I guess it's time," she said.

Halina, out of breath, declared, "It's time."

Thant was all she said. The woman removed her apron and threw it on a chair, then she removed the pot from the stove and put it on the slate floor and followed us out the door.

She could not run as fast as we did. On the way, she asked Halina some questions that I did not understand, nor did I understand Halina's answers.

We ran ahead, and the woman followed as fast as she could.

A few minutes later, we were home. Upon entering, we found my brother Niniush (Israel's nickname) sitting on the kitchen floor, crying bitterly, and my aunt Reizl in the bedroom with my mother behind closed doors.

Halina scooped up Niniush and tried to console him. He finally calmed down, pointing to the closed bedroom door.

Suddenly, I heard my mother scream. I froze, pulling at Halina's skirt and looking at her frantically. She reassured me that everything would be all right. The midwife, out of breath, entered hastily and, on her way to the bedroom, checked the large pot of water on the stove.

I wanted to enter the bedroom to comfort my mother, but most of all to find out the cause of her pain.

Nothing and nobody was making any sense. No one was telling me what was going on, why Mother was sick in bed all of a sudden and how they all knew that she would be well soon. Why didn't they call a doctor? How could this woman help my mother? Why was my crying brother and I not allowed in the bedroom?

A short while later, my father arrived. He looked concerned but did not go into the bedroom to see how my mother was. That surely did not make sense. I noticed when I slipped into the bedroom.

Suddenly, my mother arched her body in the air and gave out a piercing cry. I was terrified and ran to her as her body dropped. Aunt Reizl caught my hand and ordered me out of the room immediately. I began to cry, wanting my mother, wanting to help her. Why were all these people surrounding her, and why was I not allowed to be near her? Halina grabbed my hand and escorted me out of the room into the care of my father, who already had his hands full trying to console my brother Niniush, who was also frightened by Mother's screams. Father decided to take us both outside in order to distract us and calm us down. He tried to make us play with our dog Rex, we fed the chickens, and we went to the garden to watch things grow.

Outside, I tried to extract some answers from my father about Mother's illness, but he was not forthcoming.

The women must have closed the bedroom windows, because nothing could be heard outside. We were kept busy by Father for quite some time because it felt like an eternity. My concern for Mother and curiosity were intense, but I should have been used to my parents keeping secrets from us.

Suddenly, Halina came running toward us, yelling excitedly, "Panie Herszku, Chlopczyk." Mr. Hersh, it's a boy.

Father picked up Niniush and briskly ran toward the house. I followed right behind him.

All of us ran straight into the bedroom, where we found Mother still in bed, propped up on pillows, holding a small bundle wrapped in white. She looked pale, her hair wet and a faint smile on her lips. I ran in front of Father, jumped on the bed, and wanted to hug her. I was so happy that she was feeling better. She cautioned me not to hurt the baby. What baby? Where did she get a baby?

Father bent down to kiss her forehead, then my aunt Reizl hugged him and wished him Mazel Tov. Everybody seemed to be in a happy mood while I was befuddled. Father took the baby in his arms and examined him closely. "He is beautiful," Father declared. "He looks just like me." Mother instantly protested and reassured everyone that the baby resembled her family 100 percent. Aunt Reizl, the pragmatist, announced that the main thing was that the baby was healthy. All agreed.

Now Mother called Israel and me over to her bed and told us that while we were in the garden, a stork came in through the bedroom window and brought us a little brother. We should thank the stork for bringing us such a beautiful, healthy boy.

So why was Mother screaming and looking sick? I asked. She answered that she was very surprised to see the stork in the middle of the day because storks usually delivered babies at night. I had no choice but to accept her answer, though I was not completely satisfied with it.

Life began to revolve around the new baby. He cried at night and woke us up many times, but the inconvenience was compensated by the fact that I was allowed to sleep with Halina in the kitchen, which was always a treat for me.

I was quite happy with the whole affair because I was still the eldest and still the only girl. My value went up—at least that was what I was told.

David was a wonderful, beautiful child and quite smart.

Many years later, I asked my mother about the day David was born. She was stunned to learn how much I remembered.

The Package

A few days before my brother David took sick, we received a package from my aunt Mollie in America. To receive any mail from abroad to the USSR, especially to Siberia, was extremely rare, but to receive a package was nothing short of miraculous.

My father had to get special permission from the nachalnik to leave camp and go to the main post office to fetch the parcel and lose several hours of work that had to be made up that week. We were flabbergasted that the package even reached us and was not stolen on the way. To our great surprise, however, the package was squashed, but the content was untouched. The appointed day arrived, and Father went to fetch the parcel. We were breathless with anticipation. It goes without saying that such news spread throughout the barrack and everyone wanted to learn of its content. I was praying there would be something for me in it too.

In the afternoon, Father hitched a ride with the bread-delivering wagon but walked back home the three kilometers, carrying the package weighing twenty-two pounds.

It was dusk when he returned, and the work contingent was leaving the forest at the end of the workday. Some offered to help carry this found treasure, but Father refused the help. As exhausted as he was, he ran the rest of the way. He entered and threw the package on the bed, and Mother quickly locked the door behind him.

We could hear voices in the hallway and a crowd gathering; everyone was curious to see what this was all about, but their curiosity was not satisfied.

Father untied the string very carefully and proceeded to open the carton. The treasures we found inside were beyond our wildest dreams. There was a mixture of canned foods that we had never seen before and clothing. I vividly remember two striped wool hats, which I claimed immediately, and slacks for my father, which he desperately needed—Mother had run out of patches to sew on his. There was a dress for my mother and some things for my brothers too. Our joy was indescribable. We blessed our aunt and uncle in America, who found us in this godforsaken wilderness and sent us help when we so desperately needed it.

When we returned to reality, our concern was how to hold on to this found treasure.

From the stamps we learned that the package was four and a half months on its way.

Mother promised to fix and adjust all the items that needed it.

We quickly returned the beautiful gifts to the carton and placed it under the bed, and Mother got busy preparing our evening meal.

This generally did not take very long, for there was not that much to prepare. The summer was easier to bear for there were berries and mushrooms in the forest that we picked daily.

I am sure that our neighbors were curious about the content of the package, but they were gracious enough not to bother us with questions.

About an hour had passed since the great commotion when there was a knock on the door. Our cousin Isaac (Itchi) walked in with a smile on his face. "So what was in the package?" he asked nonchalantly. My father looked at him questioningly. Isaac repeated the question.

"That's my business," Father answered.

"Oh no, it's not!" retorted Isaac. "It is also my business. Since the parcel came from my brother, it belongs to me too and you must share it with me or you will have nothing." His words were measured and precise, and the smile was erased from his face. We were stunned and speechless.

My father said that his sister Mollie had sent the package to us; it was addressed to us and for us, and nobody had any right to demand anything. Father told him that if he wanted to be generous, he would share the contents with his own sisters and brother and especially his mother (my grandmother Leah).

Isaac retorted angrily, "We'll see." He walked out and slammed the door behind him.

We sat without saying a word for a while. Mother was the first to recover from the shock and started arguing with my father. My parents decided not to use any of the clothes. Father would write a letter to his sister in America, requesting exact instructions regarding the parcel. The clothes were mainly children winter clothes, anyway, so we could wait. We ate the food that came in cans. This was the first time we ever saw or tasted food from a can. When you're hungry, everything tastes wonderful. There were about six or seven cans of foodstuff. I only remember the contents of one—sweet condensed milk.

Initially, we were afraid to eat the food for fear it might be spoiled. Mother tried some first and assured us that it tasted good and was safe to eat. Every morsel was consumed. Our joy was marred by Isaac's pronouncements and threats. Father told us not to worry and assured us that he would take care of everything. I couldn't fall asleep that night for a long time. My parents were up too, discussing in a whisper what they were going to do and how they would handle the problem. It was easy for me to hear them talk. I slept at the foot of their bed, and the boys slept at the other end. I always liked to stay up and listen to my parents' whispers. Though my knowledge of Yiddish was limited at that time (the first language I spoke was Polish), I understood enough to figure out what they were saying.

Discovery of Zakavrashyna

Translated from Mother's Diary

One day, my neighbor Hadassah and I were working in a different section of the forest. At around noon, we heard some voices. In the beginning, they were not audible; we were sure these were some of our people working in the area, but as we came closer, we heard Russian spoken, not Yiddish or Polish. We were intrigued and went closer to where the voices were coming from.

To our great surprise, we saw two Russian women picking blueberries in the forest. At first, we didn't know what to make of it and were afraid to approach them, but we mustered up some courage and quietly came from behind. They were startled, but when they saw that we were also women, they regained their composure and addressed us in Russian. Our knowledge of the language at that time was negligible, but somehow, with the aid of our hands, we were able to understand one another. It turned out that these women came from the nearby village called Zakavrashyna, about eight kilometers away, to pick blueberries and mushrooms in the forest. The inhabitants of these villages or collective farms were also deported by the authorities from other parts of the country.

They were also not allowed to leave their designated areas without a permit or mingle with other deportees. They were just as afraid of us as we were of them. After a somewhat short and strained conversation, the wall between us disappeared and they told us about their village, their people, and their lives. Though there was a language barrier, we learned quite a bit about their lives. They told us that they lived in a collective farm, Kolkhoz.

They were primarily farmers and owned some livestock. The government gave each family a house (a little hut) and some land surrounding it. They usually had no problem with lack of food because they were allowed to grow their own. They also had to work on the government land, planting and sowing whatever they were ordered each year. The crops were sent to government storehouses and distributed from there. The villagers were told how much crops each acre must yield. They had to deliver the prescribed norma by hook or by crook.

This was music to our ears. People who grew their own crops knew no hunger.

They gave us directions to the village and said that we could surely buy or barter some fruits and vegetables from the local people.

There was one problem—we could not tell a soul about our meeting or our conversation. If we did decide to take the risk and go to the village, it must be at night or on Sunday only, when most people were indoors and not out working in the fields. These clandestine meetings were against the law, and if caught, we could all be severely punished. They also warned us against wild animals, like wolves, hyenas, and black bears, especially in wintertime, when food was scarce and the animals were hungry.

The following Sunday at dawn, when it was still dark, my neighbor Hadassah and I quietly sneaked out of the barracks and into the woods so as not to be noticed by anyone. We walked out separately and met in the forest at a predesignated spot. It was late spring. The evergreens emanated their intoxicating fragrance. The snow had melted in most places, the ground was covered with fresh moss, new grass, and spring flowers, and many other plants were returning to cover the forest floor. Under the cover of darkness, carefully walking through the forest, we began our maiden excursion to Zakavrashyna.

There were about three kilometers of forest to navigate before we reached the clearing. We were shivering, not as much from cold, but from fright. We held hands and walked as quickly and as quietly as we could, listening to the sounds of nature and more keenly for sounds of animals.

As the first sunrays pierced through the branches, the stillness was interrupted by the occasional chirping of an awakening bird. The birdsongs intensified as the sky brightened. Each of us carried a long stick for "protection" from animals in case one decided to attack us. We were breathing harder and harder as we proceeded. We both decided to go forward no matter what. Eight kilometers did not seem too far to walk to get sustenance for our loved ones. It seemed that our survival instinct and hunger were stronger than our fear of animals.

When we reached the clearing, the sun was already rising and a wave of warmth and yellow light enveloped us. We stopped to catch our breath. We looked around and back into the dark forest, but not a living soul was in sight, with only the birds singing and chirping. I smiled and said to Hadassah, "See? We are as free as the birds."

"Don't be so sure," she answered. "We can still be caught and shot, then what will our children do without their mothers?"

I assured her that I was only joking.

"A fine time to be joking!" she retorted.

She had definitely put a damper on my mood.

We eventually found the path, which made it much easier for us to walk. We continued walking in the direction of the rising sun. The earth was flat as far as the eye could see. About an hour or so of walking through the steppe, we discerned a thin thread of smoke and then another and another. My heart began beating faster at the realization that we were nearing the village.

Soon we approached the first hut on the outskirts of Zakavrashyna. This part of the journey was much easier. I regained my good mood because I had the feeling that this adventure would be an interesting and hopefully a productive one. We did not know what to expect, but we had a little money, so we were at least hoping to buy some food and bring it back to our families.

We were exhausted, with aching feet and backs, but we were full of excitement and anticipation. At first, we saw only roofs made of straw, but as we approached the first hut, we realized that it was built of logs. Siberia certainly did not lack wood. On the way we tried to rehearse what we would say, what we would ask of the people, provided they were not afraid of the authorities and would talk to us. Our knowledge of the Russian language was negligible. Though I had lived in the Ukraine for ten months prior to arriving in Siberia and picked up some of the language, we were still not sure the local people would understand us. As I mentioned, it was Sunday, a day of rest. Most people did not work on Sunday.

We finally approached the first house with great trepidation and lightly knocked on the door. The chimney emitted a grayish smoke, and the aroma escaping the front window was unfamiliar to us, but we understood that something delicious was cooking inside. My heart was pounding in my chest. The moment between my knock on the door and the inquiring voice from within felt like an eternity.

All I said was "Da." Yes. Hadassah was a basket case, so I became the spokesperson for both of us. The door opened with a creak, and a kindly, wrinkled female face appeared in the open door. She was a short woman, possibly forty-five to fifty years old, but under the burden of years of hard work, she looked more like seventy-five. Her head was covered with a colorful kerchief, babushka-style. She was wearing a dark gray dress with rolled-up sleeves, and her waist was gathered by the straps of a clean long apron of a nondescript color. Her vivid blue eyes, a faint smile, and a hand gesture invited us inside. That dispelled most of our fears. She later told us that they had heard about us from those women we had met and actually were expecting our visit. She did not think it would be so soon. After all, if any of us were caught, we would be severely punished, most likely jailed. She was happy to see us.

We asked her if she had any spare food she would like to sell or knew someone else who would.

"First, you must rest," she said. "You have come a long way. It must have taken you several hours to get here. You probably have small children to feed, otherwise, you would not risk your lives and leave the camp." We answered in the affirmative and proceeded to tell her about our families.

She pointed to the table and asked us to sit down, and we did. First, she poured each of us a tall glass of milk and then pulled out of the hot oven a *tsugun*, a black iron pot. I think everyone in Russia owned a tsugun, the most efficient iron pot in the world. The aroma of the dish was intoxicating. We had not eaten since the evening before. The woman placed a bowl in front of each of us and filled it with the most delectable potato stew I havehas ever tasted. As we were devouring the delicious dish, I asked how she made it. Well, it was very simple. It consisted of potatoes, milk, a pat of butter, and some dill. Years later, I repeated the recipe many times. She refilled our bowls and went to the next room to call her husband.

The whole house consisted of two rooms, the larger being the kitchen, where the family spent most of their time; the second room must have served as the bedroom. A few moments later, a tall middle-aged man, neatly dressed in slacks and a typical Russian shirt, entered the kitchen. A wide leather belt completed his outfit. He greeted us with a warm smile and kind words. We could feel the compassion in his words. He sat down at the table and began questioning us about our lives, where we came from, how many were in the camp, the distance from the village, how we were treated, etc.

At first, we were reluctant to talk; after all, these people were strangers to us and they could have been planted there by the authorities. He put us at ease by telling us that he and his wife were also repatriated from Charkov. He used to be a priest, but the revolutionary government considered him an enemy of the state when they outlawed religion and there was no need for priests. He might be spreading anti-Soviet propaganda. The authorities decided that he and many others like him should be put to work in other fields and become productive citizens. Thus, he and his family, as well as thousands of other "enemies of the state," were resettled to Siberia, where they could do no harm to the government and build and develop that sparsely populated wilderness.

Hadassah and I realized that we were in friendly territory and in the same boat.

Our hostess kept bringing one delicious dish after another to the table, and we devoured them to the last crumb. With every morsel I consumed, my heart went out to my children, knowing they were home hungry.

Our hostess noticed my sighs and wanted to know the reason. I reluctantly confessed my thoughts to her.

The popova—that was how I called her because she was the pop's (clergyman) wife. She came over to me, put her hand on my shoulder, and said, "Enjoy the food and I will give you plenty to take home for your children."

I thanked her with tears in my eyes, and I silently prayed to God for His benevolence.

As the conversation continued, the pop asked if we had any professions. I said that I was a seamstress. A broad smile lit up his face, and his wife wrung her hands with joy.

"Do you know how happy this makes us?" she said. "There is no seamstress in the whole village at this time. If we need something sewn or fixed, we have to travel all the way to Suzun, and it's not easy to get a travel permit or transportation. My mother was a seamstress, but she passed away four years ago."

The pop went to the next room and single-handedly dragged in an old sewing machine operated by a foot pedal. His wife disappeared for a few minutes and returned with a small package wrapped in a newspaper.

She unwrapped the package and revealed two pieces of fabric. She asked me if I could make a blouse out of one and an apron out of the second piece of fabric. I answered with glee, "Probably yes, but first I need to know how much fabric you have, so I need to take your measurements."

As we cleared the table of the utensils, I could hardly get up after the unexpected feast I consumed. I asked what style of blouse she wanted. We discussed it for a few moments, then she asked me what tools I would need.

I told her that I needed scissors, a tape measure, and if she had them, a needle and thread.

Again, she went into the next room and soon returned with the things I asked for. I smiled because I was glad that one of the threads was a close match with the fabric and was happy to again be in a familiar environment. Sewing was my favorite hobby.

I spread the fabric on the clean table and proceeded to measure and cut it.

The pop said to me, "You know, the people in this village are poor, but everyone has a vegetable garden. If you know how to sew, you will have an abundance of food. They have no money, but they can pay with food."

This was music to my ears. We had to make sure, though, that the authorities did not find out, because private enterprise and business was against the law and the punishment could be severe.

"You have to make sure that your people in the camp do not find out about this. One can never be assured of loyalty. There is no telling what hungry people might do. We all have to be very careful. You came from another country and are probably not familiar with our regime, laws, and punishment for breaking it. There are no sentiments or pity here."

I was busy cutting, pinning, and assembling the blouse. Luckily, our hostess had a few pins and a tape measure. Hadassah helped me with whatever she could, and by late afternoon, the main components of the blouse were assembled.

I realized that it was late in the day and told our hosts that we must begin our return.

I sewed together the main parts on the machine, which was difficult to operate after it was left standing idle for so long. I wanted to oil the gears to make the wheels move easier, but they had no oil at home. The pop promised that he would get some oil from the man who operated a tractor.

I asked permission to take the blouse home with me so I could continue my assignment during the week.

The popova agreed with some reluctance. She said to me, "After a whole day of hard labor in the forest, you still want to do this?" I answered in the affirmative and told her that it would be my pleasure to do it for her.

I would like to finish it and bring it back on my next visit. We wrapped the unfinished blouse in the newspaper, and Hadassah and

I rose, ready to thank them and say good-bye. The pop stopped us and told us to wait. His wife proceeded to load us up with food. We each received a bottle of milk, a chunk of butter, cheese pierogi (ravioli), half a round of delicious home-baked bread, about five kilos of potatoes, and other vegetables.

I could not believe my eyes looking at all this food I would be bringing to my family. We thanked them both and kissed the woman's hands as we said our good-byes. She withdrew her hands and said, "There is no need for that. We are all human beings and, according to the Bible, are obligated to help one another."

The pop, upon seeing the bundles on our backs, stopped us and told us to wait. He went behind the hut and returned with a tired old horse and a two-wheeled buggy. He helped us get in and insisted on driving us to the edge of the forest. He would have liked to take us all the way to camp, but if anyone saw us and found out about our escapade, surely, all of us would be in trouble. The man took the risk and drove us to the forest line.

There we got off, thanked him again, and started walking toward the woods.

The sun was hiding behind the trees as we approached the forest line. We left the flat plateau of the fields behind us and entered the woods. Though it was still daylight, it got considerably darker around us. We felt safer now being surrounded by trees, but we were not protected from the wild inhabitants of the forest.

We knew we could not be seen in the camp area with the sacks on our backs and had to find a hiding place and leave our treasure trove in the forest until nightfall then come back to retrieve it under the cover of darkness.

We got off the path and soon found a large craterlike hole and decided that it was a good hiding place. We put down the potatoes, carrots, and onions and hoped that the animals would not be interested in these vegetables. My companion and I covered them with soil, branches, leaves, and grass, which were abundant in the area. It was a pretty good camouflage. We took the bread, butter, and other perishables with us.

After we secured our priceless possessions in the hole, we resumed walking toward the camp.

It was getting darker, and it was relatively quiet. We could hear our own footsteps and listened attentively to our surroundings.

I was delighted with all the nourishment I was carrying for my children but afraid of being discovered by the authorities or being attacked by some hungry animals. As always, I put my trust in the Almighty.

I could hear Hadassah's teeth chattering. Her whole body was shaking as we approached the camp. I did my best to calm her fears and told her to pray. Prayer always eased my mind.

Since the path led to the clearing, we decided to circle it and arrive through the woods closest to our barracks. We saw the outline of the barracks in the moonlight but did not notice anyone outside. Quietly on tiptoe, we made the last part of our excursion undetected. The door to the barracks was open. There was a cool breeze, and the door moved slightly back and forth. Luckily, it was suppertime and there was no one in the corridor either. We entered it swiftly and moved toward our rooms. As we entered the small hallway of our quarters. We closed the door behind us and both let out a deep sigh of relief. Hurriedly we entered our respective one-room apartments.

Upon seeing me, my children jumped off the bed and hugged and kissed me, demanding to know where I had been all day. I had told them the night before that I would be away for a while but I didn't know how long the voyage would take. They wanted to see what was in the bundle I was carrying. Before I opened the package, I made them swear that they would never tell anyone what I brought and not even that I was out all day. I knew I could depend on my daughter to keep a secret; she was already ten years old, and life had conditioned her quite a bit. She was clever and was beginning to learn that many people could not be trusted and one must be careful with offering information. But I was not so sure about the boys. They were very anxious to be part of the secret and promised to keep it. Over the years in the Soviet Union, we had to reinforce the lesson that no information or discussion that took place in our home was to be revealed or discussed beyond our family.

As I unwrapped the bread, they smiled and were happy, but when they saw the chunk of butter, they started questioning me where I got it. My daughter observed that the bread resembled the one I used to bake at home and it had a similar aroma.

They didn't ask for any as, apparently, they had eaten not too long ago. Their dinner consisted of a slice of bread and tea brewed from dried leaves. But when I unwrapped the rest of the gifts, they began shouting and jumping for joy. This was how I pictured their reaction in my mind on the way home. Now I saw that the risk was worth taking. Seeing my children happy was my greatest joy.

They wanted to finish all the pierogi, but I persuaded them to leave some for the next day and some for their father. They reluctantly agreed and wanted to know how often I would bring these delicacies. Only then did I realize that my husband was absent. When I asked where he was, my daughter informed me that he was very nervous and said he was going to visit his family who lived in a nearby barrack. I decided to wait until he returned in order not to stir up any suspicion.

When he came home a short while later, I proudly filled him in about my day's accomplishments.

I put some of the provisions into a small sack and asked him to take it to his family. My husband took it to them and returned quite late. The first thank-you he brought back from his family was anger. They ganged up on him and shouted that how dare I take a stranger with me to such an incredible source of food and not take them into my confidence or take any of them along. I was sure my husband explained that Hadassah was with me when I met those women in the forest, the danger of being caught, and of course, we didn't know what, if anything, the venture would produce. But they would not listen. Their argument was that I cared more for strangers than my own family. Well, my blood boiled. They did not realize, nor did they care about it, the danger I was in. The family consisted mostly of young men who were hungry. My husband told me categorically that if I went to the kolkhoz again, I must take at least one member of his family with me.

It was not out of selfishness or meanness that I was opposed to telling them but simply out of fear. I had no idea what to expect, whom I would meet, and how the people would react to my and Hadassah's visit.

I realized that I had no choice but to divulge my secret to them.

First, I had to consult Hadassah since she was my partner. At first, she objected, but when I explained the reasons, she understood and consented. I told my husband that I would tell only one person and he or she must be the most reliable one to keep the secret. I also could not betray the trust of my benefactors and promised that when we went to the kolkhoz next time, I would speak to the villagers and ask their permission to bring another person or more with me.

The following Sunday, it rained and we stayed home.

Two weeks later, Hadassah and I set out on our pilgrimage to the village, the kolkhoz.

The road was familiar to us already, and we arrived much sooner and without trepidation.

Our hosts welcomed us with warmth and plenty of food.

It was October, and we could feel the approaching winter in the biting, cold wind. I told the pop and the popova what took place with the family, and they reluctantly consented that we bring one more person with us on the condition that not a single additional soul would find out. Their lives were on the line, just like ours.

I also said that one of my sisters-in-law was a very good seamstress and she would welcome some work too. The popova promised to ask some women in the village if they needed anything sewn or altered, but I would have to be in charge of the work. It meant that I would deal with the customers directly and my sister-in-law would do the sewing. I thanked her and assured her that everything would be fine.

I knew my sister-in-law was an excellent seamstress and that my clients would be very happy with her work.

That Sunday, I did some sewing on the popova's sewing machine and was introduced to their neighbor Masha.

Masha was a lovely young woman who was thirty or forty years old. She had a beautiful piece of fabric that she received as a birthday gift from her husband and asked me if I could make a skirt out of it. This was an easy assignment, and I finished it that day. Masha was thrilled.

To show her appreciation, she took Hadassah and me to her home, opened a large storeroom filled with all sorts of provisions, and said, "Take! Take! Anything you like and as much as you like!"

My heart pounded with emotion. I had not seen so much food in many months. It reminded me of my own storeroom back home after the harvest. However, I could not take advantage of Masha's generosity. I told her that we would be happy with whatever she deemed appropriate payment for my work. She filled our backpacks to the hilt and handed me an extra small sack of flour. "After all, you did the sewing," she said. "You deserve more."

We both picked up our bounty and started our return home. The way home was uneventful. The air was chilly, but we didn't feel much of it due to the heavy load we were carrying.

Again we buried part of our gifts in the same crater and arrived home at dusk.

My husband walked in about twenty minutes later, clearly agitated, demanding to know what took me so long and what I had accomplished. I filled him in on the day's activities.

I remembered that there was still a sack of vegetables hidden in the forest that we had to bring home.

I entered Hadassah's room and saw the end of a similar scene that took place when she displayed the foodstuff she had brought for her family. Her two boys were older than my children; they were teenagers and hungry all the time.

We mutually decided that she would accompany her husband and mine to the hiding place and bring the rest of the food that we had buried in the crater. I would stay and put my children to sleep.

Again, they devised a plan on how to leave the barracks so as not to be detected. One of the men would carry a pail as though he was going to fetch some water from the brook, and the other would accompany him while both would be engrossed in a heated discussion. Hadassah was going to carry a night potty, as though she was going to empty it in the woods. They would meet at a designated place in the forest and continue from there.

The plan worked well. There were only some children playing in the corridor. The wind was picking up speed, and the sky was clouding over. Most of the time, the moon shone brightly between the clouds and lit their way. The three *conspirators*, carrying big sticks to scare away any animals, made their way to our hiding place and dug up the sack with the provisions. They divided the bounty between them and very cautiously returned to the barracks. Now it was the men's turn to be afraid, for they knew quite well what the consequence might be if they were caught. About an hour or so later, they returned undetected.

It was about 10:00 p.m., and most of the people had gone to bed. There was nothing to do in the evening except talk to one another. Those who worked were tired and had to get up at the crack of dawn ready for roll call at 6:00 a.m. They needed the rest.

My husband finally arrived carrying the bundle in front of him.

Seeing him enter the room, I let out a sigh of relief. He quickly put the sack down on the bench and sat next to it. He was pretty much out of breath, not so much because of fatigue, but more so of fright. "How did you do it?" he asked after a few moments.

The children were fast asleep already, their bellies full, so I felt comfortable telling him about the day's adventure.

We were both concerned about the children being able to keep such secret and for how long.

My other concern was how and when I would be able to sew. The third and most important concern was how to go to the village and not get caught. We were both physically and emotionally exhausted and decided to call it a night. We had a whole week to think about it. The only day we could venture out of camp was Sunday. We worked twelve hours each day, six days a week.

As I lay in bed, I couldn't help but think about the possibilities this enterprise opened up. It meant food for the children and us. What mother wouldn't risk her life, if necessary, to feed her hungry children?

Every evening during the week, after a day's work, I sat near a kerosene lamp and sewed by hand. I did this after the children were sleeping. I could not risk telling them what I was doing.

A few days later, a dusting of snow covered the ground.

What if a heavy snow came down, which I knew it would, and I wouldn't be able to go to Zakavrashyna?

I shunned people so as to avoid questions. I was really getting nervous.

Winter arrived on schedule. Snow was falling day and night, almost nonstop. By January, there were about eight feet of snow on the ground, with temperatures well below zero to negative twenty degrees Celsius, with no plows or any other means except shovels for clearing the paths. Certainly no chance of melting anytime soon. When the snow was too high to work in the woods, the people were assigned different jobs. The workers received quilted wool jackets (*kufayka*) and warm winter boots made of pressed sheep's wool called pimy or valenki. The boots were very warm, as long as they stayed dry.

The snow that fell was pretty dry and fluffy and glistened in the sun. We realized that we would be cut off from the village as well as the rest of the world if the snow kept falling. Women were assigned to basket-weaving. Men cut down trees after clearing the snow from the surrounding area and performed other odd jobs. The barracks were not insulated and were drafty and very cold. The wood-burning stoves were aflame twenty-four hours a day to keep the rooms warm through open doors and for boiling drinking water. We had no tea or coffee, so we drank hot water all day to keep our insides warm.

Naturally, we were cut off from Zakavrashyna. The snow was too high to venture out anywhere, and we were afraid that the tracks would expose us. We braced ourselves for the Siberian winter, dying from hunger or freezing to death.

If we did survive the winter, we decided that come spring, we would approach the nachalnik and ask him for a permit to leave camp once a week and go to the village to buy food.

In our minds, it was not an outrageous request.

The Siberian winter was harsh and long.

There were days when the horse and buggy could not navigate the slippery or snowed-in road and did not arrive with the daily portion of bread.

The inclement weather made the narrow road impassable.

One day, Hadassah and I decided to approach the nachalnik and ask him for a permit to leave camp on a Sunday and go to the village. This was the only way out. He knew we were starving. He was human too and hopefully would understand.

We figured that he and his family didn't have that much to eat either. We would tell him that we met people from the kolckhoz in the forest, which was true, who told us that there was a kolkhoz within walking distance. Naturally, no one wanted to be the one to ask—we were both afraid. But since I was the one who discovered Zakavrashyna and my children needed food, I decided to take the chance, go before the nachalnik, and ask for a permit.

Toward the end of March, when warmer rays of sun began to shine upon the frozen wasteland, I mustered the courage to confront the nachalnik and ask, beg, or do whatever it took to obtain permission to leave the camp once a week or once a month and go to the village to buy food. It was not an easy mission. We all knew the overseer's disposition. Not too friendly, not too kind. I guess that his job and the need to save his own skin were instrumental in shaping his behavior. I had all winter long to think about it to rehearse, to rehash, to change my lines again and again until I was sure I had it memorized.

Under the circumstances, one also had to make allowances for the unexpected. Well, I decided that if I was refused, I would continue going to the village without a permit, as I did in the past, and whatever would be would be.

That would be even more dangerous, because the nachalnik would figure it out and keep a keen eye on my movements.

We didn't have too many options, but starving was not one of them.

One sunny Sunday morning, I dressed warmly and ventured out. The glare of the sun's rays hitting the white snow was blinding, and the air was crisp, fresh, truly invigorating. I straightened up my bent body and took a deep breath. It made me feel really good. All my fears were washed away, and I felt free and even happy as I marched on the narrow path toward the nachalnik's log cabin.

He and his family lived in a separate small barrack strategically located so that he could easily observe the whole camp from his window.

I knocked lightly on the door. His wife pulled slightly back the white curtain to see who it was.

The nachalnik himself opened the door and invited me in.

I entered a very hot cabin. It took a minute for my vision to adjust. I did not see their children; they must have been in the next room. I said "Good morning," removed my wool shawl, and unbuttoned the kufayka.

They were both startled.

It was rare that an inmate dared to come and visit the overseer unless it was an important work matter. There was a deafening silence in the room for a long moment.

"What brings you here on your day off?" he finally asked and gestured for me to sit down at the table. "Is something wrong with your work, or is anyone sick in your family?" Then he said, "Don't worry, the winter will be over soon and you will go back to your old work in the open air."

I smiled as though I was anxious to go back to the backbreaking work in the forest. I sensed that he was in an unusually good mood. *I am lucky,* I thought to myself. To catch him in such a friendly mood was a rarity.

His eyes were questioning me.

I gathered my wits, took a deep breath, and began. "Comrade Nachalnik, I came here with an unusual request. My family is fine, and I am not complaining about my job. I did not come to complain."

A faint smile brightened his face. I wanted to keep him interested. I could not afford to lose momentum.

"Comrade Nachalnik, you know that where I came from, the winter is not as harsh and not as long. We owned land and grew our own food and had enough to last all winter long. My children never knew what hunger was. I know very well that this is Siberia, and you also know that we did not ask to come here. It's possible that you yourself came from another part of this vast country. You are doing your job and serving your country. By working here, we are also serving your country."

My Russian was poor, but I hoped he understood the gist of my tirade. He was listening very attentively.

I finally came to the point. "There must be villages or collective farms in the area, and I am sure they are growing some kinds of crops during the short summer. As you know, we get very little food and people are hungry. A hungry worker cannot fulfill his or her prescribed norma."

"How do you know all this? Did anyone complain to you? Did you have any contact with anyone outside the camp?"

"No," I answered quickly, "but it is reasonable to think that there must be life beyond this camp. I am sure there must be fields in this area, not only forests. Where do you get your supplies for the soup kitchen?"

"You are a clever woman," he said. "Yes, there are several collective farms in the area and they supply us and other camps in the area, but you are prisoners here and are not allowed to leave the camp."

"Yes, I know," I replied. "Maybe I am a prisoner. I committed no crime, but why are my children being punished? I assure you that my children did nothing to harm the Soviet Union. I would like to get some food for my children. You have two lovely children yourself. Could you and your wife watch your children go to sleep hungry night after night? The soup we are getting from the soup kitchen is not very nourishing. The bread is also too heavy for its size. My children still remember the abundance and variety of food they had at home. They are too young to understand that we are in Siberia now and the food is different. I am sure you can understand my predicament. I don't have money, but I am sure the people might want to barter some cloths or labor for food. All I am asking for is your permission to leave camp on a Sunday, go out of the camp area, and see what I can find. You know I would not run away and leave my children and husband behind. Where would I go? I don't even know where I am. All I see is forest and some animals, which we are all afraid of."

I thought I had said enough. I took a deep breath and waited for the verdict.

His wife poured two glasses of hot tea (real tea) and placed them on the table in front of us. She even brought sugar. The nachalnik listened attentively to every word I said. It took a lot of nerve for me to approach him with such an outrageous request. He took a sip of his tea then slowly, with a determined, low voice, declared, "You know, I can have you arrested for trying to break the law. Nobody is allowed to go anywhere beyond the set boundaries without a reason and a permit. Since you are fairly new here and unfamiliar with our laws, I can understand this."

The tea was still hot, and I sipped it very slowly. I was silent and scared. The nachalnik raised his head from the glass and stared into my face. I could not return his look. I lowered my brows and continued sipping the tea, waiting for the verdict.

"You see, I am human too and have two children of my own, so I understand your concern. The problem is that, as I said, it's against the law to venture out beyond the camp proper. If this gets out of hand and the authorities find out, we will all wind up in jail. If I give you permission, I must give it to all."

I was stunned at his frank declaration and was silent, waiting to hear his confession till the end.

I was silent, but my whole being was bursting with pleas and entreaties. I was afraid that one wrong word out of my mouth might ruin everything. Though my heart was pounding, my hands were steady, and I decided to be quiet and wait.

He assessed the situation and said, "Against my better judgment, I will give you a pass to leave camp on one condition: nobody—and I mean *nobody*—except your husband will know about this."

I opened my mouth and swore that I would never, ever betray him. God would repay him for his kindness.

I burst out crying, but these tears were a release of my pent-up anxiety.

His wife came over and put her arm around my shoulders, trying to calm me down. It took a while for me to regain my composure. All my pain and suffering were released in those tears.

I resumed sipping my tea while the nachalnik gave me instructions about Zakavrashyna, how to get there, who could be trusted, and who could not. I thanked him for his kindness and guidance.

Naturally, I never divulged anything about my trips to the village in the past. I was afraid and ashamed. What would he think of me if he found out I was concealing this truth from him and breaking the law?

I continued sipping the tea, waiting for the next step.

I had not had real tea with sugar in many months, and I truly enjoyed it.

He took out a notebook from the table drawer and began to write. The note was for my protection, he said, in case I was seen leaving the camp by someone in authority. He did not think any of our own people would want to do me harm. The nachalnik warned me to be very discreet and not to mention today's meeting to anyone except my husband.

"You know," he said, "your husband is a good worker and a smart man. If anyone saw you coming here and asks why, you will tell them it was regarding a work assignment."

I thanked them both again, bundled up, and left the cabin with a big grin on my face.

I did not feel the cold or the wind; I was oblivious to the world. All I thought about was the valuable piece of paper in my hand.

When I entered our room, my husband said, "Well?"

All I did was shake my head in the affirmative, accompanied by a broad smile. He grinned in response.

After the children were sound asleep, I quietly recounted to my husband what had taken place in the nachalnik's cabin. He was happy to hear that the nachalnik was human after all.

All we could do now was wait for the snow to melt and spring to arrive.

,Being the pragmatist that he was, my husband declared that came spring, we would be able to resume our trips to the kolkhoz, but we must involve the family and give them the opportunity to ease their burden if we could.

The only logical person to be taken into our confidence would be his brother Leibish. He was sort of the head of the clan and could be trusted.

We called him for a meeting into the forest so no one would hear our conversation.

I explained everything in detail. He understood all our instructions and warnings and agreed to follow them to a tee.

Winter was cold and harsh, but we survived it. The hungry wolves and hyenas would howl half the night under the window. The children were afraid to go to sleep. We had a hard time convincing them that the animals could not breach the walls or the window and enter the room. Eventually, they would calm down and fall asleep. The fear in their eyes broke my heart.

The first nice spring Sunday, Leibish joined Hadassah and me when we resumed our trips to the village.

I introduced him to the villagers, and they welcomed him as they did us. After a long winter, their storerooms were depleted, but they did share what they could. We all bought provisions and returned to camp in the evening as usual.

The fear of being discovered constantly hovered over my head. I also felt guilty knowing that all the others were deprived of this bonanza.

I had a permit to leave camp, but what about the others? I knew this idyllic situation could not last forever. Someone would eventually discover our enterprise and report us to the nachalnik.

I certainly did not want to betray or hurt him in any way.

What would the nachalnik do to me when he found out I betrayed him and took along Hadassah and Leibish?

A few days after my trip to the village with my brother-in-law, I met one of my husband's sisters. She attacked me verbally with such ferocity that, at first, I thought she had lost her mind, but after a few sentences, I realized why she was shouting at me with such anger. She was accusing me of being selfish, of being inconsiderate, and used a few other choice words because I didn't immediately tell the family about my food source.

"Aren't we your next of kin?" she screamed.

I tried to explain the reason, but she refused to listen. She kept accusing me of all kinds of transgressions.

All this was supposed to be under wraps. Apparently, my husband's brother could not keep the secret very long and told the family about my connections with the villagers, which created an uproar.

We were not even supposed to know that there was a village in the area. The authorities told us we were hundreds of kilometers away from the closest town. This was not far from the truth. The nearest town, Suzun, was about thirty-five kilometers from our camp. No one told us about the surrounding collective farms, villages, and numerous labor camps. We only knew about number 85, which was the center. That was where the school, police station, a small jail, and other administrative offices were. In addition, there were four other satellite camps like ours, all surrounded by many kilometers of thick forest.

Little did I know that my euphoria would end in heartache and suffering, but for the moment, all my problems had been solved. At least I thought so. Food is life, and I found a way of getting it. This was the only thing that fully occupied my mind.

But at night was another story. What if someone would see me leave the camp or come back and reported us? What if the children boasted about having extra food or someone could smell something cooking? People would start asking questions and be suspicious. Someone might actually go to the nachalnik and snitch. I thought, *Who would do a thing like that to us?* Snitching is against the Jewish code of law, but one can never know what people may be capable of when they are hungry. The thought kept me awake at night.

It was also possible that the nachalnik might change his mind when he realized that he had broken the law, which could mean big trouble for him and his family.

My husband never looked through rosy glasses. His glass was always half-empty. He was a realist. All his arguments made sense.

Winter was long and harsh, but we survived it.

Toward the end of March, the days became a little longer and warmer. It still snowed occasionally, but not as much as in previous months. There were days when the sun was warm enough to begin melting the top layers of the frozen white mass. We even heard an occasional bird chirping.

I waited impatiently for the winter to end and the snow to melt so I could resume my excursions to the kolkhoz. Although I had a permit now and could go to the village, I was uneasy and did not feel right. I felt guilty because I knew that all the others were in the same predicament and could not get extra food and I could not help them either. My husband and I decided that when I went again to the village, I would take my brother-in-law with me. By the time the paths in the forest were passable, it was April.

I took Hadassah into my confidence and told her what I was going to do. She reluctantly agreed.

The first relatively warm Sunday, we resumed our escapade. We decided to leave camp separately through different parts of the forest and meet at the beginning of the fields.

I explained to my brother-in-law how to get to our meeting place.

We met about an hour later and together marched toward the village. On the way, I told Leibish what we did in the past and how to behave. He was a little annoyed, accusing me of treating him like a child, but after I explained the reason, he understood and accepted my instructions.

As we neared the village, I asked Leibish not to enter the popova's house together with us until I explained to them who he was and why he came with us.

Our kind benefactors did not object; they only asked to be discreet.

The popovs were happy to see us after such a long absence, but they warned that during winter, nothing grew, so they would share with us what they had left over from last year.

These were the kindest words I had heard in a long time.

I had been weaving baskets all winter, so I made one for the popova and brought it as a gift. She was very happy that I thought of making it for her. First, she sat us down to a hot potato soup, which we enjoyed thoroughly. Leibish gulped it down in two seconds. He was hungry and had not tasted anything so delicious in a long time. I asked if she had any work for me. She did not, but during the winter months, she had a chance to speak with some villagers about what I did, and quite a few had fabric and were looking forward to our return to give us the sewing assignments. I reminded the popova that my sister-in-law Chanah was also a very good seamstress and that maybe I could bring her with me the next time. She was happy to hear this and asked her husband to call one of the neighbors who had work for me. During the winter, the word went out in the village that there were expert seamstresses who would sew for food. This was the beginning of our sewing enterprise, and our food situation had improved considerably.

I can't recall when Passover fell that year, but the worries began way in advance. Where would we get matzo for the Holiday? The authorities would certainly not supply us with any religious needs.

On our next visit to the kolkhoz, I asked if we could buy some flour. This was one of the staples that rarely spoiled, so we were able to bring to the camp two sacks of flour. We sold some to other families and baked matzo for Passover. There was a hearth in one of the other barracks, and in the evenings, we baked matzo. Unfortunately, there was not enough flour for everyone, so only the religious adults ate matzo.

My children were happy the eight days of Passover because they could also have our portion of bread during the holiday. The flour was the thing that did us in. This could not be a secret any longer.

We had to divulge the place of the village, and many of the people went and bought or bartered whatever they could.

I knew I was in trouble and it was only a matter of time when the nachalnik would come and mete out his punishment.

I was resigned to accept what was coming to me, but I hoped that a mother of three small children would be spared.

Mother in Jail

It was a warm summer afternoon. The sun was just setting. My parents had returned from a hard day's work, and we sat down to dinner, which consisted of a bowl of berries with milk and a slice of bread.

Each worker who fulfilled his/her daily norma, the daily assignment, received a kilo of bread per day, and most of the time it resembled a brown brick. Those who did not fulfill their norma received half a kilo, including children under the age of sixteen.

Today, dark bread is valued higher for its nutritional content, but not in those days.

There was a knock on the door even though the door was open. Father said "Come in" in Yiddish, thinking it was one of our neighbors, but to our great surprise, it was the nachalnik, the overseer.

We were all in shock. He did not visit or socialize with any of us. There were two separate entities in the camp that were well-defined—the nachalnik and his family and the rest of us—and the two did not mix.

He walked in slowly, his large frame filling the entrance. Without as much as a hello, he addressed my mother. "Rosina"—that was how he called her—"you have broken the law, and I am arresting you. You will appear before the judge and defend yourself, if you can."

Needles to say, we were all stunned, unable to say a word, not having the vaguest idea what he had in mind.

Mother thought she had not filled her norma that day or had done something else wrong at work.

He took Mother by the hand and told her that she was going with him to jail at camp 85. She looked at him and asked, "Why? What did I do?"

"You will tell the judge what you did," he answered.

"I don't know what I am being accused of," she said, and they walked out.

Even Father was speechless. It hit us all like thunderbolt.

The nachalnik and Mother boarded the bread wagon and left.

Soon after the three of us were in bed, but only David fell asleep. A short while later, my father walked out, but this time, he didn't go far. He called for our neighbor Hadassah, and I could hear them whispering. When Father returned to our room, he looked at us and thought we were all sleeping. He turned around and left the room again, very agitated. After he closed the door behind him, I began interrogating my brother Israel and tried to find out if he had betrayed us by divulging our secret. He swore that he did not.

I was usually with both of my brothers since it was my job to take care of them while Mother was working, and I could not recall Israel talking to anybody about Zakavrashyna.

When I had to go to the forest to pick berries or get the soup from the soup kitchen, I occasionally took them with me, but not always. That was the day I had left them home alone.

Many times I went to the forest with Hadassah's son Meir. He was about my age and had a jolly disposition. He was fun to be with.

Father returned maybe an hour later. I peeked from under the covers and could see his face. This time, he was livid. His eyes were wild with anger. He paced back and forth and smoked nervously, emitting clouds of smoke from his mouth and nose. Then he sat down at the table near the window and swayed backward and forward.

It was dark in the room. I got off the bed and lit the kerosene lamp. Father was surprised to see me awake. None of us uttered a word. David woke up and asked for Mother, so I went to calm him down. We crawled back into bed like little mice. When I told them that Mother was arrested, my brothers asked me in a whisper what would happen to Mother and to us, but I had no answers for them. David fell asleep, but Israel and I stayed awake late into the night.

Father sat in the chair, smoking one cigarette after another. We heard him whimper as he swayed back and forth. He must have been crying but didn't want us to see or hear him. His face was turned to the window.

We heard a commotion outside. It was the nachalnik returning from delivering my mother to jail. When Father realized what the noise was, he flew out the door without even closing it.

Our neighbor Hadassah must have heard the noise of Father's rapid departure and seen the open door, so she came in and asked me what had happened.

I answered that I didn't know anything. I just knew that the nachalnik took Mother away. I began to cry, and Israel followed. Hadassah sat down on the edge of the bed and tried to console us. A short while later, Father walked in, this time slowly. He looked pensive. Father didn't expect to see Hadassah in our room. She quickly explained that she had heard us cry and came to calm us down. He called her out into the hallway, and they were whispering for a long time. I later found out that they were discussing my mother's predicament.

We all finally fell asleep, including Father.

Early the next morning, Father went to work as usual. During roll call, he got questioning looks from some of the people. Everyone knew what had happened to my mother the day before and why she was missing from the lineup. The news had spread like wildfire.

He just stood there as though the questioning looks were not aimed at him.

Father went to work as usual. A few hours later, the nachalnik caught up with him in the forest and began talking to him. Father questioned him, asking why he singled out our mother, what she had done, what her transgression was. The nachalnik spilled the beans. He told Father that one of our relatives went to him and told him that he saw Mother leave the camp and go beyond the allowed borders, which we all knew was forbidden. The relative had followed her one Sunday and saw her go beyond the end of the forest.

The nachalnik remembered giving Mother the permit, but the deal was that nobody was to know about it. He could not divulge to anyone that he had given Mother permission. If the word got out and reached his higher-ups, he and his family's life would be in jeopardy.

The two men sat on the ground and talked for a long while. Father realized that this man was very understanding and even kind, but the circumstances and his position forced him to be strict and obey the rules. The nachalnik reassured Father that the judge, after hearing Mother's plea, would be considerate and most probably free her. He himself would try to help but couldn't do it openly. He had to do what the law dictated.

Father and I had a discussion, and he let me in on some of this conversation with the overseer.

We decided that I should go visit Mother at the main camp, number 85, where she was jailed. I should bring her a comb, a piece of soap, her toothbrush (we had no toothpaste), and a slice of bread. We had no idea if they fed her in jail.

The following day, I did just what Father told me, and on the way, I picked some berries for her. Camp 85 was about three kilometers away.

I walked briskly through the woods and walked mainly on the path or stayed close to it. The birds accompanied me with their song. An occasional rabbit crossed the path, but I was grateful that there were no snakes or wolves visible. I was terrified of those two animals, and still am. About an hour later, I reached the camp. It was situated in a clearing, just like ours, but this clearing was much larger, and so was the camp. There were many more barracks. Most of the barracks were oblong and constructed of fresh logs. I could tell they were fresh because they were much lighter in color and they had not withered yet. In the middle stood a square building, and close by was another small square structure. All the structures were raised and stood on logs.

I was told that the larger square building was the main office, where the commandant and other officials had their offices. The smaller one was the jail. I was instructed to go to the commandant first and ask permission to see my mother. I walked into the first room and saw a man behind a desk reading a paper.

I introduced myself in broken Russian and told him I came to bring a few things for my mother and asked permission to give them to her. He said that I could see her from the outside but was not allowed to go in. No one except the officials was allowed inside. He asked me who my mother was, and I told him her name. He asked me if I was sure because the woman whose name I had given had dark hair and mine was blond. I answered that I was positive and that I resembled my father's family. The commandant told me that I could see her only through the window. He asked me what I had in the bundle I was carrying. I opened it in front of him on the table, and he examined every item. He said these items were permitted, so I could go see my mother and give them to her. I thanked him and left.

As I mentioned, the small building was elevated and the windows were small and too high for me to reach.

I began calling my mother. She heard me and recognized my voice instantly. After a few moments, I saw her face in the window. First, she had a smile on her face, but the smile soon changed into sadness and she had tears in her eyes. I could not hear well what she was saying and realized that I had to get closer to her. I looked around and saw logs and rocks thrown all around. I guess some previous visitors were in the same predicament. I gathered several logs and made a pile right under her window. I climbed on top of them with great care, hoping the mound would not fall apart. I raised myself on my toes and reached the bottom part of the window.

By now, Mother was really crying, and so was I. She calmed down after a while and began bombarding me with questions about my brothers: What were they eating? Did they miss her? Were they behaving? What was my father doing and saying? She asked me about myself, how I was managing and what the neighbors were saying. She also asked if they were helping me.

It took me a while, but I gave my mother a detailed report about everything and everybody. She complimented me on being responsible and observant. I gladly accepted the compliment. I showed her the things that I brought for her but couldn't give them to her. The window was locked, and she couldn't open it. We had a long conversation. Mother gave me all kinds of instructions on how to take care of my brothers, how to make some food from the "groceries" we had, and so on.

Then she said it was time for me to go back home. She didn't want me to go through the woods in the dark. My brothers were with neighbors who kept an eye on them. Father was at work. I wanted to give Mother the few things I had brought for her.

I sort of liked the commandant—he had a kind face and was kind to me—so I decided to go back and ask him to please give the few items to my mother. Mother and I said a tearful good-bye, and I returned to the main building. It was a short walk, but it was enough time to plant an idea in my head on the way to the commandant's office. I decided to plead with him concerning my mother's release.

As I entered the small corridor, I went directly to his closed door. I knocked gently, but there was no response. I waited a few seconds and knocked again, this time more forcefully.

"Enter!" came a friendly response. I opened the door slowly, shaking with fear. After all, this man was a commandant with great power over hundreds of people, and I was only a ten-year-old kid, a daughter of a gulag inmate.

I thought to myself, *What can he do to me for being so daring? Send me to Siberia, to a labor camp? I was already there. They can't put children in jail.* I was sure the Soviet government did not do things like that. They must have some compassion for children. The trouble was that I had very little time to think about all this. I had no time to rehearse what I was going to tell him. I decided to do it, and whatever would be would be.

As I entered his small office, I walked slowly toward his desk, where he was sitting. I still thought he had a kind face. As I reached his desk, I picked up my head in order to face him. He could plainly see that I was crying; my cheeks were still moist, and my eyes began filling up again.

"What's the matter now? Didn't you see your mother?"

"Yes, I did," I answered, "but I couldn't give her the things I had brought for her. I couldn't go inside. I couldn't reach the window, and the window was shut. I came back to ask you to please give her these few things. These are mere necessities." Then I continued, "While I am here in your office, Mr. Commandant, I would like to convey a plea from my young brothers and from myself. Please let our mother go. She committed no crime. All she wanted was to take care of us, like any other mother. She works all day and is a good worker. You can ask our nachalnik. I am sure he will attest to that. Both my parents are very good workers, and they fulfill their assignments every day. I would like to go to school and learn Russian, but I must take care of my younger brothers because I am the eldest. Please, Mr. Commandant, free my mother. My younger brothers and I will be forever grateful, and so will she."

He listened to every word I said. When I ran out of words, I stopped and took a deep breath. When I saw no reaction from him, I thought all my pleading and explanations were in vain. My anger returning, I almost burst out with accusations, but he shifted in his chair and asked me if I was finished. I nodded, ready to burst into tears. He stood up (now I could see that he was a short man) and came around his desk. He took the small bundle from my hand and assured me that Mother would get it that very day.

"And you, young lady," he said, "relax and calm down. I don't intend to keep your mother here very long. She arrived only yesterday, and we must go though due process. If we find that she is innocent, we will send her home to her family right away."

"I swear to you, Mr. Commandant, that she is innocent."

He looked at me and said, "You will see your mother in a few days, and I want you to know that your brave and emotional plea has a lot to do with my decision. We need many brave children like you here in the Soviet Union. Now go home before it gets dark. Aren't you afraid to walk through the forest alone?"

"Oh no," I said. "I go to the forest every day to pick blueberries and mushrooms. Would you like me to pick some for you?"

"No, no," he said. "My wife does that."

He walked me out of the building, and I ran down the few steps and headed toward the jail. I called Mother, and she came quickly to the window. I climbed on the heap of logs and told her quietly what I had just done. She must have heard some of it because she shook her head in the affirmative.

I said good-bye, threw some kisses in the air, and ran to the path toward the way home. I ran most of the way. The sun would set very soon, and I would really not be happy walking home through the forest in the dark. I was elated. I was happy because I truly believed that the commandant would free my mother very soon.

Yes, my mother stayed in jail a whole week while the hearing took place. The nachalnik testified, but there were no other witnesses. There was sort of a trial that took place in the commandant's office on the fifth day. It must have taken two days to contact our nachalnik, and they mutually agreed that my mother's transgressions were not that grave.

Mother came back to us before dusk on the seventh day of her imprisonment. Father was home from work already, and we were just sitting down for our evening meal, which consisted of a bowl of blueberries with milk and a slice of bread. As the door opened and Mother walked in, we all jumped on her to hug and kiss her. Father waited for us to finish our joyful reunion then stood up and hugged Mother. I immediately got Mother's bowl, filling it with blueberries and milk, and we all truly enjoyed our dinner. We bombarded Mother with all kinds of questions, which she promised to answer one by one. Father's main concern was if there would be any repercussions in the future. Mother reassured him that we were all free and clear of any accusations.

Our neighbors heard the commotion and stuck their head in the door to find out its reason. Mother promised to fill them in at the appropriate time. Now she wanted to be free to enjoy her family. I'm sure that Mother talked about her experiences in the jail for weeks after. We were just thrilled to have her back home.

Life resumed its usual course, but my parents were bothered by the thought that the authorities had been notified by one of our people.

Freedom at Last

On a September morning, not too long after the above incident, all the able bodies lined up for the usual roll call and work at the usual place. The nachalnik was usually the first to arrive to set an example. On this fateful day, he was not there when the workers took their usual places, some still yawning. When he walked out of his cabin, he walked slowly toward the assembled folk on the field. Some noticed his slow pace, his expressionless face, and the absence of his rifle. A murmur was heard among the workers. They didn't know what to make of it. The guess was that he was either sick or fired.

This was not the man they had gotten to know over the past eighteen months. The tension and fear were intense.

As he reached the assembled, his expression did not change. He climbed on his wooden box, and instead of the regular roll call, he surveyed the group with a keen eye then made the following announcement.

"As of today, you are free. You have two choices: you can remain here and continue to work as usual and receive more food and wages or leave and go wherever you want within the borders of the Soviet Union."

He did not elaborate but only added that we should be thankful to Comrade Stalin for his generosity, for he was the one who granted us our freedom, and said the order came directly from Moscow.

He made this announcement with a straight face and no emotion in his voice. It was probably not the first time he was the bearer of such good news. The camp was not new by any means, so he must have overseen other inmates in the past.

For a moment, the people were silent—they were stunned. They didn't know what to make of it.

After over eighteen months of slave labor in the Siberian wilderness, we were finally free.

The provisional Polish government stationed in England convinced Stalin, through diplomatic channels, that we were not the enemies he thought we were, after all. The reason he could be persuaded was that Hitler betrayed him and declared war on Russia June 22, 1941. The so-called Hitler-Stalin pact was a convenient ploy devised by Hitler, who wanted Stalin on his side while he occupied Poland and other European countries and prepared to wage war against Russia as well.

When Hitler's other schemes were fulfilled, it was time to declare war against Russia, and so he did. After six years of bloodshed and millions of victims, he was ultimately defeated by the USSR and the Allies in 1945.

The time we spent in Siberia taught all of us to be skeptical of good tidings. Things did not always turn out to be what they seemed. This was the first time the nachalnik appeared without his rifle. At first, the people were stunned, numb, but after the nachalnik left the soapbox and went back to his cabin, the hush turned into an explosion of joy. There was hugging and kissing and plenty of happy tears.

Many pronounced the Shehecheyanu blessing. It took a while for the people to realize that this ordeal was over, that they were free to go. But go where and how?

One of the men decided to go see the overseer and ask him some questions. The nachalnik did not know much more than he told us. He said he was expecting further instructions in the next few days and, when he did, he would relay them to us. He said we would continue receiving our daily portion of bread even though we didn't have to work anymore, even though the popular motto in the USSR at the time was "Kto nie rabotayer tot nie yest." One who does not work does not eat.

Freedom was effective immediately. We knew the war with Germany was on, though very few details were available. We had no radio or newspapers. We had to depend on rumors and information that trickled down to us from the village and occasionally from the nachalnik himself.

Our people were happy. They were relieved of the heavy twelve-hour-a-day labor routine. The mood throughout the camp changed from sadness to guarded joy. There was a lot of talk, mostly speculation. We didn't have any idea where we were on the map, nor had we seen one since we left home.

The overseer told us we were in Siberia, and that should be enough. We knew we were not too far from Novosibirsk, which we passed on the way in and was quite a large city, but how far or in which direction, nobody knew. Eventually we found out that it was not only our satellite camp that was freed but also all the Polish citizens who were forcibly taken to the Soviet Union in the summer of 1940. They were freed in 1942. This was a monumental achievement. The question remained: where to go from here and what to do?

One thing we knew for sure was that we could not go back home for the time being. The Germans had conquered Poland in September of 1939, then most of Europe, and now their objective was to conquer the USSR. We had no idea what was happening on the front. The Soviets made sure that only good news from the front was broadcast on the radio and written in the newspapers.

There were no reports of defeats, only victories.

Though we were kept in the dark, the farmers in Zakavrashyna occasionally received newspapers and, once in a while, passed on some news to us.

The information they brought from Suzun was not necessarily always true.

The following day, most of the adults went to the village to get food. My parents also went, and Mother visited all her friends and told them the good news. They were very happy for us and wished they could join us and leave too. They were deeply rooted in the area and had no permission to go anywhere. We and a few other families were invited to come live with them and join the kolkhoz.

Everybody wanted to be where the food was. Naturally, the villagers could not accommodate all the people of our camp, but many came almost daily to buy or barter food.

Before we left the camp, my parents went to visit the grave of my dearly departed brother David. It was a heartbreaking scene. Mother cried for days. She repeated the same sentence over and over: "How can I leave my baby in this godforsaken wilderness?"

About two weeks later, we received directives. Each family received a *comandirovka* (travel documents), which entitled us to travel by train or bus for free within the USSR. In Communist Russia, no one was allowed to travel anywhere without a permit. We were given some money and a three-day supply of bread and were told that we now could go wherever we wanted within the borders of the Soviet Union, except to the western parts, where the war with Germany was in progress.

It was akin to Yitziyat Mitzrayim, the Exodus from Egypt many centuries ago.

Though the word *freedom* sounded great, some thinking and preparation were necessary before we could undertake another trip within an unknown country.

Winter was not too far away, and the farmers had to harvest the crops as soon as possible. This was a time when everybody worked in the fields. The family asked if the people in the kolkhoz needed help with the harvest. They welcomed us with open arms. They put us up in the community center until better accommodations could be found.

All the adults went to work in the fields, and I stayed behind to watch my brother.

My aunt Reizl prepared lunch, and I, together with my cousin Etky, would bring it on horseback, with no saddle, to the workers in the fields.

Our people got paid very little for their work, but it meant a lot. For eighteen months, they had worked for Stalin and got a piece of bread and stale soup; now they worked and received real wages. This was a big improvement.

By the end of September, or possibly the beginning of October, most of the harvest was gathered and stored away. It was time for us to move on.

We were told by some villagers that if we went south, we would find a warmer climate. That sounded very enticing, and that was what we decided to do. Any warm place sounded much friendlier than this frozen Siberian wilderness.

Freedom was just an illusion. Yes, we were freed from the labor camps, but where would we go from there? What would we do? We did not know Russia at all. We only knew that it was a vast country and the capital city was Moscow. Where or how far Moscow was, none of us knew.

We hired two horses and two wagons and asked to be driven to the nearest railway station. Our belongings were very few. My grandmother and the young children were to ride.

My brother Israel, my cousin Zippora, and I were the only children in the family. The other cousins were young adults and could walk, but when they got tired, they would hop on one of the wagons to rest.

Nineteen of us came to Siberia, and when we left, there were only eighteen of us. My brother David was the first casualty. There would be other members of the family who would not make it.

Some rode and some walked, and they changed places every so often. It took almost a whole day to get to the railway station. It was Cherepanovo again. It was the same railway station where we disembarked when we came from Poland. The station looked the same; nothing had changed except the color of the leaves on some of the trees. The majority of trees were evergreens, mainly pine trees, but there were also other species, like white birch, growing among them.

We found out that there would be a train coming through early the next morning going in a southerly direction. We were greatly relieved that we didn't have to wait very long.

We showed the stationmaster our documents. He looked at them with a smile, as if to say, "You lucky people, you can leave and go wherever you want while I am stuck in this frozen wilderness!" He offered us some hot water, as that was all he had to offer, and invited us to spend the night inside the station. It was very kind of him.

He knew where we came from and what we had been doing all this time.

I guess he pitied us. I am sure he received a nice tip for his kindness. We had to learn quickly that one gets nothing for nothing in the USSR. You can call it payola, tip, or whatever you like, but it was an integral part of life in that country as well as in many other places, and it still prevails today. It's also called corruption.

We had bread and other provisions that we had brought with us from Zakavrashyna. The women prepared the evening meal for the family and invited the trainmaster and the two drivers to join us.

One thing was missing, though, without which a meal in Russia wasn't complete: vodka. But the trainmaster supplied a bottle. This was his contribution to the feast. The men shared the bottle, while the women stayed away. It was an interesting and gay evening. We were thankful for the hot water for we could have tea (pieces of dried bark of the birch tree sweetened it a little). We also learned to drink plain hot water when there was nothing to put into it. Everyone seemed to be content and in a jovial mood.

We had our blankets and quilts, which we spread out on the floor, and everyone went to sleep. The trainmaster promised to wake us in time so we could get ready to board the train. We were all tired, so sleep came easy.

The two drivers also stayed until morning. It was too dangerous to travel through the forest at night. There were wolves and bears on the lookout for a good meal. The trainmaster's name was Gregory. (Funny how I sometimes remember certain things or names from my childhood but not what took place yesterday.) Gregory woke us at 4:00 a.m. The train was to arrive at approximately 6:00 a.m. We had plenty of time to gather our belongings, grab a cup of hot tea/water with a slice of bread, and wait for the train. We were not assured seats on the train, however; after all, it was wartime and many trains were used to transport soldiers, food, and equipment to the front. Many times these trains were full to capacity and didn't make unnecessary stops.

Father must have promised Gregory a good tip for his extracurricular services.

The few rubles Father gave Gregory, the trainmaster, must have had the intended effect, for he told us not to worry, that he would make sure we got on the morning train.

Soon we heard the train approaching and the whistle blowing louder and louder.

Gregory positioned himself in the middle of the tracks, waving a red flag.

The first sunrays brightened the sky, and soon we were able to discern the gray smoke of the locomotive.

The train was moving rather fast, and we were worried that it would not stop, but soon it became apparent that the engineer must have noticed the red flag and began slowing down. Minutes later, the train came to a complete stop. It was a passenger train, and we could see some heads leaning against the windows. Most of the passengers were still asleep due to the early hour.

As the train stopped, several faces were visible, looking out some open windows.

When it came to a full stop, Gregory approached the engineer and conversed with him, then he put something in his hand. A few moments later, the engineer climbed down from the locomotive and went looking for one of the conductors. They must have also been asleep, but soon one was found. A short conversation ensued, and we were told to go past the third train car and board the train through the open door. As we dragged our bundles toward the open door, Gregory came over to my father and whispered in his ear, "Make sure you take care of the conductor." Father motioned in the affirmative.

After we had all boarded, the doors were locked and the train began to move again.

My father walked over to the conductor and "shook" his hand. I am sure he deposited some rubles in the conductor's palm.

We encountered some difficulty finding room for all of us in one railcar, so we had to split up and found room in the adjacent railcar.

The whistle blew, and the train began to move to parts unknown.

For a while, we passed familiar sights: forests, clearings, small villages, and some small towns. We probably saw them on the way in too. But who remembered?

After a while, Mother wanted to stretch her legs and check out who else was riding the train. She decided to explore some of the other train cars. Of course, curious me tagged along.

Soon we heard male voices singing. My ears perked up.

I asked Mother if we could find out where the singing was coming from. She smiled, and we both followed the music until we arrived at its origin.

It was coming from the next train car, where a large contingent of soldiers accompanied by an accordion was entertaining themselves as well as the other passengers. The railcar was stuffy and reeked of alcohol and cigarette smoke. I did not want to go any farther or go back where I came from.

I wanted to listen to the soldiers sing.

Mother was invited to sit down and join them in a song. This was a strange environment for her and me.

She politely declined, took my hand, and said we were going back.

I wanted to stay and learn their songs, but Mother would not hear of it.

One of the soldiers stood up and made room for me.

He promised Mother that nothing would happen to me. He said he would take personal responsibility for my welfare, but Mother was not convinced and she dragged me back to where the rest of the family was.

I was angry with her for depriving me of such an opportunity to sing and possibly learn a new song.

All the railcars were full to capacity, and even though some windows were open, it was hot and full of cigarette smoke and all kinds of odors.

We passed the big town of Novosibirsk, which we remembered stopping on the way to the labor camp.

As we continued our journey, the weather changed for the better. It was getting warmer day by day.

On the train we met several other families who were also freed from camps and were looking for a warmer place and a better life. They had no more information than we did.

Two or three days into our journey, we arrived at a major train station of the sprawling city of Tashkent, the capital of Uzbekistan. The family decided to get off and try our luck. It was reasonable to assume that such a big city would have many opportunities. We removed our possessions from the wagon onto the burning-hot concrete platform.

There was a myriad of other refugees with bundles, without bundle, young, old, with or without children.

In other words, there was a multitude of humanity. First thing Mother looked for was some shade, but this was hard to come by. It was primarily an open area with not a single tree in sight. Luckily, my aunt Chana noticed in the distance some people picking up their bundles, about to leave. Quickly she alerted the family to grab what they could and follow her. We were lucky to take the spot against a southern wall.

There was protection from the hot southern sun and also some protection from thieves, who were on the prowl day and night.

Tashkent

The family was in a quandary about what to do next. They had constant discussions on the subject, but they soon realized that they could not make any decisions until they had lived in Tashkent for a while and gathered more information about the city, about the war, about life in the USSR, etc., etc.

For me it was fascinating to listen to the men discuss and argue about all these things. I learned a lot from these discussions.

Before the question of living accommodations could be resolved in this beautiful, vast metropolis, the question of making a living came first. Aunt Chana and my mother were seamstresses. Aunt Cha-Golda and Aunt Reizl had no usable skills. Though as housewives they knew how to do many things, none could be used as a profession or moneymaking tool.

The men were not much more talented. My father managed Horodynski's estate and was his bookkeeper but did not know the Russian language, so his skills were of no use either. What was left for them to do was wheel and deal with whatever they could find, but this kind of business was illegal and the competition was fierce.

The city was overrun by refugees of every kind and from every corner of the Soviet Union, but mainly from the west. Our family soon realized that this beautiful big city might not be the place for us.

Father liked to explore, so he either walked or took the tram in different directions in the hope of finding something to do.

One day, he returned from his daily excursions and told us the following story.

He was riding the streetcar to no particular place (he did not know the city), but he was tired and needed rest. It didn't turn out to be the ideal place to rest, but it led him to an adventure that otherwise he would have missed. The tram was pretty full, but he got on anyway, hoping that after a while, someone would get off and relinquish a seat. Sure enough, two stops later, a woman got off and he took her seat. It felt good to sit down after several hours of walking. He told us that he saw beautiful buildings, Metchets, Muslim houses of worship, long tree-lined streets, and lots of people.

He asked where the bazaar was and was told it was several stations ahead. Father was hoping to buy some fruit for us at the bazaar. Next to him sat a slim young man. His face was pale, with dark expressive eyes. He was wearing a hat on this hot day, which was also unusual, and it was not an embroidered skullcap like the Uzbeks wore. The youth was very restless. My father thought he looked peculiar, nothing like the locals or Russians. Father figured this young man must be a Jew.

After a short while, Father dared to whisper in his ear, "Amchu?" A Jew?

"Yes," answered the young man in Yiddish. My father was pleasantly surprised. He began speaking to the young man in Yiddish, but the fellow cut him off and said, "Follow me when I get off."

At first, Father was reluctant, thinking it might be a trap, possibly one of the government informants that were dispatched daily by the KGB to gather information. They did not trust all those foreign refugees invading the city. But his curiosity got the better of him, so he decided to follow the young man.

Father dared the authorities; he figured, what could the KGB do to him, send him to Siberia? He just came from there. I must say, Father was a brave man. Not once did Mother scold him for endangering himself and the family by venturing "outside the law."

Father got off the tram at the same station as the young man and followed him. After a short walk, they entered the basement of a small apartment building in a beautiful residential area. Father was right at the heels of the fellow, whose name turned out to be Boris, Berl in Yiddish. Father followed him down several steps into a darkened foyer. Berl immediately closed the door behind them and apologized for his rudeness on the streetcar. He explained in beautiful

Yiddish that he was a Yeshiva student of the Lubavitcher Chassidim and it could have been dangerous to reveal his identity to a stranger. Religious study was forbidden in the USSR, and if the authorities uncovered this Yeshiva or any other religious establishment, the students, along with the teachers and their families, would be arrested and most likely sent to Siberia.

When Father's eyesight had adjusted to the darkness after the bright sunlight of the street, he noticed a gray door. The same color paint covered the walls in this small hallway. Berl opened the door slowly, and immediately a murmuring sound was heard. As the door opened, the sound became louder. When they entered the large room, a strong odor of cigarette smoke laced with perspiration greeted them.

The room was full of men of all ages, mainly young, sitting on benches in front of long tables along all four walls. They swayed and bowed their heads in front of open books. These were books of the Bible and Talmud that the men were studying in secret in this underground classroom.

Father, though a smoker himself, took a moment to adjust to the environment. He followed Berl across the large room. Some of the students raised their eyes from the books and glanced at the newcomer with curiosity. Several older men were sitting on the opposite end of the large room, also swaying and murmuring as the others did. One older man with a graying beard raised his head and looked at the two newcomers without stopping his swaying and murmuring for an instant.

"This is the rabbi, our teacher," Boris explained in Yiddish without giving his name. He approached the rabbi and introduced my father. The rabbi's first reaction was that of suspicion, but after a few moments, he stopped swaying, stretched out his hand, and welcomed my father with the usual greeting of "Shalom Aleychem."

The rabbi stood up and motioned for my father to follow him. He reached for a knob right behind him that opened a door, and the two of them entered a small room. This room had air one could breathe. The only furniture was a small table and several chairs. The rabbi sat behind the table and motioned for my father to sit opposite him. During the long conversation, in Yiddish, Father told him everything about our lives, where we came from, and of course, about our sojourn in the labor camp in Siberia. Apparently, the Soviet population knew nothing about the thousands of Polish citizens, mainly Jews, being sent to labor camps in Siberia.

My father was just as curious about life in the USSR and especially about these houses of learning, which must have existed throughout the land. What Father wanted to know was how they were able to flourish under the noses of the authorities without being discovered. What Father learned was just as astounding.

After the rabbi realized that he had nothing to fear, he told my father that there were many such establishments, primarily in large cities, with large Jewish populations. Some of the students were former or even current police or KGB members.

The rabbi mentioned that there were two such officials sitting and learning in the adjacent smoke-filled room. Their cooperation and protection were badly needed, and they obliged. Father was truly amazed at this revelation. The rabbi invited him to join the group and study with them if he wished.

Father gratefully declined, explaining that he was only passing through Tashkent and didn't know how long he would remain. He obtained a lot of useful information about Tashkent, Uzbekistan, and the USSR. He thanked the rabbi, asked him to thank the young man who had brought him there, and stood up to leave.

He was directed to a different door, which led from the small room directly to the street.

Father walked into a sunlit courtyard surrounded by a stone wall then through a wooden gate to another street. A short walk brought him to a main street and a streetcar stop. His head was full of impressions and useful information that he could not wait to share with the family.

In the evening, he gathered all the males in the family and very quietly recounted his unique experience.

Before he began, he made sure that there were no strangers in the vicinity who could overhear the story.

I knew from past experience that whenever there was a meeting of the male members of the family, it must be important. I followed the men while hiding among the people walking on the wide platform. When I saw them in the distance standing in a circle away from the crowds, I hid behind a nearby large tree and listened.

I didn't catch every word but heard enough of the conversation to get the gist of the story. It sounded like a fairy tale. I was thinking, *How could so many people engage in subversive activities under the noses of the authorities and not get caught?*

I began to realize that one must always stay one step ahead of the police or KGB.

When I saw the men disperse, I ran as quickly as I could to our place on the platform.

Mother didn't even notice my absence because she was busy putting my brother to "bed." He couldn't fall asleep due to the constant whistle blowing of incoming and departing trains and people on the move.

I quickly lay down in my spot but couldn't fall asleep either because that strange story kept repeating itself in my head. I visualized all kinds of punishment those people would endure if caught.

My father kept this secret to himself for many years. He only revealed it to Mother after we returned to Poland from the USSR.

One evening, Father came back from a day of "business ventures" and handed Mother something for safekeeping. Father had no profession, so finding any kind of work among this myriad of people was virtually impossible. Like most of his counterparts, he was wheeling and dealing.

Mother went under a streetlight to examine the $20 bill he had given her. She quickly returned, white as a sheet, unable to catch her breath. With glaring eyes, she confronted Father in a whisper, mocking him about his big business deal. She put the banknote in his hand and told him to go under the light to examine what he had bought. When he saw the $2 bill under the street lantern, he was as shocked as Mother was. He came back, his head down, smoking nervously, and said to Mother that he would find the man the next day in the daylight and exchange the note for a $20.

Mother laughed hysterically and then began to cry.

She accused Father of taking the bread out of his children's mouths and giving it away to a stranger. Father did not want to listen to her accusations and went for a walk. He was hurting inside.

She did not mince words. Our relatives heard the commotion and wanted to know what had happened. Mother explained.

All this went on in a whisper. One never knew who might be listening.

Now everybody was whispering. My cousin Victor went to look for my father. They must have returned late, as I was asleep and didn't see them return. Years later, whenever my father lost money in a business venture or made a bad business deal, Mother would remind him of that incident.

He tried to make other business deals, but nothing seemed to work. There were too many people in search of all kinds of deals and plenty of swindlers.

There were hundreds, if not thousands, of people living in the street in such close proximity with no sanitary facilities to speak of, inevitably leading to vermin and illness. The heat was of no help either.

Our bodies began to itch, and Mother soon discovered that we had lice. They invaded not only in our hair but also our clothes. She panicked and ran to the authorities for help. To her amazement, there was none. She was reminded that she was not the only person in the area and many others had the same problem.

She was given a small bottle of kerosene to wash our hair with a bar of smelly soap and was told to go to the river and wash our bodies and clothes. And so we did. We went down to the river, one family at a time, while the others watched the belongings.

The river was about half an hour's walk from the station. It was shallow and wide between two steep, sandy banks. The water was clear and warm. On the sandy beach, there was a multitude of people bathing, sunning, and washing clothes. As we neared the water, the sand turned into pebbles and hurt the soles of our feet. Naked children were running in and out of the water. To us it looked like the most wonderful discovery, the answer to the lice problem, not to mention the fun of playing in the water. None of us knew how to swim, but immersing in the clear, warm water was sheer joy.

Well, we had plenty of company with the same problem. There was no place to get undressed, and I flatly refused. My brother did it right away and ran joyfully into the water. Mom held a towel around me to shield me from onlookers, and I reluctantly undressed down to my underwear. There were lice crawling all over the place. We took our clothes to the water and removed the little critters from the folds and seams then threw them one by one into the flowing river.

We thought we were getting rid of the vermin, but it was only temporary. The people around us were doing the same thing. The water was full of lice, and we watched them swim away with the current together with other debris.

Mother washed our clothes and other articles of clothing she had brought with her. We got a good scrubbing. It felt really good. Mother washed our hair several times and, at the end, poured kerosene on our heads, hoping to kill the lice.

She did the same to herself.

Father had very little hair to worry about. We liked the water and the fun and had not had a good bath in quite a while. We didn't want to leave, but as all good things must come to an end, so did this adventure.

When we returned to our spot at the train station, other members of the family went down to the river until everybody was bathed and deloused. We knew that if we remained in this place much longer, the lice would come back and we might contract diseases ranging from dysentery to typhoid. The family decided that we must move on. Where would we go from there? Only God knew.

We stayed about two weeks under the stars on the platform of that train station in Tashkent.

The money we received for the work in Zakavrashyna was quickly disappearing, and there was no other income in sight. There were just too many refugees in one place looking for the same thing: how to make a few rubles.

The family decided to move on.

To get ready for the next leg of our trip, one of the necessities was food, so the men went to the market to buy food for the journey. We also needed to know when there would be a train out of Tashkent going south or west. We really didn't know where we were going, but southwest sounded good.

The following morning, we all went to the public baths, luxuriating in a tub of hot water, and everybody got another dose of kerosene in their hair as a preventive measure against a lice attack. We also could not know when we would next have the pleasure of a bath.

Feeling clean and refreshed, we were ready for our adventure to the unknown.

The following morning, Mother made sure we had a good breakfast. Mother was a strong believer in good nutrition, though nutritional standards during the war in the early 1940s were very different from today's. In the USSR, nobody knew when and where the next meal would come from.

Mother's pregnancy was showing, and she was getting tired very often. The heat was a great contributor to her discomfort. I saw her enlarged belly and thought she had gained some weight lately. She didn't work for several weeks, so she put some flesh on her bones. I had no idea she was expecting, but I wouldn't have understood the concept anyway. I still thought that a stork brought babies in the night.

The next day, our train arrived around midmorning. It was quite full, but we found enough space for the whole family and luggage in two adjoining cars. Tashkent was an important stop, and the people had enough time to get food and drink. Some passengers even found time to buy or sell all kinds of wares. Every large train station became a mini bazaar every time a train stopped for a while.

It was a slow-moving passenger train, stopping often in the middle of nowhere to allow oncoming trains to pass.

As we continued our slow journey in the southwesterly direction, the climate became even more oppressive. The hot air coming through the open windows gave us an indication that we were far from Siberia.

We advanced two or three days, passing empty trains on their way to pick up soldiers and war supplies. We passed enormous steppes, small and large villages, and quaint, odd-looking settlements. The majority of structures we saw were one-story stone or stucco homes surrounded by high stone or clay walls and fences. To us, they looked very odd. We had not seen these types of developments or houses before.

Eventually, we found out that we were passing Soviet Republics inhabited mainly by Muslim populations and that this was their architectural building style. These types of structures were supposed to stay cool in the hot summers and warm in the winter. Sometime later, we learned that this entire southern part of the Soviet Union was annexed in the late nineteenth century. Prior to the Russian occupation, these were independent, self-governed Muslim states.

One day, we stopped at the station of a sprawling metropolis called Bukhara, an ancient city in the republic of Uzbekistan. We stopped at the central station and found out that the train would spend the whole day there. All the adults scattered to look for acquaintances, relatives, information, food, and anything else they could find. My uncle Baruch (Aunt Chana's husband) spotted a close relative on the platform, a brother-in-law or a cousin, who told him that many Jews had recently settled in Bukhara after being released from the Siberian camps. There was also a large local Jewish community that had been living in harmony with the local Uzbeks for many generations.

Southern Republics

Uncle Baruch wanted to take his wife, Hannah, and daughter and join his relatives, but the rest of the family objected. They claimed that they must stay together in this vast, unknown land.

Uncle Baruch and Chana remained with us for a short while, but on the way back from Turkmenistan, they did get off the train and join their relatives in Bukhara for a few months.

We continued our journey on that train going southwest. We started our journey in search of a kolkhoz, which we thought would be our source of livelihood. But who knew where there was a good kolkhoz? A good kolkhoz meant one with a lot of land and good management. The family decided to stop at the next city and ask around about a kolkhoz.

Grandmother Leah was very thin and frail. Siberia did not do her well, and all this traveling and heat did not help either. One morning, Aunt Reizl noticed that Grandmother was listless, sitting on the bench in the train. Aunt Reizl touched her forehead, and it was hot. She alerted the family, and they decided to get off the train at the next stop. They were hoping it would be a town where a doctor and medicine or a hospital could be found. The next stop was Churzuy in the Republic of Turkmenistan, a small dusty Muslim town. We all got off the train not even knowing where we were. It didn't really matter because we didn't know one town from another. We had to take the chance, and Grandmother urgently needed medical attention. It was still harvesttime in the southern parts of the country, so we hoped that the farmers would need a helping hand. Some areas in those republics were called the breadbasket for their fertile soil and abundant crops. This particular one was the sand basket, arid and mercilessly hot.

We decided not to travel any farther for fear of it being even worse. We got off at the first stop as soon as we saw some houses. It was a suburb of Churzuy. We didn't know that there was another larger, central station in the heart of town. The area was sparsely populated with small clay and stone huts scattered in every direction with no particular order. There was lots of sand and hardly any vegetation. At the slightest breeze, the sand would form clouds, obstruct visibility, and burn our eyes. The sand would penetrate every nook and cranny. Rain must have been a rare occurrence.

There were narrow winding alleys leading in every direction. This place would probably be as good or as bad as any other. We brought our belongings to the nearest tree, in search of shade and some relief from the oppressive heat. It was October and late afternoon, but the sun was still high and the ground was parched and burning hot.

One could not walk barefoot for fear of burning one's soles. Mother said, "I could cook an egg in the sand if I had one."

Two or three of our men went in search of fresh water and anything else they could find. They were also hoping to find a doctor.

The sun was beating down mercilessly, but we had no choice. We did not know where else to go.

About an hour later, the men returned with pails of water from someone's well and several large flatbreads. These natives did not bake loaves of bread as we knew them. They baked flatbreads—we know them today as pita bread, *lepioshka* in Russian. It was new to us at that time. It was food to eat, and it tasted good.

The men told us that the area down the road was much more densely populated and that they had also found one of the markets. That was where they bought the bread. They learned that the market was active twice a week in the summer, only in the early morning, due to the intense heat. They found out that the locals were primarily Muslim, but now, since the war began, many refugees from the west were flocking in and settling in the area.

We were not used to such a climate. Mother could not stand the heat. My grandmother Leah was also showing signs of weakness. We learned that if we continued traveling southwest, we would come to the Persian border. This was an intriguing thought. Maybe we could cross the border and go live in Persia, another exotic country. All this was conjecture, a pipe dream. No one was leaving the Soviet Union that easily.

The next day, we found a doctor. He examined my grandmother, and the diagnosis was dysentery.

I remembered my bout with the illness when we first arrived in Cherepanovo. It was a nasty and dangerous sickness.

Grandma Leah's condition deteriorated, and we hoped she would be admitted to a hospital and receive badly needed care and medicine. We asked the doctor if he could refer her to a hospital where she could have a better chance of surviving. The doctor told us that there had not been empty beds in the hospital for weeks already.

There was an influx of refugees from all over the country, and many brought diseases with them, so the small hospital was filled to capacity. There were patients lying in the corridors and even on the bare floors.

There weren't enough mattresses to accommodate all the sick. A woman her age didn't have a chance of being admitted. The doctor prescribed a medication that we were able to buy in town and told us to give her lots of tea or boiled water. We were warned to stay away from her, if possible, as it could be typhoid and very contagious. We started a bonfire, boiled water, and spoon-fed her. She was so weak that she couldn't sit up and drink from a cup.

There was an abandoned passenger railcar nearby, and Grandma was transferred there to stay out of the burning sun. The women made a makeshift bed for her on one of the benches.

Some of the windows in the railcar were open, and some broken, so the sand had blown in, but they were able to clean an area, spread a soft blanket on one of the benches, and make Grandma a little more comfortable. The women cared for her, in shifts, day and night. Unfortunately, though, Grandmother's illness was too advanced, and two days later, she passed away.

According to Jewish law, a corpse must be buried within twenty-four hours. My aunts washed the body according to ritual and stayed with her all night according to the law. They also hand-sewed the burial shroud from a white sheet and dressed her in it.

Early in the morning, the men scattered in search of a *minian* (quorum). Ten Jewish men were needed for burial and the recitation of the Kaddish (prayer for the dead). We had no knowledge of a Jewish community or Jewish cemetery in Churzhuy.

My grandmother was carried to the outskirts of town and buried there with a stick as a marker on her grave. The obligatory seven days of shivah were observed, and my father, as the eldest son, recited the Kaddish three times a day.

While the family was sitting shivah, several local Jews came to talk to us. They apparently found out that we were Jewish refugees from Poland recently released from labor camps in Siberia. They told us that there was an influx of refugees from the west and that food was becoming scarce and lodging almost nonexistent.

Once again the thought of life in a kolkhoz became appealing.

After some inquiries, we found and were accepted in a kolkhoz by the name of Kizyl-tepe.

The family was in mourning.

We also learned that we were not far from the Persian border, so they began to explore this possibility.

My father, though, did not completely give up the idea of crossing the border into Persia (Iran).

One day, he and one of my cousins took the train to Ashgabat, a big city right on the Iranian border. They met Jews and non-Jews trying to find a way to cross the border and leave the USSR. There were guides who, for a fee, guided people through the mountains to Iran. There were rumors that some people actually succeeded in crossing the border. The validity of the rumors was never established. Father also learned that there was a Jewish scout from Palestine gathering Jewish youngsters and smuggling them to Palestine via Iran.

Father decided that he wanted to save at least one or two members of our family, namely me and possibly one of my cousins. He found one of those agents, paid him his fee in advance, and told him to include us in the next transport to Palestine.

When he returned that evening and told this to my mother, she fell into a rage. She accused him of being callous and heartless. How could he decide to send his child to unknown lands without even consulting the child or mother? She refused to let me go. She stated categorically, "If we survive, we survive together, and if we perish, we perish together. I already lost one child in the wilderness of Siberia. Don't make me lose another."

That was the end of the conversation, but I must admit that the thought intrigued me. Everything surrounding me since we arrived in the USSR was new and interesting to me, whether it was good or bad.

The following day, Father took the train to Ashgabat, found the agent, and got his money back. His intensions were good; he wanted to save at least one child. At that time, we did not think we would ever return home alive.

Kolkhoz Life in Turkmenistan

After more inquiries, a decision was made to remain where it was warm and where there was food. It was autumn, time for harvesting crops. A kolkhoz was a good place to settle in, at least until things became clearer. A day after my father's adventure in Ashgabat on the Iranian border, we hired a coachman with a horse and wagon with large rubber wheels, probably lifted from a truck, and about twenty minutes later arrived at the nearest kolkhoz, named Kizil-Tepe.

This village/kolkhoz looked totally different from the one in Siberia. The terrain was somewhat hilly, and there were narrow dirt roads and one stone or stucco hut after another surrounded by stone or cement walls and wooden gates. Dogs barked everywhere. They must have smelled strangers. The man whom we hired wanted to unload the wagon immediately and return to town, but Father asked him to stay a little longer and not to worry, that he would get paid for the additional time.

We arrived unannounced and didn't even know if we would be accepted. Two of our men went to find the office of the *predsedatel* (chairman). He would know if they needed help with the harvest and if there was room for us to stay in. Luckily, the predsedatel was in his office, arguing with another man in their native tongue.

After a short question-and-answer period, he agreed to receive us. They needed people to pick fruit and cotton. He couldn't make any promises as to the future. He needed the help for four to six weeks, and we were very happy to oblige.

The whole family was ushered into the community center until better accommodations could be found. This was not a very large collective farm, maybe three- or four-dozen households. The members of this kolkhoz were farmers in the past, so the transition, however painful, from private to government collective enterprise was easier than teaching how to farm people who had other professions in the past.

Farming in the forties was the number-one priority in the USSR. Most of the crops went to the front. In exchange for wheat, corn, and other staples, the collective farms could receive seeds, machinery, fertilizers, or any other equipment they needed. The amount of crops they had to relinquish was decided by the state.

This was the cotton-picking season, so all the men went to the fields to do just that. Our men already had some experience working in the fields from their previous job in Zakavrashyna.

Most of our family members were born and bred in villages and were familiar with farming. Cotton-picking was not very different, but it was backbreaking work. The workday was from dawn to dusk, which meant ten to twelve hours. They made a deal with the predsedatel (chairman) that they would be willing to work Sunday instead of Saturday. The local people, being primarily Muslim, observed Friday as their day of rest. Sunday was the government's day of rest. Our men were asked to work only half a day on Friday and rest on Saturday, which suited them fine. We settled down in the community hall as best as we could—we were given some mattresses to sleep on. We did not need blankets in that heat. But more importantly, they promised us abundant food.

In front of the building, there was an area designated for a kitchen, meaning there was something that resembled a stove/oven, namely a square made of rocks with a place for logs in the middle. So we almost had all the conveniences.

The next morning, Mother set out with a pitcher and a basket in search of food. The main objective was to find milk. Mother believed in milk as the best nourishment for children. Though we were not babies anymore, she tried to give us milk whenever possible.

We still had some money, so she was sure there would be someone who would be willing to sell some milk and other provisions.

She went directly to the predsedatel's office to ask him where she could fulfill her objective. He welcomed her to his office, and after Mother told him that she had two small children who were hungry, he told her to wait and left the room. He returned a short while later with a substantial sack of flour and another with dry corn. He asked her to follow him to the adjacent building. This turned out to be his private home, and he filled her jug with milk. He also told her to come every day for fresh milk.

Mother took out money and wanted to pay him, but he refused to take it. He said to her, "We were blessed with an abundant crop this year, and you are giving me an opportunity to share it."

Mother was awestruck. Words of gratitude were stuck in her throat, and tears welled up in her eyes. She finally regained her composure and thanked him. "Thank God for people like you. There is hope for humankind." She was so thrilled with the provisions and the whole episode that she almost ran back to us even though she was carrying a heavy load. She wanted to share her experience with the family. Mother shared everything she brought.

Right outside the hamlet, there was a large grindstone where the neighbors ground their grain into flour. My aunt Channah and my mother ground the corn into flour, mixed it with wheat flour, and baked delicious flatbreads. They learned to improvise and found out that bread could be made without yeast and that its shape didn't matter. It really tasted delicious.

There were three of us who enjoyed the extra attention and privileges of our age: my brother Israel, my cousin Feyga, and I were the youngest in the family. The other cousins were already teenagers or grown adults.

The first experiences in the kolkhoz were favorable, and we even thought of remaining there, at least until the war was over.

Mother did not feel comfortable getting milk and other food from the predsedatel daily, so one late afternoon, she set out in search of milk and any other provisions she could buy. She tried to find another source for milk, but there was hardly anyone in the narrow alleys. Most men were still at work, and the women stayed in their homes, behind the stone walls.

She knocked on one gate, and a few minutes later, a man opened a small window in the wooden gate and asked her what she wanted. She told him that she wanted to buy some potatoes, flour, milk, or anything else he could spare. He asked her to step into the yard and wait. The man entered the limestone hut, and a few minutes later, a woman came out and invited Mother to come inside. Mother gladly followed her hostess. She was curious to see how these homes looked inside and how these exotic people lived.

The lady of the house showed Mother into a large square room in the middle of the house. There were benches along the walls covered with what looked like woven or embroidered colorful cushions. The walls and mud floor were decorated with rugs of every color and design. In the middle of the room stood a low square table also covered with an embroidered cloth. The room was cool even though it was hot outside. The man of the house appeared from one of the openings and asked Mother to sit at the table. He seemed nervous for some reason. There were no chairs, so Mother sat on the floor. He disappeared again into the adjoining room and swiftly returned carrying a very large bowl of steaming food. The woman, who must have been his wife, and two little girls followed him. He placed the big bowl on the table while his wife, a beautiful, dark-haired, and dark-eyed young woman, placed a bunch of warm round flatbreads on the table. The enormous bowl contained steaming rice with pieces of meat on the surface.

The aroma was foreign but very pleasant. Mother had never smelled anything so delicious. She had forgotten what good food tasted and smelled like. They gestured for Mother to start eating. There were no visible plates, forks, or spoons on the table.

Mother tried to explain that she only came to buy milk and did not expect to be invited to a meal. She ate only kosher food and thanked the family very much for their kind invitation but said that, according to our law, she was not allowed to partake of this food. She hoped they would understand her broken Russian.

Mother had no idea that refusing such an invitation was a grave insult to the host. She also didn't realize that they had never heard the word *kosher* and didn't understand what Mother was talking about.

After several attempts at trying to make her eat, the man became very agitated and began shouting at Mother in his native language, which she didn't understand. Mother, seeing his reaction, decided to leave. He grabbed her by the arm and forced her to sit down. Now she was really frightened.

His wife sat there and watched while the children ate, picking up the thick rice with the flatbread. They all ate from the same bowl. This was another thing Mother was not used to seeing or doing. While the host walked over to one corner of the room, Mother stood up and swiftly ran to the gate. He ran after her with a long stick. Mother made it through the gate and kept running while he remained inside. He didn't follow her.

She ran all the way home, and when she arrived, totally out of breath, she collapsed onto a chair and burst out crying. We all surrounded her, asking what had happened to her, but she couldn't speak until she had completely calmed down. It took a while for her to regain her composure, and only then did she tell us the story.

When Father came home from work and heard the story, he decided to go to the precsedatel (manager) to lodge a complaint against the man. Other members of the family were against it for fear of reprisals. Father decided to tell him anyway. "It should be known," he said, "what kind of violent people inhabit this village and how they treat newcomers."

The next day, Father went to lodge a complaint with the predsedatel, but the man, instead of showing anger, was amused. Now Father was angry and demanded an explanation. The manager explained to him that it was the custom of the Muslim people to be hospitable and invite any stranger who came by to join them at mealtime. Refusing to eat was an offense and a grave insult to the host.

Every day we learned something new.

We were unfamiliar with all these customs and were not sure if we could or wanted to get used to them. This was a good place for us (the climate was warm); there was enough food, and we were treated with dignity. The people and their way of life were strange to us, but we were sure we could learn their customs if necessary. We were the only Jewish family in this kolkhoz. The question of a minyan (quorum) came up. Where would the men pray during holidays? Where would we find kosher meat? We survived eighteen months in Siberia without meat, but we were hoping that the future would be different, better. The family decided to stay, finish the cotton and fruit harvest, and then move on. This place paid well, and there was enough food.

I brought up the question of food very often, but this subject was utmost on our minds. It meant survival! We were not sure they would keep us after the harvest was finished.

Our accommodations had not been changed, and we all lived in that one room for almost two weeks. There was no indoor plumbing or running water where we stayed. Each house had a well and an outhouse.

Soon, a neighbor gave us permission to draw water from his well and use his outhouse. It was not ideal, but it was better than Siberia. Soon the family realized that we also had social and religious needs.

Though it was the middle of October, it was still hot during the day but cooler at night. It was quite pleasant, and we still wore summer clothes. The earth was still so hot at midday. Those of us who had remnants of shoes had to preserve them for the winter, so we wrapped our feet with rags in order to not burn our soles or injure our feet. The roads and alleys were not paved and were full of stones, broken glass, and other debris. Though our bellies were full, our spiritual life was empty—actually, nonexistent. We were taught that a Jew must have nourishment for the body as well as for the soul.

At the end of October, it looked like the harvest was finished. We thanked the predsedatel and the other members of the kolkhoz for the opportunity to work and all the good things they had done for us.

We hit the road again. We really didn't know where to go, but it was decided to settle in a larger place where other Jews lived. My cousins and I had not attended a school since 1939. This was October 1942. Mother was pregnant, and she hoped to give birth in a hospital, or at least be assisted by a doctor or midwife, and not in the desert.

She also worried about our education or rather the lack of it. My older cousins were also still young and in need of schooling. We knew we would find schools in cities.

We loaded our belongings and plenty of flour, potatoes, onions, cabbage, carrots, and whatever else we could buy or barter. This time, our direction was east, as to the west was the Iranian border and a little more north the war with the Germans. The oxen-drawn wagon took us slowly into town and the rail station.

The family was very sad, and my aunt Reizl cried. We were leaving this region of Turkmenistan where my grandmother was buried, not knowing if we would ever return to her grave. We never have.

My parents also remembered the day we left the camp in Siberia and my brother David's grave, which we would never see again. We had already parted with two members of our family, Grandmother Leah and my brother David.

As we arrived at the train station in Churzuy (I think this was the name of that small town), we saw other families in the same predicament. Everyone was on the move, natives as well as refugees. As the Germans advanced, Stalin resettled the population from Europe to Asia. Some people were fleeing the Germans of their own free will, primarily Jews.

We spent another night in the train station and, the following morning, boarded a passenger train going east. We remembered the stop in Bukhara and hoped to settle there or in another town along the way.

We didn't know the difference between the towns. We were glad to be free and able to travel freely and knew that somehow we would find a place to settle down in and survive until the war was over.

Two days later, we arrived in Bukhara, where we had made a stop on the way to Turkmenistan. In Bukhara, my aunt Chana, her husband (Baruch), and their daughter Feyga left us and joined Uncle Baruch's family. While in Bukhara, we found out that there were many thousands of refugees and it was almost impossible to find lodging or work. Even Aunt Chana and her husband could not find work and joined us in Dzhambul a few months later. At that time, we were unaware that my mother's sister Blima also lived in Bukhara. She remained there until the liberation in 1946. Her tall, handsome, and learned husband died in Bukhara. It must have been during the typhoid epidemic, which spread like wildfire throughout the region.

We kept traveling northeast through Turkmenistan, Uzbekistan, Tajikistan, and Kyrgyzstan and finally wound up in Kazakhstan. The vast distances between towns were mostly steppes and parched fields, some dotted by small villages and collective farms surrounded by agricultural activity. The towns that we did travel through were quite similar in terms of architecture. The names told us nothing.

One day, we pulled into a station of a large, sprawling city by the name of Dzhambul.

DZHAMBUL

The first thing the men did was get off the train in search of information, friends, relatives, etc.

My father had this ability of asking the right questions and getting the right answers. He always knew what was happening. As he walked on the platform along the train, he spotted a close relative, a second cousin named Layzer. Cousin Layzer and his family were also in Siberia, in the central labor camp not far from us. They had left the labor camp before us and wound up in Dzhambul.

Father was very happy to see a familiar face, especially this relative, for he and his family were the finest people we knew. Dzhambul was a sprawling city with many collective farms and factories surrounding it. There was also a sizeable tannery in the center of town, a sugar factory on the outskirts, as well as other enterprises.

A very important piece of information was that there were many Jewish families in town and in the surroundings. Mr. Layzer and his sons quickly acquired a new profession—they and their neighbors became shoemakers. They manufactured shoes and boots by hand for the government. They also found a way to make some for themselves and were even able to sell some. Though legally they were not allowed to do this, in the USSR everybody found a way to do some kind of business.

Father immediately saw the possibilities. He came back to our train car with Layzer and convinced the family that Dzhambul was the place to stay in.

Among the Jewish population who had lived in the area for generations were recent refugees and possibly thousands who were recently freed from the labor camps.

We gathered our belongings, and by afternoon, we were walking behind a wagon, carrying our bundles and following our cousin Layzer to his home.

When we arrived, there was a lot of hugging and kissing, laughing and crying. It was a happy reunion, and we were all glad we had found one another again. Our cousins had come to Dzhambul directly from Siberia and had lived there for a few months already. They had time to acquire knowledge of the town and its possibilities. There was a thriving Jewish community and culture even though it was frowned upon by the government.

Layzer's wife, Reiza, got busy in the kitchen and began serving food.

It had been quite some time since we had eaten a home-cooked meal. It was a very welcome sight and tasted delicious. There was no room in their home for all of us, but somehow we managed that first night. We slept on the floor and wherever there was a vacant spot.

The next morning, my parents as well other members of the family went scouring the city in search of living accommodations. By the day's end, this was accomplished. Mother found a one-room, freestanding little house with a wide entrance foyer and a wood-burning brick oven. She rented it from a native Kazakh woman. Mother was particularly happy with the large yard in the back of the house, which in the spring and summer became her lovingly cared-for garden and food supplier. Mother was very good at gardening; she toiled many hours each day, and it paid off. Our new address became 38 Menzinskaya Street.

The rest of the family needed a larger home to accommodate their ten members, and they found one in a farming area across the river on the outskirts of town, a distance of about three kilometers from where we lived.

Life began to acquire some semblance of normalcy and stability. Soon my brother and I were enrolled in school, and we began learning Russian in earnest. Mother gave birth to my sister Leah on November 22, 1943 in the hospital, just as she wanted it to be. Children were not allowed to visit patients in the hospital, but one day, when I brought my mother her food, she was nursing the baby and she showed me my newborn sister, Leah, through the window. She was wrapped in a white blanket. The only visible parts were her beautiful round face and two lively big black eyes. She looked just like a little doll. Mother stayed in the hospital a whole week. My aunts prepared our hot meal, and either Father or I went to get it. We were all thrilled with the new baby, who became the center of everyone's attention. In the beginning, Mother would not allow us to handle her, but after a while, she realized that I could be trusted with the baby's care and allowed me to take care of her whenever she had to go somewhere. This made me feel grown-up and taught me responsibility.

The house Mother rented was one of those typical limestone homes. It measured approximately ten by twenty feet. The front foyer was about six by ten feet, running the width of the structure. The main room had three windows, two in the back, overlooking the garden, and one placed higher, facing our next-door neighbor. The foyer had two small windows perched high, facing the street. A flat roof covered the whole building.

The outside walls were made of something resembling cinder blocks covered with gray stucco. Inside, the walls were fairly smooth and whitewashed.

Near the entrance to the room, there was a wood-burning stove that was connected by the same chimney to the brick oven in the foyer. Above the stove was a built-in concrete shelf. This shelf turned out to be very useful; we could dry laundry on it and store pots and pans, and on occasion, on very cold nights, I even slept on it. The shelf kept its warm temperature many hours after the fire in the stove was extinguished, emitting warmth throughout the room.

Mother was happiest about the large garden in the back of the house. She had great plans for that piece of land came spring and summer.

Father was hardly ever home. He was always out, trying his hand at business, doing his utmost to keep us fed.

I was happy to be back again in school, to be with other kids, learning and making new friends.

The school was about half an hour's walk. The L-shaped gray one-story school building was fairly large, constructed of cinder blocks. The rest of the square property was designated as a playground, where the pupils exercised in the morning and played during recess. The classrooms were spacious; each class had thirty to thirty-five pupils. The makeup of the pupils was quite varied. Many ethnic groups were represented, though the majority were local Kazakhs.

In the twenties and thirties, the Communist regime uprooted thousands of families from the European parts of the USSR and resettled them in Siberia and the southernmost republics in the east. Their crime was being either rich or other fabricated, stupid reasons. The wealth was confiscated and occasionally divided among the poorer citizens, but generally, it was just taken in the name of the state and most of the time wound up in the hands of the new and "deserving" leaders. Some were uprooted for no reason at all.

After Germany attacked the USSR in June 1942, there was a new influx of refugees from various western republics, like the Ukraine, Belarus, Latvia, Estonia, Chechnya, and others.

The schools became overcrowded and integrated, and there was a great mix of nationalities. We all had to learn the Russian language no matter where we came from. I was enrolled in second grade again because of my lack of knowledge of the Russian language. I wasn't happy about it, but I had no choice. We had no money for a tutor. I caught on quickly and soon became one of the best pupils in class.

One day, Mother walked out the door and saw, a few houses away, a family being thrown out into the street with all their belongings. There was crying and screaming. Neighbors and passersby began gathering around them to see what was happening. Mother walked over as well. She addressed the woman who seemed to be the mother of the children. A tall, husky man was arguing with the landlord in broken Russian. Mother knew right away that this was a Jewish family. There were clothes and pots and pans thrown all over. The landlord was evicting them and throwing their possessions out into the street. People helped gather their meager belongings and put them in a pile next to an old woman who was sitting on a suitcase numbly, with tears flowing from her eyes. There were two girls, one of them about my age, with straight dark-blond hair gathered in a ponytail. The other was taller and looked older. She had a shock of curly dark hair and dark, lively eyes. It was also obvious that the short woman was expecting a child. Mother soon found out that they were being evicted for nonpayment of rent. The man claimed he was only a few weeks late with the rent and made a solemn promise to pay by the week's end, but the landlord would not even listen.

When all the things were thrown out, the landlord retreated into the house and would not listen to any pleas or promises. By that time, a large crowd had gathered and surrounded the homeless family.

My mother, the avid humanitarian, invited them to stay with us until they found other suitable accommodations. The old woman stood up for the first time and kissed my mother's hands. She also said that God was watching and would surely repay the kindness. Though we had only one room, it was a large one compared to the one we had occupied in Siberia. We moved the bed and other items to one side and invited them to occupy the other side of the room. Slowly they began dragging their things into our house. They had a large bed, which was in pieces, which they had to put together again. They also had a small oblong table and five stools. The rest was bedding and some rags they called clothing.

A few pots and pans and several metal plates completed their possessions.

Suddenly, we were ten people living in one room. We had one large bed made of wooden boards and a long wooden table with benches on each side. There were some shelves near the stove that my father had put up, and that was where Mother kept her few pots and pans.

I became friendly with the girls, Helen and Deborah. We went to school together, and for a few weeks, things went well. But soon, Mother noticed some unpleasant traits in their behavior. She feared their behavior might negatively influence my brother and me. She decided that they had overstayed their welcome and should look for their own place.

One evening, Mother asked Solomon, the head of the family, how he was doing with searching for a place to live. He answered that he was not looking for any other place to live in; living right here with us suited him just fine. Mother was shocked! Father was home, too, and he was always hot under the collar and short-tempered, and a shouting match ensued. Mother realized that her generosity had backfired. She felt totally defeated. After the shouting between the families, there was a big argument between my parents. We, the kids, went under the covers, afraid to breathe. Father realized that arguing with our squatters would lead nowhere, so he resigned himself to living together with them, but they would have to pay half the rent. Sol's answer was "When I'll have money, I'll pay."

Both my parents were livid, but there was not much they could do. The only thing they could do was throw them out, just like the Kazakh did. This was not in my parents' nature.

We wound up living with them for about two years. There were many arguments between us, but somehow, we survived the inconvenience and hardships.

This was a time of a great influx of refugees trying to settle in Dzhambul as well as in other Asian towns.

Finding an apartment or a job was like looking for a needle in a haystack. There was no new construction to speak of. Many families were forced to live together for more than one reason mainly because of lack of accommodations and lack of money. Many wound up living in the street.

After a few months of Sol's nonpayment of rent, Father decided to take him to a rabbinical court, where it would be decided if they should pay their share of the rent or not. Our tenants were not very religious and didn't abide by too many Jewish laws, but they had no choice. The head of the family was summoned by a messenger, and he had to appear in person. Three days later, the rabbinical court ruled that they had to pay half the rent retroactively and every month thereafter.

The court also ruled that they would have to share all other mutually incurred expenses, like coal and wood for heating, any needed repairs, etc. They were not thrilled with the verdict, but they didn't want to lose face in the Jewish community.

After the big fight, Mother fully understood why they were thrown out of their previous apartment. It was a very unpleasant atmosphere, and there were weeks when we didn't talk to one another.

It became very difficult to live with them. We had to watch everything day and night. We contemplated moving out, but the town was so overcrowded that finding another apartment we could afford was almost impossible. We were compelled to live with them for almost two years.

One of their daughters was my age and we were in the same class in school, but we didn't always get along. We fought often and called each other derogatory names. Her sister, Deborah, was two or three years older, and the two of us had a more amicable relationship. She and I were often sent on errands together.

Father realized that if he worked or did business with our tenants, at least he wouldn't report us to the authorities, and they could not claim being penniless when father knew when Sol was making money.

After assessing the situation, Father decided to take Sol on as a partner. If you can't beat them, join them. We already knew the taste of Siberia, so we had to be very careful with what we were doing and whom we were doing it with. There were no jobs to be gotten in this overpopulated city. Despite the great risks, many people had to find other ways of making a living. I would say half the country was wheeling and dealing under the noses of the authorities and trying to stay one step ahead of them.

Most of the KGB and police were on the take and looked the other way, but occasionally, they would arrest someone, guilty or not, to show to their superiors that they were doing their job. This was another way for the KGB to make money. Their salaries were low, especially for the lower ranks, so many of them supplemented their income by taking bribes. Some of them took the bribes openly, while others did it in a clandestine way, but everyone in town knew who could be bought.

The price was set by the taker according to the "crime" committed.

Over the four years we spent in Dzhambul, my father bought and sold everything, from condoms to meat, leather, wheat, shoes, and everything in between. Most people who couldn't find work did basically the same with some variations.

There were three fairly large markets in Dzhambul with distinctive names, the flour market, the green market, and the coal market, each specializing in different merchandise.

They were supposed to offer specific items connected with their names, but during the war, you could buy almost anything at any market.

Father primarily frequented the flour bazaar. First, it was closest to where we lived, and second, it offered a vast variety of items. There you could usually buy or sell flour, beans, a pair of shoes, a cow, a sheep, and anything else anyone was selling that day.

In the beginning, Father's business resembled many others. He would buy an item at one bazaar or market then take the item to another one and sell it at a small profit. It didn't matter what the item was as long as there was a customer who would buy it and a few kopeks could be made. Sometimes he would buy an edible item, which was difficult to sell. If it could not be sold at a profit, we ate it. The idea was not to keep any merchandise at home in case someone squealed to the police. The police could come in the middle of the night and search, which they often did. If they found anything they thought was not a 100 percent kosher, they would take the man of the house (along with the merchandise) to the police station for interrogation. God help those who showed fear or did not give the right answers. Many times the police would search people in the street or in their homes without any permit or reason. They didn't need a reason or a search warrant to do their job. Many innocent people went to prison for many years on trumped-up charges.

I recall an interesting enterprise my father was in, which included other members of the family. One winter evening, I can't recall the month, Mother told me that I would be awakened in the middle of the night to go somewhere with my father. She did not elaborate, so I knew it was a secret mission. She also said that Sol and Deborah would go with us.

At about 2:00 a.m., Mother woke me and told me to get dressed. I obeyed as usual. The kerosene lamp was lit, and I saw Father dressed already, and on the other side of the room, Deborah was getting dressed and Sol was sitting in a chair. Mother urged me to dress well because the night air was freezing. Before I put on my coat, Mother put something that resembled a quilted vest on me, but it was empty—there was no filling in it. She also gave me a very loose pair of pants and instructed me to tie them at the waist and at my ankles as tightly as I could.

This was a strange and unfamiliar outfit, and I asked Mother for an explanation. She said it was to keep me extrawarm. I noticed that the others were also wearing the same outfits. They were made of burlap, and I was glad to wear it on top of my clothes. When we were all ready, we stepped out into the street on a moonless night. It was very cold, but not windy. That was a big help. We walked together as quietly and as fast as we could. After a while, my breathing was labored and Father was already sorry that he included me in this escapade.

About half an hour later, we arrived at the railroad depot. There was a large yard surrounded by a high metal fence and, next to the gate, a small hut. A faint light came through the dirty tiny window. Not a sound could be heard. Father knocked on the window, and a moment later, a hunched man came out, opened the gate, and showed us in. We all entered the tiny hut. A kerosene lantern hung over a small square table, supplying a very dim light. The shadows of our bodies made it even darker. The hut was so small that the five of us barely fit standing up.

We all removed our coats and held them in our hands, except Father, because the man asked him to go out with him. He and my father went outside and, about ten minutes later, returned with pails full of grain. Both men picked up scoops and began filling the empty tufts of our specially made garments.

After he showed us how it was done, Deborah and I continued filling our jackets and pants while the two men went out to get more.

The wheat (I think that was what it was) was moist and felt cold at first, but our body heat warmed it quickly.

When our garments were full, it felt heavy, and the bulky slacks made it difficult to walk. When we were all filled up, my father paid the man and we were off on our way back home. Going back took much longer because we were all carrying heavy loads on our bodies and we were forced to walk much slower. The night was cloudy and dark. Occasionally, the moon peeked out from between the clouds and lit our way. There was not another soul on the road, but occasionally, a dog barked as we passed their homes.

When we returned home, it was about five o'clock in the morning. Mother had hot tea ready for us all. We hadn't felt the cold coming back because the heavy loads of grain hugged our bodies and kept us warm.

These escapades were repeated several times that winter. Father said the wheat was rotting anyway so some people might as well put it to good use.

There was a mountain of wheat at that depot delivered during the fall harvest from the collective farms. It was awaiting transport, to be delivered to the army at the front and distributed in towns and villages. Because of the war, many trains delivered war materials and other goods and services, so wheat for the masses took secondary place.

The grain was exposed to the elements of winter, namely rain, snow, and wind.

The birds helped themselves too, as well as the watchman. Everybody had to eat.

Father began to make a living day by day buying and selling whatever he could get his hands on. The first few months were difficult. We had arrived in November and had nothing prepared for the winter.

Most locals had gardens around their houses and grew their own fruits and vegetables. We were new in town and didn't have the time or opportunity to prepare.

We had very little money, clothes, or valuables left to sell in order to exchange for food, and many days we had only one skimpy meal. Mother always believed in good nutrition and always tried her best to have milk for us.

That winter, my parents and I owned only one pair of shoes between the three of us. The shoes we brought with us from Poland were long torn and discarded. I had outgrown my BATA lace-up shoes, but they still fit my brother Israel, so he had a pair of his own. Father had bought a pair of army lace-up shoes at the bazaar, and the three of us shared them. No socks or stockings. We wrapped our feet with rags cut up from torn old clothing or a piece of a torn sheet. After a while, Mother bought some wool yarn and knitted socks for all of us. Eventually, I learned to knit and became proficient at it and was quite creative. Early in the morning, Father would go to prayer and wear the shoes. When he returned, it was my turn to wear them to school, and if he had to go somewhere, he wrapped his feet with rags. There was no shame in it; many people did the same.

I wrapped my feet with many rags so the boots fit better and kept me warm. When I returned from school after twelve noon, the shoes came off and the next person, usually my father, would wear them and go out to the market or wherever his business took him. Before he left for the day, he would usually bring a pail of water in from the well across the street or anything else Mother needed. She also walked around the house with rags wrapped around her feet.

Though Kazakhstan was in the south of Russia, the winters were cold at times, with snow and howling winds. The summers, by contrast, were hot. On cold winter days and nights, we used to bundle up and sit as close to the stove as possible to keep warm. My brother and I would recall poems, say our prayers, or do homework.

The clay floor stayed cold winter and summer. The windows were not insulated and drafty. At night we would hang blankets on the windows to keep the wind and cold out. During the day, we replaced them with sheets so the light of day and sunshine would seep through. As I mentioned before, we were very lucky that Mother took the down quilts with us when we left home. It was Mother's idea, and she was right. They saved us from freezing to death in Siberia, later on in Dzhambul, and even after the war. When we had heat in the apartment, we still used them in the winter. I think quilts are the greatest invention since electricity.

Father said down quilts must have been invented before electricity.

Oblava (Roundup) in Dzhambul

Every so often, the police would conduct an *oblava*. These round-ups and searches were authorized by the government. Whenever men were needed for work behind the front lines or any other venue, the authorities would send a contingent of policemen to catch men in the streets. The police looked primarily for men with menial jobs or no jobs at all. A person without a legitimate job was called a parasite, and there were plenty of those in our town.

People who had important jobs, if caught, were released and returned to work.

An oblava was simply the action of searching the streets and catching able-bodied men.

All those unfortunate ones who were caught had to pass a physical examination. If the outcome was satisfactory and they were more or less healthy, they were sent behind the front lines to work in factories or wherever else they were needed.

The police in Dzhambul would go out and search homes, bazaars, trains, and fields and then catch and deliver the men to a large hall in the community center. There, they would be *sorted* and given a physical examination, and those who passed would be sent to a designated location. Only healthy ones were needed, and age didn't matter much. The sick or disabled were released. The authorities did not draft non-Soviet citizens, but many volunteered and fought alongside the Russians.

One summer day, there was an oblava at the flour bazaar. My father was there at that time. The flour bazaar was on a hill, so it was easy to see anyone approaching. Someone noticed a large contingent of policemen walking swiftly in the direction of the bazaar. Everyone knew what it meant when a large group of police was moving swiftly. Someone yelled "Oblava!" and instantly, all the men began running in all directions in order to hide from the police. Many succeeded, but many were caught, among them my father. He had tripped on a rock and fallen, and by the time he was able to stand up, two policemen had grabbed him under his arms, stood him up, and put handcuffs on his wrists. That afternoon, they caught about forty-five men. All the men were hurled into this large community room to await their destiny.

It took several hours to process the multitude. There were men of all ages, most with family responsibilities. None of this mattered to the authorities; according to them, if those men were not at work during the day, they were parasites. The prisoners were to remain under lock and key overnight, and the following morning, they would undergo a doctor's examination and the able-bodied would be sent to where they were needed.

Those who escaped made every effort to notify whomever they could about the oblava.

Toward evening, a boy came running and told us that my father was among those caught that day and that his father was too. His mother had sent him to tell us. Someone else had told her. It worked like a relay race. Mother began to wring her hands and cry. "What are we going to do?" "We will surely die of hunger if Father is sent away!" and so on.

First, she wanted to see him and she also wanted to notify our relatives—maybe they could help. She left me in charge of my brother and little sister and ran as fast as she could to the community center. It was getting dark and she was afraid that the police would not let her see him, but there were also many other women trying to see their next of kin. The police had no choice but to allow them to see the detainees through the windows. No one except those in authority was allowed inside. Mother stood in line and waited her turn to see my father. When her turn came, a policeman asked the name and went inside to find my father and told him to get close to a window. The windows in the building were high, and my father was short, so he could hardly see my mother. She stood on a big rock that someone had put there for that purpose. She began to cry and asked him in Yiddish if she should try to rescue him from the police. She would tell them that she had three small children, that he was their father and the only breadwinner. Father knew that this would not work. It would incriminate him even more if they found out that he wasn't working. He didn't have a *legitimate* job.

The authorities had a quota to meet, and they had to deliver a certain number of men or face consequences. There were no sentiments. My father told Mother (in Yiddish) that he would try to fool the doctors during his examination and hopefully obtain his freedom. He told her to go home and come back early in the morning with some bread and a bottle of very strong coffee.

Mother hurried home with the intention of carrying out Father's instructions and with hope in her heart that it would have the intended effect.

The authorities allowed food into the compound. They were supposed to feed the prisoners, but many people ate only kosher food and wouldn't touch any nonkosher food that the police had provided. The less food the men consumed, the more was left for them to steal.

The medical examination was supposed to start the following morning at 6:00 a.m. Mother woke up very early, made the strongest coffee she knew how to make, cooled it a little, poured it into a quart bottle, wrapped a large slice of bread, and before 5:00 a.m., went to see my father in the temporary jail, which was about two kilometers away.

I couldn't sleep that night, thinking all kinds of frightening thoughts. How were we going to survive without Father? I was thinking of dropping out of school and possibly finding a menial job. I could take care of my little sister while Mother got, if possible, sewing jobs, like in Siberia. If not, we would probably have to beg in the streets like many other kids. This was one thing Mother abhorred; she always took pity on the beggar and gave whatever she could. Father sometimes objected, claiming (and rightfully so) that we were one step away from being the beggars. But Mother always had her answer ready: "If we give when we can, God will spare us and we will never need a handout. If God forbid we do, God will repay us in kind."

Mother arrived at the community center at about 5:30 a.m., and she asked the guard to see her husband and give him his breakfast. They called Father to the window, and she gave him what she had brought. The guard examined the contents of the bag, and he found nothing unusual—the bread and a bottle of warm black coffee. Only then was she allowed to give it to him through the open window. Many men yelled all kinds of messages in the hope that Mother would deliver them to their families. It was early in the morning, and very few visitors were present. The police allowed an exchange of a few sentences between my parents, and then Mother was ordered to leave.

Father slowly drank the whole liter of strong black coffee and saved the bread for later. He didn't want to dilute the effect of the coffee with the bread. At about 6:15 a.m., he was called to the examining room. He was told to undress the upper part of his frail body, which was bent over since his youth. His face was pale, and his whole body shook with fright. The examining doctor took one look at him and saw right away that this was not a candidate for the front or any other hard labor. As he put the stethoscope to Father's chest, he heard his heart racing like a locomotive. He couldn't believe his ears, so he called the other doctor to listen to my father's heart. They looked at each other, and the first doctor said to my father, "You are going straight to the hospital. Your heart is in a very bad shape!" Father pretended to look alarmed and asked what to do. The doctor told him to get dressed, and with the note he wrote for him, he ordered Father to go straight to the hospital for tests. Father's inner joy was indescribable, but he could not show it.

He got dressed and walked out holding the doctor's note in his hand. He showed it to the guard, who in turn told Father to go to the administrative office.

There, Father received his dispensation. He received a very valuable document that stated that due to poor health, he was released and was not allowed to perform any kind of hard labor. That meant he could not be sent to the front or forced to work. This note served him well during future roundups; all he had to do was show this note to the policeman and he was freed on the spot.

We had no knowledge of this. Mother returned home that morning in a somber mood and urged my brother and me to pray to God for our father's release and safe return. We took the prayer book and did not stop praying until Father walked in the door a couple of hours later.

Though he knew that the coffee caused his heart to race, he was a little anxious and went to the hospital. As time elapsed, his heart beat much slower. On his way to the hospital, he stopped in a *tchaichana* (teahouse) and ordered a strong cup of coffee. He needed the coffee effect in the hospital. His heart took on some speed, and he quickened his pace to aid it. I guess Father knew the workings of his heart and the influence of strong coffee on it. When he arrived at the hospital, he was told that the doctor was not in that day and was asked to come back the following day. He was glad about this turn of events because his nerves were on edge and he preferred to deal with this matter another time, when he had more time to think about the situation and give his heart time to rest and his mind to clear.

From the hospital he went directly home. When he opened the door and we saw him, we ran to embrace him and kiss him. Mother burst out crying, and so did we, but those were tears of joy. Father said jokingly that he didn't know we cared about him so much. Mother told us unequivocally that our prayers went straight to heaven. God heard them and facilitated Father's release. She said, "Every child needs a father. That's why God helps in time of need, but only when prayers are sincere."

Father always drank several cups of coffee to accompany his cigarettes, but this was one day he had enough. We all sat around the table, and as he told us about his adventure of the past twenty-four hours, we hung on every word. At one point, when talking about the effect of the coffee on his heart, Mother winked at him as though to stop him from talking about this so openly. We might want to show off and brag about it to some friends, and that could be dangerous.

Father looked at us and said firmly, "Nothing said in this house is to be repeated beyond these walls." We understood very well what he meant.

The following day, he drank the strong coffee again, went to the hospital at the designated time, and was examined by the doctor and given medication to slow down his heartbeat. The most important benefit of the last thirty-six hour's episode was the note stating that he was not allowed to do any hard labor. During future roundups, he did not have to run and hide.

When he was approached by the catcher (policeman), he presented the note and was released on the spot.

This was a tremendous relief for all of us. The possibility of our father being taken away didn't hang over our heads any longer. We grew up very quickly and took part in most aspects of our family life. Father's freedom was one worry we didn't have anymore, no doubt a very important one, but all the other problems still remained. We strongly believed that with God's help, in time, all our problems would be solved. The expression "With God's help" was part and parcel of our vocabulary, especially Mother's. God's help was always invoked no matter the problem.

This episode was soon forgotten, and we all returned to our daily lives. Father continued making efforts to make a living, Mother took care of little Leah and everything else a household needs, and my brother Israel and I made every effort to be good students.

My brother was a very smart boy; he was an A student, and so was I most of the time. Two years in a row, we both received what they called in Russia Pochvalnaya Gramota, something like a certificate of excellence. Our parents were very proud. At the end of each school year, there was a ceremony in front of the faculty, pupils, and parents, and the best students were recognized and awarded certificates. This certificate of excellence entitled the student to be the head of the pioneer group, and I became one the following year. Naturally, there was a lot of jealousy among our classmates, and some of my "friends" distanced themselves from me. The rumor was that I was chosen because I was Jewish and so was our teacher, and that was why the honor was given to me. Of course this accusation could not be further from the truth. There were many Jewish pupils in my class as well as in all the other classes. I was very proud but also hurt that my Christian classmates reacted that way.

Dzhambul, Our White Puppy

One warm summer afternoon, while we were living on Menzhynskaya Street, Father came home cradling a little white puppy. We were anxious to know what this meant. Father was not in the habit of bringing gifts, especially live ones. The story goes like this: Father was on his way home, still about half a mile away, when he felt something soft moving and touching his feet. He looked down and saw this dirty white ball of fluff squealing and rolling in the dirt. He looked closer and saw this adorable little puppy rolling in the sand. Father let it stay on the road and continued on his way, but several minutes later, he heard a squeal and the little bundle of fluff was under his feet again. He tried to shoo it away, but to no avail; every step he took, the puppy was right behind him, limping and crying. Father noticed that the little dog had a slight limp.

Two men passed him, and Father asked them if the puppy belonged to them, but they knew nothing about it. It must have belonged to someone. But to whom?

Raising a puppy, not even a watchdog, was another mouth to feed and an additional burden on the family, but Father took pity on the little animal and carried it home. He knew we would all be thrilled to have it.

After hearing the story and warning us that if the rightful owner showed up, we would have to return it, we agreed on the spot. We named him Rex. The first thing Mother did was give him a bath. The puppy turned out to be as white as snow. Mother dabbed some iodine on his wound, and the poor animal squealed with pain. She bandaged his foot with a piece of rag and poured some milk for him into a saucer. He drank it ravenously while we all stood around and watched with glee. We were all very happy—even Mother didn't mind the extra responsibility. She made a leash out of a string, and we loved to walk him in the street a few times a day, whether he had to relieve himself or not. We covered one corner of the floor in the hallway with newspapers, and he slept there at night. Though we wanted him to sleep with us at night, Mother didn't allow it. She argued that there was hardly any room for all of us in the one bed we all slept in.

Rex turned out to be a beautiful bundle of joy; he ate all kinds of scraps, and on occasion, we would share our food with him when Mother didn't look. When we were in school, he stayed tied up in the hallway on the newspaper. We used to run home from school so we could walk him and play with him. We taught him some tricks and had lots of fun with little Rex.

A few weeks had passed, and with our excellent care, he even grew a little. We loved him and were hoping that nobody ever showed up to claim him.

One day, while we were in school, he was crying and Mother was sure he needed to relieve himself. She was busy and couldn't take him for a walk, so she let him out of the house and saw him run into the garden.

About half an hour later, she remembered that she had let him out and hadn't heard him scratch the door, which he usually did when he wanted to come in. She called from the window, "Rex! Rex!" But the dog didn't respond. She dropped what she was doing and went outside to look for him, but the puppy was nowhere to be found.

Every day when we came home from school, Rex was there to welcome us, but that day, Rex was not there to do it. We guessed from Mother's sad face that something was wrong. She told us that she had let him out but he didn't come back. We spent several hours looking for him in the whole neighborhood and asking every neighbor and passerby, but no one had seen our little dog.

My brother and I returned home crying. When Father came home in the evening and heard the story, he tried co convince us that Rex's rightful owner must have found him in the street and had taken him home. Since the dog was outside, he didn't know whom to thank for the care the dog had received, so he just took him home. This was the most natural and convincing explanation, and we should be happy that we had Rex for a while and that now he went home and was in good hands again.

A week or so later, Mother opened the window to let some fresh air in, as she did every morning. As she opened the window facing our next-door neighbor, her keen sense of smell caught a foul odor. She was not sure at first what the odor was, but after a few whiffs, she realized that it was of a dead animal or rotten meat.

True, sanitary conditions in town were very primitive, almost nonexistent. Poverty in our neighborhood was a way of life, and Mother realized that nobody could afford to throw out meat, so it could only be a dead animal.

She put on a sweater and went out to investigate where the foul odor was coming from. She followed the smell and soon enough discovered its source: in the ditch (irrigation / sewage canal) adjacent to our house. This ditch was part of a canal where rainwater ran off. This water was used for laundry, irrigation, and sometimes for drinking and cooking.

In this ditch she saw a mound covered with leaves and other debris, and it smelled terribly. She removed the upper layer, and lo and behold, there was the beautiful white skin of our beloved puppy, Rex, rotting in the ditch. Mother was shocked. She put two and two together and soon she realized what had happened. We knew that our next-door neighbor, whose husband was at the front, fighting the Germans, supplemented her income by preparing all kinds of food at home and selling it at the bazaar. To think that someone ate our puppy made Mother sick. She came inside, took a spade, dug up the skin, and buried it in a deep grave at the very end of our garden. The thought of someone being capable of such an act made her cry. Mother did not tell us about this.

At night, when my siblings were asleep and I was still awake, as usual, I heard my mother tell the story to my father. Though I slept on the opposite end of the bed, I overheard many things my parents talked about at night. I was always an insomniac. Many times I would pretend to be asleep so I could hear my parents whisper. Sometimes they tested me if I was sleeping by tickling the soles of my feet, to see if I would react. Though I was ticklish, I would dig my heel into the mattress in order not to move my foot. I was always interested in what they were saying. They always made sure our "roommates" were fast asleep as well. Most of them snored, so it was easy to discern. After a while, we even recognized to whom a particular snore belonged.

The next morning, I waited for Mother to say something to us about the puppy, but she didn't say a word. After school, I went to check out the garden, and sure enough, there was a fresh mound of earth in the corner at the very end. I had no doubt about the validity of her story, but as always, I liked to check things out for myself. I didn't say a word to my brother. I didn't want to divulge how I obtained the information. I was sure that an opportunity would arise for Mother to tell us. She told us many months later.

We had no positive proof, so we could not accuse the neighbor, but from that day on, whenever I saw her, I avoided her like the plague.

THE REASON I FEAR DOGS

There was a rule in every class of our school that a different student was chosen daily by the teacher to act as monitor for that day. His or her duties included cleaning the blackboard, making sure all the pupils left the class during recess and were in the yard, making sure the class was clean and the floor free of debris, and probably some other chores.

One day, it was my turn to be monitor, and I took my duties very seriously. All the pupils went outside except one boy. I didn't notice him at first because I was busy cleaning the blackboard. When I finished and turned around, I noticed him sitting at his desk. I asked why he was still in class. He answered with a smirk on his face and said that he did not take orders from a dirty Jew.

My blood began to boil, my face turned red, and I ordered him to leave.

"Make me!" he retorted.

I walked over to his desk, grabbed him by the wrist, and pulled him toward the door. He was a husky kid, much stronger than I was, but somehow I managed to drag him to the door and push him out. As he found himself in the corridor, his anger was at its peak. He slammed the door in my face while hissing, "Zydovka!" A derogatory name for Jew. "I will repay you for this! You just wait."

The doorknob hit my mouth and broke half of one of my front teeth. I covered my mouth with my hand as the sharp pain brought tears to my eyes. Then I saw blood on my hand dripping from my mouth, and I ran to the principal's office.

Everyone was outside, pupils as well as teachers, and no one witnessed the episode. The principal was sitting behind her desk and stood up immediately. Upon seeing my bloody face, she ran toward me. She asked what had happened, but I was unable to speak and cried uncontrollably. She brought cold water in a bowl and began washing my face with a wet handkerchief. After a long while, I calmed down and told her what had happened. She left me sitting on the chair in her office and went to tell my teacher about the incident.

The boy, when confronted, denied the story, but when he was questioned where he spent the first ten minutes of recess, he fabricated a poor excuse and the teacher was reassured that he was the culprit. He was ordered to come to school the next day with his mother or father.

At the end of the school day, my teacher herself walked me home and told Mother about the incident. Mother was beside herself, but the teacher reassured her that the boy would be punished.

In the meantime, my mouth was swollen, I was missing a piece of my front tooth, which occasionally scratched my tongue, and I was in pain. I could not eat and could hardly drink. I didn't go to school the next three days, and that added to my misery because I loved school. On the fourth day, when I arrived in school, my classmates told me that the following morning, the boy came to school with his mother and she was told what her son had done.

We all lived in close proximity, and a neighbor of this boy told us that his father had given him a severe beating. Not necessarily because he hurt a classmate but because his mother had to appear in school and lose half a day's work. My classmates surrounded me and told me that my enemy threatened to teach me a lesson for what I had done to hm.

He was on his best behavior until the end of the school year. On the last day of school, he approached me and said, with hatred in his eyes, that I would pay for his embarrassment. I turned and walked away, but his threat registered in my memory. There was a constant fear in the back of my mind until a few months later, when the threat was fulfilled.

That summer, we had moved away from the house on Mendzynskaya to a two-room apartment on Stalina Street. I was going to a Polish school then and hadn't seen this boy or any of my former Russian classmates since the end of the previous school year.

I might have mentioned earlier that one of my chores was to visit some of our customers once or twice a week and collect payment for the meat we had delivered. Very few paid on the spot.

One summer day, my parents sent me to our old neighborhood to collect some debts.

We could ill afford to extend credit for more than a week or two. It was late afternoon, and there were few people in the street. I was walking along Menzynskaya Street, not far from where we used to live.

Menzynskaya Street was wider than most alleys in that neighborhood.

Suddenly, I heard a whistle behind me and then a dog barking. I turned around and saw that about one hundred yards away, that boy, my sworn enemy, was urging his dog to go after me. He was yelling, "Get the Jew! Kill the Jew!"

The dog was running toward me, barking loudly. It was a medium-sized dog with an off-white hide and black spots. I started to run away, but the dog was quicker than me. He caught my left leg just below the back of the knee and bit a chunk of flesh. I screamed, and suddenly, two women appeared and chased the dog away. Hearing my screams, a former neighbor came running too. He took me in and cleaned and bandaged my wound with a clean rag. The pain was excruciating, and I couldn't stop crying.

Another woman who was passing by heard me scream and came over to see what was happening. She recognized me, knew where I lived, and volunteered to take me home. I could hardly walk but was too big to be carried. The woman took me by the hand and walked me slowly home. I was limping and sniffling because my shin was hurting terribly.

Mother met us at the door. When she saw my contorted face and tearful red eyes, she scooped me up into her arms and questioned the woman about the reason for my sad state. The woman, who saw most of what happened, told my mother every detail she knew.

At that point, Mother started crying. She pulled me closer to her chest and began murmuring, "My poor child! My poor child! What is her sin? Why is she punished so? Where is God? Does He not hear our children cry? Does He not feel our children's pain?"

The woman exchanged a few more words with Mother and left as Mother thanked her.

Mother held me on her lap until I was completely calm, then she took out an aspirin from the cupboard and made me swallow it. She promised it would ease my pain.

When Father came home in the evening, she began yelling at him, "Why do you send her on such dangerous missions?" Though she knew well that sometimes there was no other way. He let her vent her frustrations and didn't say a word. That was not like Father, but he assessed the situation and decided that this was the best way to handle it. He knew that Mother was hurting inside, and so was he. Many times there was no other choice but to use us children as messengers. We, at our tender age, understood that we must participate in the bread-earning process.

The next morning, Mother took me to the clinic to have my wound checked. They redressed it with real bandages and gave us some ointment and clean bandages to use at home. I also got a tetanus or rabies shot—I really don't know which, but it hurt a lot. When they removed the bandage, only then did I see how deep the wound was. I limped for about a week.

To this day, I have a scar the size of a dime on my left shin.

Since I am on the subject of dogs, I might as well relate another encounter with a dog that also took place in Dzhambul. It could have been the same summer or the one following it. My chronology during those war years may not be precise, but the incidents are quite memorable.

Very often, people react to my fear of dogs in a negative way. They automatically think that I hate dogs.

No, I don't hate dogs. As a child, I had several dogs; as a matter of fact, when I was five or six, I had a dog and loved him. After I tell you about my second encounter with a dog, you will understand that my fear is justified.

I never went to psychotherapy to get rid of this fear, and I must say, I have come a long way since that incident. The fact that I no longer run from dogs at a mere bark as I did for many years is a sign of tremendous progress. Occasionally, I even allow some small dogs to come near me and smell me. Years ago, I would have shaken with fear.

The second incident, which also took place in Dzhambul, was also in the summer.

Father had sent me to deliver the skin of a cow to a Kazakh on Furmanova Street. This Kazakh, whose name I have long forgotten, owned a tannery or worked in one. He produced fine leather from all kinds of animal skins. He was an excellent craftsman and made the skins soft and supple. This was another enterprise my father was involved in as an extension of the meat business. The hide removed from a slaughtered cow or calf would be made into fine leather and usually sold to a shoemaker. One of these raw skins at times weighed twenty to thirty kilograms. They were very heavy when fresh, especially for someone my age. In the summer, the skins that were several days old had a foul odor.

I was about thirteen or fourteen years old at that time.

Furmanova Street was about six kilometers from our home. Carrying such a heavy load was hard enough, but I also had to make sure I was not caught by the KGB. And yes, I walked both ways. There were no buses or any other public transportation that went to those parts of town. I don't think there was public transportation in Dzhambul in those days. And even if there was, I would not have used it. One, it cost money, and two, it would have been too risky.

Don't forget, all this business was illegal; that was why, in many cases, children were used to do the dirty work.

Well, I finally arrived at my destination, with the heavy skin on my back, and knocked on the wooden gate. I knew these people had a very large dog, almost the size of a pony. Not only I but also everyone in the neighborhood, including the lady of the house, was afraid of this monster dog. The only one who could handle him was his owner. His bark was deep, loud, and scary.

That day, the proprietor was not home. I stood and waited behind the gate until his wife came and saw me through the small opening. She knew who I was, opened the gate, and asked me to come in. I mentioned the dog, and she assured me that he was tied to a tree with a chain at the far corner of the yard. Yet the dog did not stop barking and jerking at the chain. I was terrified. I wanted her to take the bundle from me, but she told me that she was pregnant and was not allowed to carry anything heavy. I reluctantly stepped into the yard with the load on my back and walked as fast as I could. My heart was beating like a hammer. The dog was jumping and barking furiously.

The lady went ahead to open the door for me. My eyes were on the dog, and I didn't see the concrete step of the open porch. I tripped and fell forward on my hands and knees. The bundle fell next to me. As I tried to rise despite the pain, I suddenly heard the dog's bark right above my head. He jumped on top of me and went straight for my head. He pulled the hair on the back of my head. I gave out a terrifying scream. The lady turned around and saw what was happening.

The woman also screamed as I felt the dog's teeth on the back of my head. He tore a clump of hair, including some skin. He would have probably eaten me for dinner if the woman had not intervened. She grabbed a broom and hit the dog. This made him even angrier, and he turned on her as she kept hitting him with the broom.

We were both saved by her brother-in-law, who lived next door. When he heard us scream, he jumped over the wall and grabbed the dog by the chain and pulled him away from us. It turned out that the only two people the dog feared and obeyed were the owner and his brother, who lived next door. The brother took the dog away to his own yard and tied him to a tree with a heavier chain. It is very rare that a dog can break a chain, but this one must have been strong enough to do it. The owner rarely left him home in the yard. As luck would have it, this was one of the rare occasions. The lady took me in, tended to my wounds, and gave me some tea with raisins.

Tea with raisins was the Kazakhs' national drink. It took a long time for me to calm down, but the back of my head was throbbing and I could not stop crying. I had no idea of the extent of my wound, as I couldn't see it. I only knew it was very painful. The woman didn't let me walk home alone after this ordeal. She made me wait until her husband came home. After she told him what had happened, he apologized and drove me home in his horse-drawn wagon. This was a rare treat for me; I did not have to walk back the six kilometers.

As we both entered our house, my mother was in shock when she saw us. My dress was torn in the front and soiled (she had not seen the bloodstains in the back yet), both my knees were bandaged, my eyes were still red and swollen from crying, and my hair was in a mess and bloody. She still did not see the back of my head, where the dog had helped himself to a piece of it. The bleeding on my head and on the other wounds had stopped.

I ran to my mother, seeking safety and consolation. She embraced me, and only then did she see the back of my head. She burst out crying and demanded to know what happened. The man tried his best to explain my encounter with his dog. He apologized for the dog's behavior and told Mother that his dog was trained to attack any stranger who might come to his house when he, the head of the household, was not there. He had trained the dog to protect his wife when she was home alone. There were thieves and bandits in town, and many people kept dogs for protection, and Muslim men were very protective of their women.

The man pointed to me and told Mother that I would be the one to tell what happened to me since I was the injured party and he was not home at that time. He even offered to pay for my dress. Mother was tempted to accept the money, but she knew that Father did business with him, so she just thanked him for tending to my injuries and bringing me home. After the Kazakh left, I recounted the whole episode.

Upon hearing the story, Mother hugged me and kissed me, and we both cried. She promised then and there that I would never go to those people again to deliver skins or anything else. But this was not to be, as I went there again and again but never stepped inside the yard or the house. The fear of the dogs remains with me to this day.

My brother and I were very good students; we had high marks in most subjects. As Comrade Stalin's faithful and loving children, we had to belong to the pioneer/*komsomol* movement, depending on age. Once you reached high school age, they called it komsomol, and the indoctrination was much more intense. We received our share of lectures on what a pioneer was and what our obligations were toward the fatherland and fellow citizens, especially our great leader and father, Stalin.

At least once a week, we would have a lesson in citizenship. They lectured us about our wonderful father Stalin, how he loved us and what wonderful things he was doing for all the Russian people and us.

It was considered a great honor to be a part of this movement, and as a sign of membership, we wore red bandanas around our necks. As naive children, we all got caught up in the propaganda and tried to do our best to fulfill our obligations. We were taught nationalistic songs and poems and used to get assignments to write stories and poems on the subject.

School Project: Stamp Collecting

Through our creative work, they could tell how dedicated we were to the cause. The teachers knew who was not native-born, and those were automatically under suspicion. The Soviet Union was already at war with Germany, and that added fuel to their insecurity and suspicions. As a matter of fact, everyone was a suspect, native or not.

Occasionally, a letter or a postcard from a relative abroad would find its way to a next of kin in the USSR. Even we had received one or two letters from our relatives in America during those four years in Dzhambul. Our relatives in the United States were somewhat familiar with the restrictions of the Soviet regime and were very careful with the text. Their letters were very plain and benign. They asked very few questions other than about family, health, and other non-incriminating subjects. They were very careful not to put our lives in jeopardy. Our letters to them were of similar content. We wrote many more letters to them, knowing they would be censored but hoping that some would get through.

One day, my teacher announced a new class project: stamp collecting. This was a very innocent and certainly interesting enterprise. None of the pupils thought of an ulterior motive. Apparently, the teacher received orders from the KGB to find out who was receiving mail from abroad. The KGB had complete authority over the post office and its activities, so they should have known who received what. Post office workers could have slipped some mail before it was censored. As I said, for money, anything was possible. The mail was only one of the vehicles that allowed the KGB to keep an eye on the population.

The teacher promised that whoever brought the most foreign and interesting stamps would receive a prize.

Sometimes a letter would be written in a language for which a translator could not be found. The KGB also mistrusted some translators. The condition of the stamp and letter was very important. We were all anxious to outdo one another. That day, I came home from school very excited. I knew we had received a letter from our relatives in America a few weeks earlier and was sure that Mother had saved it.

As I entered the house, I immediately asked my mother where that letter was. She wanted to know the reason for my inquiry. The letter was written in Yiddish, and I could not read it. I was happy to tell her about the school project. She told me to wait until Father came home and ask his permission since the letter was from his family. When Father came home, I excitedly told him the story again.

But Father's immediate answer was "Absolutely not."

My heart sank, and I hastened to explain again. I knew he had read the letter several times and had no need for the stamps. I accused him of depriving me of possibly winning a prize.

Father said to me, "Let me eat something. I'm very hungry. Then I'll explain everything."

I waited patiently until Father finished dinner. He called me over, put me on his knee, a very rare fatherly touch, and began explaining. First, he asked me all his questions. He wanted to make sure that his explanation would be correct.

After he heard me out, he said to me, "Listen, my child, we live in the Soviet Union now, under a Communist regime, which you are too young to understand. You probably still remember being in Siberia for no reason at all. Siberia is the equivalent of jail. As foreign citizens, we are not allowed to do many things. Even native Russians are not allowed to do many things. For the smallest infraction, I can be sent back to Siberia, and you and the rest of the family will remain here. You don't want that to happen, right?"

I listened very attentively because this did not make much sense.

"One of the things we are not allowed to do is communicate with people outside the USSR. We have to be very grateful to the authorities that they do let a letter through once in a while and that we have some information from our relatives and they from us. This is very important, because when the war will be over, with God's help, we'll return home one day, and we want to have contact with our family."

Father continued to explain the dangers of the word getting out to other sources that we were communicating with foreigners. "The authorities may one day change their minds and decide not to allow any letters through or, worse, accuse me of espionage."

About two weeks later, the girl who had brought in old German stamps (from before the war) came in crying.

She told us that her father had been arrested that night. The charge: espionage. He was eventually tried in Alma-Ata but was not convicted because they were a well-to-do family and were able to bribe the prosecutor, the judge, and the other involved officials.

The reason for letting him free was given as lack of evidence. This time, it was true.

The truth is that most of the time, they did not have real evidence in order to prosecute, but they were experts at fabricating it whenever necessary.

DZHAMBUL: TYPHOID EPIDEMIC

In the spring of 1943, a typhoid epidemic broke out. There was hardly a household that was not affected by this horrible disease. People were dying in the streets, at home, and in the hospital. There was only one hospital in town for so many thousands of inhabitants.

The population had increased manifold during the war, and no new facilities were added. Not enough doctors and certainly not enough medicines were available to treat the sick. Corpses were found in homes and in the streets, and many of the dead bodies were buried in mass graves. This type of typhoid was highly contagious, and people were afraid to touch the corpses for fear of being infected.

After several weeks of this dreadful situation, the sanitation department was forced to bury some of the corpses. They used masks and rubber gloves and, under police supervision, were forced to take the corpses to the outskirts of town, where a Jewish cemetery already existed, and, with the help of the chevrah Kadisha (ritual burial society), began the arduous task of burying the dead.

This catastrophe did not spare our family.

One day, a messenger came to our door, asking for my father. He brought the news that Father's whole family was sick and needed help. Father was not home at that time. Mother questioned the man—who he was, who sent him, etc. She gave him a glass of tea and sent him on his way, stating that she would relay the message to Father.

Mother was truly worried. She knew about the epidemic and was afraid it might strike us as well. She watched us like a hawk. She would not allow us to play with other children or go to their homes. She even considered keeping us out of school, which was just as dangerous, but Father objected to that idea. He claimed that if it had to strike, it would. It was all in God's hands. We should all pray the sickness would not reach us.

Father came home late that evening. Mother hastened to tell him the sad news, but it was too late at night and too dangerous to go see his family. He decided to go early in the morning and see how he could help them. Mother claimed that he would surely catch it from them and infect us all.

Mother's objections and reasoning, though justified, had no influence on his decision. He asked Mother to prepare any food she could spare and make some hot tea with lots of sugar. He took all this and set out at dawn to see how his family was faring.

It was at least one hour's walk to where they lived on the outskirts of the city. Before he left, Mother still argued that he had no right to endanger his own family, and if he died, who would provide for his children? Father's answer was "God will provide."

Father left with the food and did not return for several days. We thought the worst. He returned on the evening of the fifth day. He looked awful. Unshaven, his skinny frame looking even smaller, his eyes red from not sleeping.

Mother didn't allow him to enter the house. She heated some water and made him remove all his clothes and wash his body thoroughly with hot water and soap. She gave him fresh clean clothes to wear and wanted to burn the ones he had worn. She was sure that he had brought all the germs home in his clothes. Father convinced her that burning his clothes was not necessary. They should be washed in boiling water with disinfectant soap, which the government distributed free of charge. Mother boiled the clothes to make sure all the germs were destroyed. She made him hot tea and gave him some food. Father had not eaten in two days. Sitting at the table, he began relating the horrors of the family's situation. Of the thirteen people in the family, six were already in the hospital, receiving treatment. He had to get the others in. The hospital was overflowing with patients. The only time they accepted another patient was when one was more or less cured and sent home or died. More often, space became available when someone died. To get someone into the hospital, one had to pay an exorbitant price (in goods or cash) to a doctor in charge or the administrator, or both, and later, if the patient was accepted, to the nurses and so on. A patient did not get his prescribed medication or even a glass of water without bribery. People with no means had no chance.

Father told us that he sold some of his family's possession in order to put some money together for that purpose. It started with one uncle, and within a few days, one after the other was infected. High fever and red blotches all over the body were the symptoms. Some of them had terrible rashes and were itching all over.

Some had a stomach virus with stomach pains and vomiting. They were lying on cots or on the floor. It was a horrible scene.

Father made the decision that the sickest person would go to hospital first. Those were the older members of the family.

The younger cousins remained, but a few days later, Father managed to get them into the hospital too.

Eventually, all members of the family were hospitalized. As soon as everybody was out of the house, Father notified the sanitation department. They came the next day and disinfected the whole house and put a lock on the front door. This disinfectant spray was supposed to have killed all the bacteria within forty-eight hours. The odor of the disinfectant was atrocious.

We heard that wine was a good remedy for stomach typhoid. Father went to market, sold his shoes, bought a bottle of red wine, and took it to his relatives in the hospital. Every member was given a few drops at a time. This was how we wound up with only one pair of shoes between the three of us the following winter. We had no money to buy any additional shoes that winter. Summer was no problem—everybody walked barefoot.

The disinfectant had a foul odor, but there were no people in the house, and it had to be done. That night, Father came home to sleep and change clothes. Mother repeated the same ritual, cleansing my father and his clothes. She did not allow us to go near him, and she washed her hands with disinfectant soap every time she touched something of his.

The shock came when she saw his bare feet. Upon her questioning, he explained why he had to do it. About a week later, my aunt Chana Golda (she was called Cha Golda for short) and her husband, Uncle Hersh Yitzchak, the parents of Victor and Aaron, were released from the hospital. They were considered cured. They stopped at our house on the way home. Father did not know they were being released, so he hadn't prepared the house for their return. They both looked horrible, like walking corpses. They were famished and would have eaten everything in sight. First, Mother gave them tea. This was her remedy for everything. She also knew that their stomachs must have been empty for days and they had to be very careful with food intake.

The first thing Uncle wanted to do was pray, which he had not done properly for weeks. Mother handed him Father's phylacteries and prayer shawl, and he proceeded to pray. He knew all the prayers by heart, and as he stood there facing Jerusalem, tears came rolling down his cheeks. His face was covered with hair, the beard slightly graying. It was a sad sight to behold.

My aunt sipped her tea at the table, while Mother prepared farina cooked in water for them. Farina was the food my baby sister ate, but Mother knew these two sick people could safely eat farina.

My uncle finished praying and quickly sat down at the table to eat. He would have swallowed the whole bowl of farina in one gulp, but Mother warned him not to hurry as his stomach was empty and sore. He asked for more food, but Mother warned them again about the dangers.

She promised to give them some bread to take home. Mother wanted them to leave as soon as possible, fearing they might infect us.

After they finished eating, she washed the dishes and glasses thoroughly. When Father came home and saw the two of them, he began questioning their health condition. He was not so sure they were well enough to resume a normal life after all they had gone through. They were probably released too soon, but there was no choice. The hospital released patients as soon as there was some improvement in their condition. The beds were needed for the gravely ill. There were times when patients slept in corridors, on the floor, and wherever there was a vacant spot.

Father told his sister that he had the house disinfected and that it was still locked. It had to be aired out and cleaned, and he needed to get some food for them. They were too weak to do anything. It was decided that they would spend the night with us and, in the morning, go home with Father so he could take care of them. There was an objection to their staying from our rooming partners. Everybody feared the disease. It was decided that my aunt and uncle would spend the night in the adjacent hallway, on a pile of straw.

The following morning, my father hired a horse and wagon and took them to the other end of town, where they lived. The house was locked. Father opened the door, and a sick odor overwhelmed them. They reluctantly walked in and opened all the windows to let some fresh air in and get rid of the stench. As they entered, they saw that they had been robbed while they were in the hospital. It looked like a haunted house. My aunt was very weak, but she did her best to bring some order to the disarray within. I don't know what was stolen; there was not much to steal, but this was a time when everything had value. Father brought in some wood and made a fire. The least they could have was hot water. He took the wagon back to town to buy some provisions for them—bread, potatoes, and anything else he could find and afford.

The following day, we received the sad news that another of my uncles died in the hospital. It was Uncle Yitzhak, Aunt Reizl's husband. Unfortunately, there would be more casualties.

Our relatives lived on the outskirts of town, across a narrow brook. Most of the family was still sick in the hospital and could not attend the funeral. Ten males were needed for the service, but that was no big problem at the cemetery. There were funerals all day long, and the men went from one to another. As days and weeks passed, other members of the family began returning home from the hospital. They were all weak, emaciated, undernourished, and unable to do any kind of work.

I forgot to mention that my relatives owned a cow and a horse. Father fed and milked the cow. He brought the milk home, Mother boiled it, and he would take it to the hospital for them. Mother also made butter and cheese when the cow was generous with production.

After several weeks, those who survived were slowly nursed back to health. Unfortunately, not all survived.

My aunt Cha Golda and her husband, Hersh Yitzhak, got a relapse of the same illness and died a short while after their release from the hospital. My cousins Victor and Aaron became orphans, as did Tzipora, Rachel, Israel (Unek), and Esther. All lost their fathers within a short period.

It was rumored that they were released too early from the hospital and had not completely recovered. The family remained together, being even more dependent on one another. Uncle Leibish, the eldest male, became the head of the family. After those who survived returned home, Father did everything he could to nurse them back to health. The survivors had to think about their future. They leased a parcel of land and applied the agricultural skills they brought from home and began tilling the soil and planting vegetables.

When the three young cousins, Israel, Aaron, and Victor, recovered from the terrible disease, they began looking for jobs. Victor and Aaron got lucky and got the bread distributorship in a certain district of Dzhambul. This was considered the best job in town. They had plenty of bread to eat and devised a way to do some business on the side. They were given a horse and a boxlike covered wagon and delivered bread from the bakery to distribution centers in their designated area.

Bread was rationed via food stamps. Food stamps were distributed once a month according to the number of people in the family. Each person received one kilo of bread per day, which wasn't very much, because the bread was very heavy. The bakers would steal some of the flour and substitute it with sand. It certainly used to grit in the teeth.

At first, Israel found a job in agriculture in a nearby collective farm. After a while, they found and rented a house closer to the city. The house was surrounded by a parcel of land that also included a small barn. The new dwelling had several rooms, so each family could finally have some privacy. They eventually bought another cow and some chickens and grew their own vegetables in the garden.

Life for them had improved considerably.

Life in Dzhambul

But life has many twists and turns, and after a couple of years, their lives were suddenly turned upside down again. Someone reported to the authorities that they were doing business, namely selling bread on the black market. This was a crime punishable by many years in prison. All three young men, Victor, Aaron, and Israel, were arrested. The police came in the middle of the night and took all three to the police station for interrogation. Though Unek was not in the bread business, the reason the KGB arrested him for was collaboration.

He had befriended a young lady who worked in a printing shop where they printed food (bread) stamps. This young woman somehow succeeded to print extra sheets of food stamps and sold them to my cousins.

There may be another version of this story that goes like this: my cousins would give her the paper, and all she did was print on it.

There was also a rumor that one of my cousins was romantically involved with this young woman. Naturally, this whole enterprise was illegal, and my cousins would have probably rottedn in jail for many years, but this young woman saved their lives. Luckily, the search of the house did not produce anything incriminating. The Soviet police, or KGB, did not need any concrete evidence in order to accuse someone of wrongdoing or put them in jail.

The authorities were specialists in fabricating and producing evidence at will. There was a long drawn-out trial with lots of publicity. The state-controlled newspapers made sure that there would be mention of the trial every day on the front page. The authorities wanted the population to see how they caught and prosecuted speculators. The public was invited to witness the trial, which was a rarity.

Everything the authorities did had a specific reason.

What saved my cousins' hide was the young woman, who denied knowing them or having any dealings with them. The prosecutor threatened and told her categorically that if she did not reveal her collaborators, she and her whole family would be jailed and sent to Siberia. She was truly brave and denied any knowledge or wrongdoing from beginning to end.

The judge might have been bribed, too—he probably was. How else would four speculators go free after such grave accusations?

Had my cousins been convicted and jailed, the rest of the family would have been without any means of support. There was no way one person could support twelve to fourteen people.

It must have been late October or November. It was a cold, rainy, windy night. The time might have been 2:00 or 3:00 a.m. We were all asleep. Suddenly, Mother heard a loud knock on the entrance door. The room was cold and dark, and she wondered what the knock was about. It was known in Dzhambul that thieves, murderers, and other criminals did their best work at night under the cover of darkness. Since this was a stormy night, it must have been appropriate for all kinds of crimes.

Mother listened attentively for footsteps or any other signs of prowlers around the house. A few minutes later, the same knock repeated itself, but this time much louder. The wind was howling, and the rain was knocking on the windowpane. Mother decided to wake up my father and send him out into the hallway to investigate. Though my father was a brave man, thieves or murderers trying to get in were too much for him to handle alone. He grabbed his pants and put them on, but the room was like an icebox, so he also put his sweater on. In the meantime, another double knock was heard from the same direction. Father quickly woke up our neighbor Solomon and told him that someone was knocking on the front door, trying to get in. By that time, due to the whispers and commotion, his wife had woken up, and slowly but surely, the rest of the household was awake too.

We sat in our beds under the covers, listening to the wind and rain and anticipating the next knock on the door. Sure enough, a few minutes later, there it was, loud and clear. This time, they came one after the other, even louder than before. When this happened, we quickly hid under the covers, shivering with cold and fear. Mother took little Leah out of her crib, held her close to her bosom, and went back to bed. Mother grabbed a prayer book and began praying.

My father and Solomon armed themselves with a stick, a cleaver, a long sharp knife, and a lantern. The two big heroes went out into the hallway to investigate the noise. Though it was a dark night due to the stormy weather, they could discern the small window high up, with rain rivulets streaming down the pane. Now their attention was on the door, the direction of the knocking. It was a thick wooden door, with several different locks and latches securing it safely.

All were intact. Every time a gust of wind descended, another knock on the door was heard, sometimes twice in a row in quick succession.

The neighbor's grandmother started screaming when she heard the knock, and we all followed her example.

Mother, trying to divert our attention, told us to pray. Since we knew most of our daily prayers by heart, we stayed under the covers and recited them. We hoped the thick quilts would protect us from the robbers or killers who were so desperately trying to get in and do us harm.

This ordeal lasted about an hour or two.

The wind slowly subsided, and the knocks were less frequent and not as loud. The rain fell steadily until morning. When the knocking stopped completely, the men abandoned their posts and returned to the room and into bed. They were both freezing and welcomed the warmth of the bed.

Nobody slept anymore that night.

As dawn broke and the gloom of night dissipated, the men were anxious to find out what damage had been done to the door. Both of them dressed warmly, unlatched the door, and with great trepidation, opened it, afraid to find someone behind it. The rain had subsided. The men theorized that whoever wanted so desperately to get in must have realized that the door was strong, securely locked, and impenetrable. As they looked at the other side of the door, all they found were two loose pieces of wood that had become partially detached from the door and were knocking whenever the wind moved them to and fro.

That was how we found the culprits of our fearful, sleepless night.

Mother's Fur Cape

While I am on the subject of thieves, let me relay an incident of a real theft.

As I mentioned, Mother liked beautiful clothes, and she had them until the war broke out. She had a beautiful black lamb fur cape that she wore on special occasions. I have a photo of Mother wearing it. It actually looked more like a very large collar that could adorn a suit or coat. I know that Father had bought it for her as a birthday or anniversary gift. When we left home, Mother took this valuable item with her despite my father's objections. She treasured it. Whenever she looked at it or wore it, which was very rare during the war, it reminded her of home and the times she used to dress up for special occasions.

She had no use for it in the USSR, but it was like an insurance policy. Over the years, we had sold most of the valuables Mother had taken along. She wanted to keep this cape as long as she could and only part with it as a last resort. We had no closets in the house on Menzhynskaya Street, so whatever clothes we had and didn't wear at that time were hanging on a nail on the wall. The fur was also hanging on the wall above our bed, covered with a sheet. In the days before air-conditioning, one slept with open windows to keep cool at night. One such hot summer night—and Dzhambul had plenty of those—we slept with open windows.

When Mother woke up in the morning, she felt a shiver go though her body. She felt something was wrong. As she was getting dressed, she noticed something missing from the wall. Her heart skipped a beat. She knew right away what was missing because the fur was the only item covered with a sheet. The cape was not on the wall. At first, she thought maybe Father took it and sold it without telling her. He knew she would not want to part with her beloved cape. She woke him, questioning him about the fur. Father gave her an angry look, told her she was crazy, and turned around to go back to sleep. Mother was beside herself. She wasn't whispering anymore and started crying aloud, looking all over for her precious fur. By this time, everybody woke up and looked for the fur cape.

We all thought it had fallen down and might be under the bed or somewhere on the floor. It didn't take long to figure out that the fur was stolen. Someone must have known about it and found a way.

The only way we figured it could have been done was through the open window with a long stick. Nobody could have climbed in through the window because our bed was standing under it and the thief would have had to step over us. We also had other theories, but no proof. The theory of the thief with the long stick was the most plausible. Mother was upset for months. She held on to it as a last resort in case we had to sell it and buy food or medicine. She never forgot this fur cape, and nor did we.

My Sister Leah's Evil Eye

One spring day, when Leah was about six months old, Mother gave her a bath and put her to sleep in her crib. One of Father's relatives came to visit on some business. It was early evening, and Father was home. The man, who always wore a black coat, also had a black beard and earlocks to match and piercing black eyes. When he looked at you, you had the feeling that he was looking through you.

He walked over to the crib, where my sister, who really looked like a little rosy-cheeked doll, slept soundly. He said to my father words I never forgot. "Heshl, how does such a beautiful child come to be yours?"

Father's answer was "Oh, she resembles her mother, not me."

The man answered, "Now I understand."

He walked away from the crib and sat down at the table. Mother gave him a glass of tea and asked Father if he wanted one too. Father never refused a glass of tea. The two men drank their tea at one end of the table, and I did my homework at the other end. They were discussing a business opportunity. About twenty minutes later, the cousin was gone. As soon as he closed the door behind him, my little sister woke up crying. She sounded like she was in pain. Only a few minutes earlier, she was sound asleep. Mother picked her up and tried to calm her. She screamed louder and kicked with her little feet. Mother gave her sugar water, which she always loved, but this time, she spit it out and continued screaming at the top of her lungs. Mother tried all kinds of things to calm her down, but nothing worked.

After a while, Mother declared, "This can only be an evil eye." She wanted my father to run after his man and bring him back to the house and remove the evil eye. Father dismissed her accusation as nonsense and naturally refused. How could he accuse anybody of such a thing? Suddenly, Leah turned blue and stopped breathing. Mother screamed and ran outside with her. Maybe some fresh air would bring her breath back. Mother blew air into the baby's mouth. The house was in an uproar. No one knew what to do. As a gust of cool air hit the baby's face, she began breathing again, and the crying resumed. Moments later, Mother came back in, asked to open the window, and handed me the baby as she proceeded to remove the evil eye from Leah. She took a glass, put three pieces of bread into it, three teaspoons of salt, three teaspoons of sugar, and three hot coals from the stove. Into this mixture she poured cold water. As the coals heated the water and it boiled over, mother immersed her finger in it and dabbed three dabs on Leah's forehead, three on her tongue, three on the palms of her tiny hands, and three on the soles of her feet, while the whole household looked on.

Slowly the baby began to calm down. After a while, Leah drank the sugar water and smiled faintly. Seeing the baby calm and smiling, Mother calmed down too and put her back into the crib. She then placed the glass with the "anti-evil eye" concoction under it. It took a while for the rest of us to calm down.

This was my first encounter with the evil-eye phenomenon, but not the last. Mother insisted that this man never enter our household again. Naturally, an argument ensued, but Father agreed and promised that when this man would come again, all business would be conducted outdoors.

That was how it was from then on.

Doing Business in Dzanbul

As I mentioned, Father was forced to take our boarder, Solomon, as a partner. If he refused, Solomon threatened he would go to the authorities and report us. This was pure blackmail, but Father had no choice. These were the kind of people we lived with. I think that war affects people in many negative ways.

Whenever I was sent on a "business" errand, one of their daughters was included. The younger one, Helen, and I were approximately the same age and in the same class in school, but she did very little to help the business. On the other hand, her older sister, Deborah, was more cooperative.

One day, Deborah and I were sent to bring home a finished cow's skin from the tannery located near the Muchnoy Bazaar.

We had a neighbor, a young couple, with a three-year-old boy. They had fled Latvia when the Germans conquered their country. One day, my father met Grisha outside, standing and smoking a cigarette. Father walked over and asked him for a match to light his own cigarette. During a short conversation, Father found out that Grisha was chief officer and manager of the tannery. He also found out that Grisha was a member of the Communist Party and that was how he landed this lucrative job. He complained about his salary. This was no news to my father as very few people could boast of a high one. That was why most took bribes in order to supplement their incomes. Father understood the hint.

Over the next few weeks, both men met several times and began talking business. Grisha warned Father that if either of them got caught doing something illegal, he would for sure get ten years in a

Siberia labor camp. Father assured him that he knew exactly what he meant. Father knew where and what Siberia was.

He offered to buy leather from Grisha because he knew whom he could sell it to.

This was an added plus because the merchandise would be delivered directly to a third party and we would avoid storing incriminating merchandise in our home.

To take it out of the factory without anybody noticing was not an easy task. Eventually, we would also deliver raw skins to be processed in the tannery owned by a Kazakh.

One hot summer afternoon, Deborah and I were sent to fetch a ready, processed skin from the tannery. We were to hide behind some bushes on top of the hill directly across the factory. Someone would bring the skin out and deposit it on top of the hill, and we would pick it up and bring it home or deliver it to a customer.

Deborah and I arrived at the appointed hour at the designated spot. We found some low-growing bushes at the edge of the steep hill and sat down on the ground and waited. The soil was sandy and hot, with very little grass growing on it. The few bushes were sparse and did not protect us very well. We lay down on the ground, each of us behind a bush, and waited.

The hill was an abandoned property where nobody walked. There were some heaps of discarded articles, mostly trash. The wind blew in our direction, and every so often, the horrible, acrid smell of the tannery invaded our nostrils. We lay there on the dusty ground, the sun beating down on us. We were sweating profusely, with no sign of a drop of water anywhere. From our hiding place, we could see the factory below across the street.

After about thirty minutes, which seemed like an eternity, a young man carrying a bundle on his back went through the gate, crossed the street, and walked in our direction. We lay low in anticipation. The young man looked to the left and to the right. It was the hottest time of day, and no one ventured out into the street. He came directly toward us. We had no idea who the young man was, but we knew he was carrying the merchandise we had come for. It took him a few moments to cross the street, then he began to climb the hill. It was not easy, especially with a load on his back and loose rocks and sand falling downward from under his bare feet. He finally made it. He came up panting, his face covered with perspiration. Upon seeing us, he dropped the bundle and, without a word, ran down the hill and back to the factory.

Before we made a move, still in a lying position, we looked around to make sure we were safe from incriminating eyes, our hearts beating with fear.

Hot, thirsty, and covered with dust and beads of perspiration, we slowly got up to fulfill the balance of our mission.

Deborah was the first to pick up the bundle. It must have weighed fifteen to twenty kilograms. We quickly crossed the flat expanse of the hill and began descending the opposite slope. We took turns carrying the load all the way home, which was about three kilometers away.

As we walked in, the first thing we did was hide the incriminating object under some straw in the hallway, then we ran into the house and filled our bellies with water.

When Mother saw me red-faced, covered with perspiration, she murmured under her breath, "How can a father use his own child as a slave?" She made me throw off my clothes drenched with sweat and wash up in cool water, which felt wonderful. When I was dry, she ordered me to lie down and rest. I fell asleep instantly.

When I woke up, my dress was washed and hung out to dry so I could wear it to school the next day.

I owned only this one dress, which I wore to school, on Shabbat, on holidays, on errands, and on other special occasions. The rest of the time, I wore hand-me-down rags.

A few months later, Mother made me another dress. She put it together from the back and other parts of her own dress that was frayed and stained in the front and many other parts.

Now the "new" dress became the one I wore to school, on holidays, and on other special occasions. I was rich now—I owned two dresses. The fabric was a thin pale-blue cotton with tiny green and yellow flowers. Mother sewed it all by hand. I was thrilled. I wore it for two to three years until I grew out of it.

Eventually, Mother bought a piece of fabric and sewed another dress for herself.

Leather was not the only type of business my father was involved in. For a while, my father was also a butcher. He had met a kinsman from Rozwadów, Poland, who was a butcher before the war. The fact that there were many observant Jews in Dzhambul who ate kosher food gave them the idea to form a kosher meat business.

It took some time to work out the logistics, find a reliable and trustworthy *shohet* (ritual slaughterer), and borrow some money, and a few weeks later, they were in the butcher business.

Our squatter, Solomon, had to be included in the partnership for security reasons.

Father found a trustworthy shohet who agreed to do his job whenever he was needed.

In the meantime, both my parents paid visits to relatives and acquaintances to tell them about our new business and take orders.

Many could not afford to buy meat during the week, but they tried hard to have some for the Sabbath.

Thus, my father became a butcher, a business that lasted a couple of years. They began with a calf once a week. When the clientele increased, they graduated to a cow and an occasional sheep. Sheep were in abundance in the Muslim republics. Lamb was the mainstay of their diet.

Our life improved considerably.

Whatever could not be sold that or the next day was either consumed by the families or given to relatives or people in need. Lack of refrigeration in a hot climate made this part of the business a necessity, and it gave us a good feeling.

My parents always taught us benevolence and sharing. They were good examples.

Our place was most suitable for the slaughtering because we had the large, empty hallway at the entrance to the apartment, so it became the "scene of the crime." That was where the animal was killed, dismembered, cut up, and disposed of as fast as humanly possible.

The major part of the procedure took place at night. The two small windows in the hallway were covered up so no light could be visible on the outside. The animal was brought under the cover of darkness and given food so it had no reason to *moo*.

Timing was of the utmost importance.

The shohet would arrive in the evening, examine the cow or calf, and make sure it had no imperfections of any kind. Kashruth does not allow for any. He was a short, stocky man with a black beard. Dressed in black with a brim hat to match. His garb was a sign of his religious affiliation.

The floor in the hallway would be covered with a thick layer of straw to catch the excrement and any blood of the animal. Though most of the blood would be caught in a pail, there was always a chance that some might spill on the floor.

All three men worked diligently to subdue the animal and turn it on its side on the floor in order to enable the shohet to do his job as swiftly as possible.

One evening, one of the partners was sick and was unable to come to assist.

I was always curious about everything, so occasionally, I peeked to see what was going on in that hallway, where I was not allowed to enter during the clandestine procedure.

That evening, all bets were off. Things had to be done no matter who did them.

Mother and Baila were called to assist, and I sneaked in behind them. They were all too busy to pay attention to me. Mother, the animal lover, always stayed away; she had no desire to watch the procedure.

This time, she had no choice.

She was told to push the pail with water right under the cow's head. While the cow was busy drinking, the men swiftly tied her feet with rope. They sat her down on her behind, and that apparently made it easier to make her lie down on her side. She did present quite a bit of resistance, but they managed to hold her down long enough for the shohet to swiftly cut her throat. She kicked several times and then was still.

Sol put the pail under her throat to catch the blood. Mother almost fainted; she could hardly make it back to the room. Beila and I were ordered to leave too. Our services were not needed anymore.

The animal had to cool down before it could be skinned and dismembered. While this was taking place, the two men were busy disposing of the blood and other incriminating evidence.

Mother and I were in total shock during the proceedings and just followed orders. We had never witnessed anything like this before.

At dawn, the third partner, the professional butcher, arrived and dismembered the cow.

The meat was cut and weighed according to orders, and the women were on their way, delivering them.

If a calf was bought, the same or similar procedure was followed. This took place as often as necessary, depending on the orders received. Usually once a week.

In the afternoon, it was my and Deborah's job to collect payment from our customers.

Our Melamed

Hebrew Teacher

One very bright, humid summer afternoon, after a short rainfall, Father arrived with a young stranger.

At that time, we still lived at 38 Menzynskaya Street. The young man was about eighteen or twenty years old. He was slim, of medium height, and had curly blond hair and smiling blue eyes. It was late afternoon, but the sun was still quite warm. Father introduced him as our melamed.

It was common in those days for a young Yeshiva student to tutor young children in the Holy Scriptures, in prayers, preparing young boys for their bar mitzvah.

My brother was about twelve years old at that time, and it was time for him to begin preparing for his bar mitzvah at thirteen. This is the age when a boy supposedly becomes a "man" and assumes all the religious obligations as an adult. Father found this young man in the marketplace. The youth was looking for work, and there was none to be found. After questioning him about his background, Father realized he was a learned Yeshiva boy from a fine home. This young man was also caught in the same predicament of joblessness, as were thousands of other inhabitants in Dzhambul.

He was introduced to us as Shmeel Zeinvel Baunvolshpiner, a long and somewhat unusual name. He asked to be called by his first name only, Shmeel. He told us that both his parents had died during the typhoid epidemic. He had a younger brother, and they both lived with relatives. Since the parents died, the boys had no income and couldn't pay the rent; they were evicted from their one-room apartment. Their relative had pity on them and took them in.

His clothing left a lot to be desired. They were simply rags. His pants had holes all over them, and his light skin could be seen through them. There was a small hole in his pants in the rear, and we chuckled when his leg was visible.

With Mother, food came first. She asked him to wash up. The truth was that he needed a good scrubbing. Mother asked him politely if he had soap at home. He said no. Mother found a partially used bar of soap, wrapped it in newspaper, and gave it to him.

Dinner was ready, and we all sat down at the table. He must have been famished, for he devoured the soup almost in one gulp. One could plainly see that the young man had not eaten in days. Mother had tears in her eyes. While we were eating, Father introduced my brother and me as his new pupils.

Father said to him, "I have no money to pay you, but if you agree to come two or three times a week to teach my children, your payment will be a meal. Whatever we eat, you eat." Father also promised to ask other parents if they wanted a tutor for their children. Shmeel agreed on the spot. It was an offer he couldn't refuse.

After dinner, Mother cleared the table and he sat down to test us, to see what we already knew. Though my brother and I had gone to a cheder before the war, we didn't remember much.

Occasionally, Father would tutor Israel because he was a boy, but I had no instruction since the summer of 1939.

We had our own prayer books, though raveled and torn in places, and the Five Books of Moses. These books went wherever we went. To Father they were more important than clothes or pots and pans. In order of priority, first came the books, then came the down quilts, and then came the rest of our possessions.

The first lesson was short, but he promised that the next one would be longer. He would bring his own books too. Before he left, Mother took him aside and asked him to take off his shirt. She would lend him Father's shirt until he came next time and would wash and mend his for him. He looked at her in disbelief as she handed him Father's shirt. He went out to change and brought back his dirty, torn shirt. Father's shirt fit him quite well. He wore it outside to cover some of the holes in his pants. As he bade us good-bye, he ran out singing, jumping into the little puddles left by the rain. We watched him and laughed. We were not used to seeing a young man as a melamed. We knew that a melamed was an older man with a beard, but this one was young, vivacious, and at times made us laugh. We liked him instantly.

We began regular instructions twice a week. I was taught prayers and Chumash (the Five Books of Moses). For a girl, this was sufficient; boys had to know much more.

My brother studied the Talmud, and he was being prepared for his bar mitzvah, which took place in the fall of 1945, on his thirteenth birthday. He had to know the weekly portion of the Torah reading and the Haftarah (a chapter of the writings of the prophets). Those chapters were usually memorized. Naturally, this depended on the ability and knowledge of the pupil.

Because my father had a considerable amount of knowledge in the field, he helped my brother Israel whenever possible.

Two days after our melamed's initial visit, Mother handed him his old shirt, all patched up, mended, and washed. He accepted it with tears in his eyes, stating that nobody had ever done such a noble deed for him and, if his religious upbringing would allow, he would have hugged and kissed my mother for her kindness. Mother asked him if he had any other clothes that needed washing or mending—she would gladly do it for him.

Next time he came to teach, he arrived in a short version of his pants and carried the long ones under his arm. He told Mother that he was wearing his brother's pants so that he could bring his own for mending. He didn't own another pair. Mother immediately sat down to the task. She found some rags and cut them to the appropriate size, and by the time we finished our lessons, Shmeel had his pants with no holes in them. Shmeel was ecstatic.

After a while, someone donated a pair of pants for our teacher, which Mother tailored to fit his slim frame. Eventually, his pants got washed too. We liked our melamed and eagerly awaited his arrival on designated days.

After several weeks, our neighbors (the Shaffers) decided that their girls could also benefit from some Hebrew instruction. They decided to engage Shmeel once a week. So we saw him three days a week and he was assured three meals.

My time after school hours became quite occupied. Twice a week I had Hebrew instruction, and other days I had to help out with my little sister. I also had to run errands for my father or go to the market for my mother and so on. I was free after school Fridays and, of course, on Saturdays, which was our day of rest, and Sundays.

We were happy to learn what he taught us. My brother was very smart and made great progress. In a few months, he was ready for his bar mitzvah and continued to study Gemarah, more advanced writings and commentaries on the law. Shmeel was also satisfied with us because we were good pupils and didn't give him any trouble. After a while, word spread that there was a good young teacher in town, and Shmeel was very much in demand.

He had many pupils and began charging a fee for his services. He was grateful to my parents for the initial start, and all he wanted from us was a good, home-cooked meal. He didn't want any money from us.

This relationship lasted until my brother's bar mitzvah.

We had also switched from the Russian to the Polish school that was organized and supported by the Russian government and the Polish Committee. The Polish Committee was organized by the Polish refugees and dealt with problems and concerns of the Polish community in Dzhambul and the surrounding area.

It must have been 1944 or 1945 when we began attending the Polish school and switched back to our original native language, which we had almost forgotten.

That was the school I attended until the war ended and we left Dzanbul.

Another Episode with the Meat Business

This time, it was on a cold winter night. Mother made sure I wore every stitch of clothing I owned to keep me warm. We left my little sister, Leah, in my brother's care—both were fast asleep.

The combination of the deep snow and cutting wind, the heavy clothes clinging to my body, plus the heavy sack on my back took their toll on my physical endurance. Emotionally, I was fine. I knew I had to help my parents with this endeavor. Whatever they did was for the benefit of the whole family, and I had to do my share.

I didn't know any better. Most kids were included in the daily activities of survival.

I was dressed to my eyeballs. Mother claimed that if I didn't wear all of it, I would catch cold and get sick again and lose school days. This was one thing I desperately wanted to avoid.

We looked like mother bear and baby bear as we walked out into the night. There was not a single soul outdoors as far as we could see. It was too early for the streets to be cleaned or for people to go to work.

The snow had been falling since the afternoon, and the accumulation was considerable. The wind was howling, and the frost was biting. Soon I was covered with perspiration and had difficulty breathing, pulling my feet out of the deep snow with every step I took. I wanted to peel off one or two pieces of clothing, but Mother wouldn't let me. She urged me on. We had to complete our assignment before daybreak. The snow was fresh, fluffy, and glistened in the moonlight. Nature supplied the beauty of the moment.

The streets stayed covered with snow unless the town officials sent out a contingent of men to clear some of them and the area in front of government buildings. The snow was usually cleaned around the KGB building, the police station, the bread factory, and some other important buildings, like schools, hospitals, and major thoroughfares. The others had to fend for themselves.

We arrived at our destination at 3:00 a.m. Father gave us his disapproving look for being late and showed us where the orders were ready and waiting for us. There were small bundles wrapped in white rags. Each had a piece of paper attached to it with a first name, the weight, and the price. We were supposed to know the addresses by heart, which we did.

The notes were written in Yiddish, which at that time I couldn't read too well. As I examined my orders, Mother came over and helped me with the language. She picked the customers who lived closest so I could finish my assignment in time for school. I also realized that none of the partner's children were there to help with the deliveries, and I asked why. I was told that on that morning, most of the customers were ours and knew us.

The room was warm, and I began shedding some of my clothes, but by the time we were ready to leave, Mother made sure that I had put back on every stitch I had taken off. As we were ready to leave, I picked up the sack, which must have weighed twenty kilograms, but I knew that with every delivery, it would get lighter.

We started out very cautiously, making sure no one saw us. As I arrived at each address, I tapped lightly on the window to wake them up. Someone would usually come to the window and ask who was there. As I identified myself, they would open a crack and I would push the bundle through. If they told me to wait, I knew I would get paid on the spot. If they closed the window, I knew the mission was accomplished for now and proceeded to the next client.

By the time I finished my deliveries, I was covered with perspiration and my clothes were wet and stuck to every part of my body. I knew I could not remove any of it (Mother's orders) to cool off. By 6:00 a.m., I finished my deliveries and headed back home. My brother and my baby sister were still sleeping when I walked in. The first thing I did was peel off my clothes. As the cool air of the room touched my body, it felt so refreshing. I crawled back into bed and fell asleep instantly.

At 7:00 a.m., the alarm went off and my brother and I got up. The first thing I did was wash my face. The cold water felt good against my still-hot face. I felt refreshed and ready to face a new day. Soon, Mother also returned home, exhausted and dripping with perspiration. She removed her coat and proceeded to make us breakfast. She made each of us a sandwich for lunch, and at 7:30 a.m., we walked out into the freezing air, bundled up to our teeth, and were on our way to school.

Again, we made more furrows in the crisp white snow, and we saw that many had done so before us.

It was about half an hour's walk to school.

As usual, we met other kids on the way and walked together. At times, we also threw snowballs at one another for fun. It was fun to walk together, but we also did it for protection.

There were times when Jewish kids were attacked and beaten by Christian boys, but when we walked in groups, they didn't always dare. They would approach Jewish kids, grab one or two by the collar, and order them to say "Kurochka" in Russian, meaning "small hen." They had the notion that Jews couldn't pronounce the letter *R* with tongue in the front as the Russians did. They were under the impression that Jews could only pronounce a guttural *R*, the way the French do. That was how they tried to identify who was a Jew. I was among the lucky ones and could pronounce any kind of *R* and, at times, was spared a beating. Some kids got a bloody nose just because they could not pronounce the letter *R* the way the Russians did.

The Kazakh boys were much more tolerant. Probably because they were also a minority. They were of a different culture and were possibly taught by their parents to be tolerant of others. All this took place in Communist Russia, where religion was forbidden and the main ideology of Communism was equality. Despite the Communist doctrines of equality being drummed into every kid, anti-Semitism and other forms of racism were rampant.

This hatred was deeply rooted and handed down from generation to generation.

The KGB

One hot summer day, as many times before, I was sent to the Kazakh on Furmanova Street to deliver a hide of a calf. As usual, it was after school. The sun was still high and hot. A calfskin was not as heavy as a cow's, but a raw skin was heavy enough for a thirteen-year-old. It was wrapped in two sacks so it wouldn't leak. That day, I made a daring decision. Because of the oppressive heat, I decided to take the shorter route: through the center of town, right under the noses of the KGB. The other and more important reason for taking that route was to avoid being pelted with rocks by neighborhood kids. Several times in the past, when I had walked through the other neighborhood, they threw stones at me and yelled "Zhydovka!" Jew. The word *Jew* did not bother me—I knew I was one—but the stones often found their mark and I would return home bruised and bleeding. I sometimes washed my wounds in a stream so Mother wouldn't see them. She used to get very upset and fight with Father for sending me on those dangerous missions. Father would answer her, "Then you yourself go and risk getting arrested!"

In case I was caught, I had two or three alibis memorized (none of them implicating my family).

I remember it was a Monday, when the KGB was not very active after Sunday drinking. Their offices were about three hundred feet past the Muchnoy, the flour bazaar, right on the main street, and if one stood on the hill of the bazaar, one could see their comings and goings. It was common knowledge that on Mondays, many of them had a hangover after Sunday's day off.

So Mondays made it the less dangerous day to carry out some illegal business.

I was still aching from the previous week's stoning incident and decided to take the alternate route, namely the street where the KGB offices were located.

That street began right at the bottom of the bazaar. This bazaar was situated on a hill in the center of town, and from there one could see the area in all four directions pretty far out. For the most part, Dzhambul was pretty flat and the houses were primarily one story.

People from the surrounding villages as well as locals would bring their wares for sale: cattle, foul, flour, beans, an occasional rug, and other dry goods. There was another bazaar called the green bazaar, where farmers would offer fruits and vegetables, milk, cheese, and the like.

The third one, situated near the railroad station, was where one could buy coal, firewood, scrap metal, some building materials, an occasional tool.

According to the law, all these businesses were illegal, but the police and other officials were bribed and knew how to close one eye.

I walked along the main road, sweat pouring from my brow. As I passed the bazaar, I raised my eyes to look ahead and saw three KGB men in uniform standing in front of their office building and talking. I was still about 150 feet from where they stood. It looked to me that they were talking and laughing. I had to think of a quick plan of action.

There was a small residential building just before the offices of the KGB. I hid behind it, dropped my load, and wiped the sweat off my face with the hem of my dress. I sat down on the sidewalk, my back resting against the wall of the building, and began to map out my strategy. First, I would rest and cool off in the shade so that when I continued on the road, the KGB men wouldn't notice that I was tired and dripping with sweat from the heat and the heavy load.

While resting, I concocted a story in my head in case I was caught. I would tell my captors that while walking from school, a man approached me (I also made up his description and address) and asked if I wanted to make some money and that, naturally, I said yes. He told me to drop off my books at home and meet him in twenty minutes at a certain intersection, and so I did. He gave me this sack and forbade me to look inside (it was tied with a heavy rope). I was supposed to deliver it to a certain address (fictitious). He promised to meet me in two hours and pay me fifty kopecks. This was a lot of money for a kid like me.

This would be my story for the KGB. I memorized it and was sure that I had an ironclad alibi. My father's instructions were quite clear: I could never divulge my real name or address to any government official. After I cooled off and rested, I picked up the sack, threw it on my back and continued on my way. When I turned the corner from the side street the three KGB men were gone and I proceeded on my way much more relaxed.

I was totally unaware of the scene which played itself out on top of the hill at the bazaar. I had no idea that my father was there and saw me from above do the unthinkable. I eventually arrived at my destination, delivered the skin and were heading back home.

When I was passing the Muchnoy bazaar, on the way to deliver the merchandise, a man who knew our family recognized me just as I was nearing the three KGB men. He pointed me out to my father who was standing next to him,

saying "Hershl, isn't this your daughter on the road?" Father followed his finger and when he saw me he fainted and fell to the ground. The men picked him up and ran for cold water to spray on my father's face. When he came too his eyes searched for me on the road. I was gone from the road and so were the three men. He was certain that I was picked up by the KGB. His mind was full if terrible things that might or could happen to us. After all his teachings and indoctrinations, how could I be so careless. He went home thinking the worse. When he came through the door he accused Mother of the terrible way she was bringing me up. Mother knew that words were useless. She put a bowl of soup on the table and pretended to be busy. She knew that if I walked in when he was in such a rage, he would surely hurt me. He was eating the soup when I walked in. When I opened the door Father was sitting at the table his eyes riveted on the door.

He replaced the spoon in the bowl, stood up, walked over to me and delivered a resounding slap on my cheek. I lost my balance for a moment, but immediately regained it.

Mother tried to protect me from additional blows and yelled "run, run" but I stood my ground and waited for more. Mother came between us to protect me but he pushed her away with such a force that she fell in the bed. He yelled "If she doesn't get it you will". I can't say I was totally surprised at his reaction to what I have done. I only wondered how he found out. I knew very well that what I did was wrong and deserved to be punished, but not my mother. He did not hit me anymore that day. My cheek was on fire, but I held back my tears. This infuriated Father even more. After a while, when he calmed down somewhat, I tried to explain why I took that "dangerous road." I wanted to avoid the thugs who yelled obscenities at me and pelted me with rocks." he ordered me to sit down and listen carefully. In a low voice he said: Which would you rather have: A bruise on your head which would heal in a few days, or going back to a Siberian labor camp for 10 years. I begged my father to forgive me and promised that I would never do it again.

No, you will never do it again, because you will never go there again. Father kept his word.

It should not be misunderstood that my brother did not do his share, he did, but this was the time when he was preparing for his Bar Mitzvah.

When he could not go I replaced him.

The Russians were not very selective about "lawbreakers." The job of the KGB was to find "criminals," arrest them, and throw them in jail. I knew very well that what we were doing was against the law.

SKIMMING FOOD FROM MY SISTER

Many times, Mother left Leah in my care when she had to go somewhere. We had no carriage for the child, and if Mother went to the market, it was too difficult to carry the provisions and Leah. Leah was easy to care for. She was a happy baby most of the time. On warm days, she would stay in the yard, playing with whatever she could find—sticks, pebbles, grass, etc. She had no toys, and at the age of two or three, she didn't need much to entertain her. When she got into trouble and cried, I would hug her and sing to her. She loved to hear me and Mother sing to her. Apparently, our voices had a calming effect on her. I must say that we all had good voices, including Leah, and all of us loved to sing.

Father's singing was limited to Hebrew liturgy, which he excelled in. He sang Cantorial pieces with such feeling and emotion that it brought tears to people's eyes.

One of those days when Mother went to the market, she tarried longer than she intended. It was Leah's dinnertime, and she was giving me signals that she was hungry. I knew exactly what to do. Mother kept some farina in a jar for Leah. I poured some milk and water into a small pot, brought it to a boil, and measured the farina into it while mixing the hot brew. At that moment, I realized I was also hungry and poured more farina into the pot. I kept stirring so it wouldn't become lumpy. When it was done a few minutes later, I saw that it was too thick and Leah would not eat it that way.

I added some milk and sugar and mixed the cereal, and we both had a great feast. While we ate the farina, I had a feeling that I was stealing from my sister because I knew that the farina was only for her. I think it was rationed for small children only. I was afraid Mother would discover what I had done and scold me for my transgression, but she didn't, and I got away with it.

The guilt hung over my head and subconsciously maybe still does. Many years later, when Mother and I had plenty of food and reminisced about those times, I told her about it. This brought tears to her eyes, and she hugged me, saying, "I hope to God that you, Leah, or any of us will never be hungry again."

I'm not sure I have told this to Leah. It is about seventy years later, and I still remember my transgression. I think it stems from my religious upbringing. Mother always used to say that people who do bad things to others are sooner or later punished. Am I still waiting for my punishment? I was told that God watches everything and everybody, writes everything in His ledger, and metes out His punishment when He feels it's the right time. The Day of Atonement is approaching. I hope I will remember to ask God's and Leah's forgiveness.

Though I do not practice all the laws of Judaism, I think that deep inside, I am a religious person. This story with the farina may be laughable in the land of plenty today, but this transgression remains with me and retains the sense of guilt.

Now began a more prosperous time for us—meaning, we had food. This was the number-one concern of the population. There was always a shortage of food in the USSR, especially during the war. We had plenty of meat and could buy other articles (if they could be found). Mother decided that we had enough of living with the other family in one room and persuaded my father to talk to our boarders about it. Father gave them two choices: either they move out and we stay in the house or vice versa. They were quite comfortable where they were and decided to stay. That meant we had to move. Mother set out looking for an apartment.

A few weeks later, she found a two-room apartment on Stalina Street.

That was also the end of the partnership with Solomon. Father soon found another partner, and our meat business continued.

Stalina was the town's main avenue, which cut through the town from end to end. It was an elevated cobblestone road, so it didn't flood in the spring.

Since it was one of the main roads in town, the authorities installed light poles with megaphones for radio broadcasting. It was a much livelier area due to increased traffic and the radio, which broadcasted news, music, new songs about the valiant Soviet soldiers, all kinds of stories from Russian literature, poems, important announcements, and much more. Everything was censored, but at least we heard some news; whether it was true or false, no one knew.

What I fell in love with were the songs. These were mainly songs about the war and heroism, and I learned many of them and still remember some.

The apartment consisted of a small kitchen and a somewhat larger room, which became the bedroom. We had one large bed (wide boards on crisscrossed legs), and we all slept together, except the baby. She was less than two years old at that time and had her own cradle. Mother and Father slept at one end of the bed, and my brother and I at the other end. As far as I remember, those were our sleeping arrangements throughout the war, possibly with minor adjustments.

In the back of the house was a small piece of land, but it was not conducive to planting. It was mostly rocks and sand. Mother was very disappointed, but she realized that having some privacy after two years was more important.

When we moved into the apartment on 24 Stalina Street, we had Jewish Russian neighbors, the Gurevich family, a husband, his wife, and a teenage boy. The Gurevichs were Russian refugees from the Moscow vicinity. They were evacuated when the German Army advanced and were close to the city. Mr. Gurevich was a high-ranking official in the KGB in his hometown and continued his high-position job in the KGB in Dzhambul.

A few weeks later, we were obliged to seek his services.

Every official was on the take, and he was no exception. We were lucky that he could help and thus save my father from a probably long jail sentence in a gulag in Siberia.

One day, a policeman caught my father selling a shirt at the bazaar. Father was arrested, pending trial. He sent a messenger to notify us.

Mother started crying and wringing her hands. "What will we do? What will we do?"

Mrs. Gurevich heard her cry and came in to ask what had happened.

At first, Mother was afraid to tell her the truth, fearing even more trouble, but when Mrs. Gurevich told her that her husband might be able to help, my mother told her the whole story.

In the evening, when Mr. Gurevich came home from the office, his wife hastened to tell him about my father. He came in and asked Mother if she had money. Mother asked him why he needed to know. He answered that there were people who might be able to help free my father, but this kind of work was not free.

Mother told him that since it was summer, my father had no use of his jacket, so she would sell it and use the money to buy him out of jail. Mr. Gurevich answered, "Do what you need to do, and I will give you an answer in a day or two."

The next morning, Mother went to the bazaar and sold my father's jacket and waited for Mr. Gurevich to come home with some good news.

Mr. Gurevich was a simple man, tall, on the heavy side, and it looked that the son would follow in his footsteps—he was sort of a bully. Though they were Jewish, they were nonobservant at all. They followed their country's custom.

Religion had been outlawed in the USSR since the revolution, so the Gurevichs discarded the Jewish religion and obeyed the law of the land.

All the beautiful churches and synagogues were used as storehouses, barns, or whatever they were needed for. Some were demolished altogether.

Mrs. Gurevich was a refined, educated lady. She was slim, of medium height, and had long blond hair worn in a bun at the back of her head and beautiful blue eyes. She kept to herself most of the time.

Two days later, Mr. Gurevich came in and asked my mother to see him in the hallway. They must have discussed my father's arrest. I don't know how much it cost—my mother never revealed—but several days later, my father was released from jail.

He came home gaunt, unshaven, and he smelled. He had not showered or shaved the whole week.

We later found out that shaving, showering, or bathing were luxuries and criminals did not deserve them.

We were all very happy to see him but did not hug him until he had washed up and changed his clothes.

Father took a short "vacation" from doing "business" at the bazaar, but we had to eat and pay rent, so soon he went back to making a living anyway he could.

We were very grateful to Mr. Gurevich for his help.

My brother befriended their teenage son, and they played ball occasionally.

Baking Passover Matza

I must have mentioned that our house/apartment on Menzynskaya Street was long and narrow. This shape was conducive to other uses if necessary.

One early spring in 1943 or 1944, Father came home with a novel idea for business.

The holiday Passover falls in the spring, and the custom is to eat matzo (unleavened bread). Father went to the flour bazaar, bought a sack of wheat flour, and carried it home on his back. Mother questioned the amount. "Well," he said, "Passover is approaching, and we will need matzo. Very few people have a baking oven like ours, which is conducive to baking anything, so I thought, why not bake matzo for us and other people as well and make some money in the process? We'll clean the oven thoroughly and make it usable for Passover."

"And who will bake the matzo?" Mother asked.

"We will!" he said. "You know how to bake other things. Why not matzo?"

There were certain laws to be observed in baking matzo, but this could be learned easily.

The following day, the room was cleared of all small items stacked up against the wall, cleaned, and scrubbed as much as possible, and in the middle of it stood a brand-new long table that my father built with the help of a neighbor and borrowed tools. I remember how particular he was about it being smooth. He worked many hours until he was satisfied with his creation. He had leftover wood and made about ten rolling pins. Mother looked at them, bewildered, but she knew that there must have been a reason for that many.

Toward evening, during dinner, Mother popped the question. "What are we going to do with all those rolling pins?"

"These are for rolling out the matzo."

She did not interrupt, and Father continued to explain to all of us.

He had decided to go into the matzo business. He would hire women who had no regular jobs, and he was sure they knew how to use a rolling pin. There were plenty of women who would be happy to make a few rubles. He would teach them the rules and regulations of rolling matzo. Mother would make the dough, the women would roll the matzo out, and he and Sol would be the bakers. Then they would sell the ready-made product or have people bring their own flour and we would bake the matzo for them for a fee.

Everyone agreed that it was a brilliant idea, and all were very excited. This must have been sometime in March. After several days, word got around about our enterprise (of course, illegal), and soon people came to us to buy matzo or brought their own flour and we baked it for them.

Though short-lived, it was a great idea that supplemented the income for both our families and enabled many people to observe an important Jewish custom.

The following year, Father repeated the business venture. This time, we had competition from similar entrepreneurs, but we still did well.

Even I helped roll out the matzo when I came home from school. I was too short and could not reach the table surface, so Father made me a special stool to stand on so I could reach it. The table was long, almost from one end of the room to the other, and it stood there for several weeks. We were not allowed to eat at this table unless we covered it with a cloth because it had to remain kosher for Passover.

Some of the women stood on their feet many hours and sang songs to pass the time. Many people were coming and going. These were exciting few weeks. I should not forget to mention that there was always someone outside watching out for the police.

The Meat Business Continues

Some time passed, and the partners had a big argument. The professional butcher was ousted, and Father and Solomon remained, but they needed someone who knew how to cut meat.

After an extensive search, they found a suitable partner who knew the business and also lived in a large apartment suitable for this kind of venture. Another plus for us was that they lived not too far from us.

I do not recall his name, but only his looks. He was a tall, slim man with a graying beard and side curls. They occupied several rooms in a large Kazakh's house. They were a large family with married children and grandchildren.

Their house became the new venue for our enterprise. The word went out that we were in business again, and orders started coming in and the business flourished.

This was already in the last year or so before the end of the war.

A few months later, we moved again. It was also on Stalina Street. A Russian woman with a child, whose husband was at the front, fighting the Germans, owned this one-story house that consisted of two apartments. She worked while the child was in his grandmother's care and supplemented her income by renting out the other half of the house.

Toward the end of our tenancy, she even sublet part of her apartment to a single ex-veteran/convict who was released from the gulag somewhere in Siberia. He was a tall, skinny man with a dark complexion and shifty eyes. He was truly a chain-smoker. He made a living by wheeling and dealing at the bazaars. We didn't know why he had been jailed, and Father was probably afraid to ask him. He appeared very nervous most of the time, and sometimes at night, we would hear him scream.

Again, we had only one room with a large window facing the street, but it was all ours, no sharing, and we had privacy for a change. Next to the entrance was an iron stove, which constituted the kitchen. We had the same table with benches on each side and the wooden platforms serving as beds. Mother made new mattresses. She sewed together burlap sacks and stuffed them with straw and horsehair. The old ones were worn and torn and probably had bedbugs inside. Mother burned them the day we left the old apartment.

What made Mother most happy about this new apartment was the garden. The owner of the house was a woman alone with a job and could not handle the whole garden by herself. She was happy to share it with us. Mother was again in her beloved environment, planting, sowing, and reaping the fruits of her labor.

I used to help weed and water the garden. Mother usually asked me to watch what she was doing and encouraged me to help her. In this respect, we were very much alike.

We both liked creative projects. I still do.

The meat business flourished, and when needed, I was asked to help. The slaughter would take place on a Wednesday or Thursday night. Our customers primarily bought meat for the Sabbath and holidays. Very few could afford to eat meat during the week.

I am not sure about the exact date but it was toward the end of summer 1945 when we celebrated my brother Israel's Bar Mitzvah.

Family and close friends got together in a nearby house of prayer to mark the occasion.

My brother was well prepared by my father and our melamed and beautifully chanted the Torah portion and the accompanying "Haftara" (writings of the Prophets).

We were all proud of him.

The week preceding the Sabbath, my mother baked cakes and cookies and father brought "shnaps" for the guests to enjoy. Everybody wished us Mazal Tov and after they partook of the refreshments they went home to have their Sabbath meal.

In those days Bar Mitzvah's were not elaborate parties like some make today. The emphasis was on the religious portion of the celebration, rite of passage, when a boy of 13 becomes an "adult" and assumes his religious responsibilities.

This euphoria did not last long, because shortly thereafter the second typhoid epidemic hit with a vengeance.

Second Typhoid Epidemic

The typhoid epidemics came in waves, and there were two or three during our sojourn in Dzhambul.

The first wave took its greatest toll. It was in 1942–1943. People were traveling to and fro. The whole country was on the move, and the disease spread like wildfire.

This was shortly after our journey through the Southern Republics and our arrival in Dzhambul. That was when the illness claimed one aunt and four uncles.

The second wave of stomach or intestinal typhoid came during 1944–1945. This time, my brother Israel became ill. It was a few months after his bar mitzvah. We kept him home despite the danger of the disease spreading to the rest of us. The hospitals were full, and the care in the hospital was poor, to say the least. My parents had no choice but to care for him at home. He was taken to a doctor and was diagnosed with intestinal typhoid fever. His fever was not high in particular, but he had terrible stomach pains, constant diarrhea, and blood in the stool. He was getting medication and drank lots of tea.

Mother tried to prepare all kinds of dishes for him so he could gain some strength to fight the disease. There were not a great variety of foods he could eat, but she tried her best. He was in bed about four or five weeks, and it looked like he was slowly recovering.

One day, he said to Mother that he would like to have a piece of white bread. We knew now that white bread had no nutritional value, but in those days, it was a luxury and more expensive.

The government bakeries baked white bread, which was rationed to the sick young children and, of course, the KGB dignitaries. My cousins were also in charge of the white bread distribution. White bread was baked in large cookie sheets, cut, and weighed according to the ration cards and entitlements.

Upon hearing my brother's request, Mother sent me to my cousin's store to buy a piece of white bread. We had already received our potion of white bread for that week. The only one entitled to it was my little sister, Leah, and she had eaten it.

I had no ration card to take with me, only money. The place where they kept the bread was on the second floor of a building about two kilometers from where we lived. It was a two-story wooden warehouse. The exterior was painted gray and bore signs of age and neglect. I climbed up the flight of stairs, knocking on the door, and my cousin Aaron answered. He opened the upper half of the door and smiled upon seeing me and asked what I had come for.

I told him. He smiled a broader smile and said mockingly, "Who told you that I have white bread? And even if I had, why should I give it to you? You already received your share."

"I want to buy a piece of bread for my sick brother," I answered. "You know he has typhoid and cannot eat much of anything."

His tone changed to anger, and he said, "I have no white bread! You have already received your weekly portion of white bread! Go home."

But he realized I had seen two large sheets of white bread on the table. He opened the bottom half of the door and grabbed me by the hand and pulled me toward him. I struggled and, after a few moments, was able to free myself from his grasp. I ran down the stairs, yelling curses at him and crying. I ran all the way home, hardly stopping to catch my breath. I felt humiliated, frustrated, and angry.

When I finally entered the house, I was a little calmer, but not much. I was out of breath, and Mother could see that I was crying. I told Mother that my cousin refused to sell me a piece of white bread.

He denied having possession of any while I saw with my own eyes that he had plenty.

I never told my mother or anyone else of the rest of my encounter with him. Mother could hardly believe her ears. How could he refuse a slice of bread to his sick cousin?

We were not asking for charity; we offered payment. Mother accused me at one point of not trying hard enough. She thought I was rude to Aaron and didn't ask politely and that was why he refused.

I took the accusation with a grain of salt. I knew the truth.

A few days later, when Aaron was confronted by my father, he changed the story and fabricated a lie.

He told my father that he had said to me jokingly that he had none. He said that I probably got insulted and ran away before he could cut a piece and give it to me. Father believed him and not me, and I was yelled at.

After several weeks of diarrhea, vomiting, and stomach pain, my brother felt better and we all thought he was on the way to recovery. At least it seemed so. He was still very weak and didn't go to school yet, but he was walking around the room and began catching up with his homework. I went to his teacher once or twice a week and brought home his assignments.

Israel had an excellent mind, had almost all As, and his teacher was confident that once he recovered, he would catch up with the rest of the class.

One day, he asked Mother if he could have some sardines for supper. Mother, not thinking twice, left me in charge of Leah and Israel and went to the market in search of sardines. My brother had lost a lot of weight due to the diarrhea and vomiting. He hardly ate anything for several weeks. Mother was very happy to hear that he had finally regained his appetite and wanted something to eat. That meant he was recovering and getting back his usual appetite.

About an hour later, Mother returned with a tin of sardines and a smile on her face. She was happy that she could get what he wanted. Her heart was in the right place, but not her mind. She did not realize that after such a horrible illness, one's stomach could not digest such heavy food. She bought the sardines from a soldier at the market. Only God knows how old the sardines were.

Israel was happy that his wish was fulfilled so quickly. Mother opened the tin and gave him a slice of bread to eat with the sardines. He wanted to eat it all at once, but Mother stopped him after only half. Only then did she realize that this kind of heavy food should not be eaten right after such a dangerous illness.

The tragedy was that by the time she realized what she had done, she tried to stop him, but it was too late. She made him hot tea and made him drink it. A short while later, he began complaining of stomach pains. His pains were so severe that Mother got scared and took him to the hospital. When she told the doctor what Israel had eaten, the doctor yelled at her, pointing out that she might as well have given him poison. They pumped his stomach, but to no avail. He ran a high fever and, two days later, passed away.

Mother never forgave herself for this. When my parents came home from the hospital, both with red eyes from crying, Father yelled at her for a long time, accusing her of killing her own son.

I sat in a corner, holding my sister Leah, afraid to breathe, and crying for the tremendous loss we suffered again. After some hours of screaming at each other and accusations, Father walked out and did not come back until the next morning.

The funeral was the next day. Father sent messengers to relatives and friends to notify them of the funeral.

My brother was buried in the Jewish cemetery in Dzhambul the following day. This time, there was (I hope there still is) a gravestone to mark the spot.

While we sat shivah (the seven days of mourning), Father kept repeating to himself in a quiet whisper, "The curse did come true! The curse did come true! The curse, the curse, the curse."

No one wanted to ask Father what he meant by the curse. He was hurting terribly, and we did not want to cause him any more pain. When Father was upset, no matter the reason, we knew not to get in his way.

A few weeks later, he was having dinner when little Leah sat on his lap. He loved that child and made every effort to be congenial when she was near him. Sometimes when he was upset, we would try to cheer him up by sending Leah to him. His mood would change instantly. I knew never to get in his way or contradict him when he was in a bad mood.

That evening, Mother decided to ask him what he meant by the curse. He recounted an incident that I had witnessed but had forgotten about.

In the back of the previous apartment we had lived in, there was an empty lot. It was hidden from the street and undesirable eyes.

This lot was occasionally (Fridays and before holidays) used as a place of slaughter. People would bring their chickens, geese, or other foul to be ritually slaughtered. There was a lot of sand, so the blood could be covered up instantly. The blood of the slaughtered foul would be drained into a pail and disposed of properly.

That particular day was Hoshana Rabbah, the end of the Succoth (Booth) holiday. Father had some business to discuss with the shohet (ritual slaughterer), and I was sent by my mother to have a rooster slaughtered. There was another woman present who also brought a chicken to be killed.

When I arrived, there was a heated argument in progress between the woman and my father. I understood that the woman owed my father money and tried to postpone payment. Apparently, the debt was long overdue, and Father insisted on payment. The woman became very angry and began yelling at my father and cursing him. At the end, she yelled out loud, "I wish you a black year!"

Father was livid but stood there petrified and didn't utter another word.

The shohet tried to stop the argument, but to no avail. When the dust settled, there were two people shaking with rage and a frightened kid—me. I was stunned and ran home, forgetting about the rooster. When I entered the house, Mother asked me where the rooster was. Only then did I realize that I ran home empty-handed. I ran back to get the rooster.

By that time, the woman was gone and my father was sitting on a rock, sobbing bitterly. The shohet tried to console him. I picked up the rooster, still dripping with blood, poured some water on its neck, and took it home hidden in a pail covered with a rag. I wanted Mother to get busy with cleaning it and not see Father in the state he was in. Father didn't come home for a long while. He probably took a long walk, analyzing the situation.

My brother Israel died on the twentieth day of the Hebrew month of Heshvan it was October 27, 1945.

It was a very difficult time for us, a terrible blow to my parents, especially Father. He walked around like in a daze. I noticed many times that his eyes were red from crying.

Father did not shave a whole month, and he looked like an old man.

Mother was busy with the household chores and the care of my little sister, and it seemed like her preoccupation with the daily chores made it easier for her to bear the pain.

The Jewish mourning period lasts eleven months. During that time, no manner of entertainment or celebrations is allowed, nothing that can bring one pleasure. Even my little sister, who was two at that time, felt the sadness that was in our hearts. She kept to herself most of the time.

A few months later, I was invited to a friend's birthday party. I asked permission to go but was refused by my father. He reminded me, in case I had forgotten, that I was in mourning. I didn't forget for a moment, and I still feel the pain of the loss of both my brothers and observe the anniversary of their deaths. I very much wanted to go to that birthday party. I sort of persuaded Mother to allow me to go, and I promised that I would leave if there would be any music or singing. Mother tried to persuade my father to allow me to go, but he refused. The party was Saturday afternoon, so Father was home and I couldn't sneak out. My friend lived on the same street very close by.

In the afternoon, Father usually took a nap, and I sneaked out for half an hour and went to the party. Yes, there was music coming from a gramophone, but when my friend saw me, she stopped the music and the party went on without it. I stayed for about twenty minutes. First, I felt bad because I felt as if I betrayed my brother, insulted his memory, and disobeyed my parents. Second, I was afraid of the wrath of my father if he found out I disregarded his will and went without permission

My friends understood my predicament and didn't mind when I left a short while later.

I had guilty feelings for many years because of that incident. The reason I remember it so vividly and am writing about it can be that the guilt is still with me.

When I returned home, Father was still asleep. Mother asked me to take Leah outside so she could also rest a little. I took her for a walk in the direction of the party, which was still in full swing.

I passed my friend's house and kept on walking.

I was fifteen years old at that time and no longer a child. My mind was quite mature for my age, but my body was not developing at the same pace. I was small and flat-chested.

Our household was under a cloud of mourning and sadness since my brother Israel had died. We had hardly recovered, if at all possible, from the untimely loss of my brother David only a few years earlier. The only one who brought a little diversion and some joy into our lives was little Leah.

She was a happy child.

She liked to play outdoors whenever possible and used to pick flowers in the garden. Though the garden belonged to our landlady, she allowed Leah to play there and pick an occasional flower or grass. Our next-door neighbor had a cow that stayed in their backyard most of the time, eating grass. Leah saw this and would pick some grass and try to feed the cow.

When she found out that a cow gives milk, she would take a cup and go to the cow and ask her for milk, and we would laugh. When the neighbor milked the cow and Leah was around, she would send Leah inside to get a cup and gave her some milk directly from the udder.

Leah was fascinated by all this and wanted to repeat the procedure again and again. She knew some words in Russian and understood everything. She was about two and a half years old at that time, cute as a button, with a doll face framed by loose dark-blond curls and had big brown eyes and a button nose. She was the one who kept us going.

Naturally, my parents and I went about our chores and assignments, but we hardly communicated.

Mother would burst into tears every so often, and we didn't have to ask the reason. Father would come home in the evenings, have his meal, smoke one cigarette after another, and go to sleep.

On rare occasions, he would put Leah on his knee and play with her a little. Most evenings, she would be asleep when he came home.

It was my father's custom, as in most traditional Jewish homes, to sing Sabbath songs on Friday evenings during and after the meal. This had also stopped after my brother passed away, and Father did not resume the singing until my youngest sister, Sarah, was born in September of 1946 and we were back in Poland.

During 1944 to 1945, the war was going pretty well for the Russians with the help of the Allies. The Germans were on the run. We used to hear the news reports through the loudspeakers in the streets. Everyone heard the same news at the same time. I must hand it to the Russians; they very rarely broadcasted bad news from the front. When things were going badly on the front, there was a lot of music on the radio, mostly propaganda stories and war songs. Some of them I remember to this day. I must admit, they were beautiful.

The people began talking about an end to the war and returning home. Nobody made actual plans, but everybody was hoping to return to his or her own home.

Dzhambul had a mixture of people. They came from Poland as well as from many other Soviet Republics. Dzhambul was not the only town to have this mixture of nationalities. Most of the Southern Republics east of the Urals had an influx of refugees from war-torn European territories of the USSR.

When the war ended, everyone wanted to go home, but no one knew what awaited them there. For one, nobody knew about the Holocaust, the horrible atrocities perpetrated against the Jews and other nationalities of Europe.

No one could imagine the horrendous destruction and the utter devastation of Europe.

That was still unknown to us.

Everybody was happy when the war was over, and when this long-awaited news was blasted through the streets of every town, there was singing and dancing in the streets. A jubilant atmosphere engulfed the population.

Even my parents lightened up and began talking about going home. But a dark cloud hung over us. How could we leave behind the graves of our two young children? One was already left behind in Siberia, in an unmarked grave, the other in the Jewish cemetery of Dzhambul. This was the most difficult pain to bear, and the loss of the other relatives and my grandmother Leah.

We knew the war had ended and the Germans were defeated, but this was the Soviet Union, and no one did anything unless the authorities ordered it. We had to be patient and wait. Everybody believed, though, that one day, we would be free to return home.

We remembered the agreement with the provisional Polish government, so we put all our hopes and prayers into their hands. Now patience was a virtue. The subject fueled the imagination of many, and freedom was utmost on everyone's mind. Everyone waited for the day of deliverance, but nobody knew when it would come and what shape it would take.

In the meantime, life went on.

On a cold, crisp February morning in 1946, an announcement blared through the megaphones loud and clear that all Polish citizens who wished to return to Poland could do so. Those who wished to remain in the Soviet Union and become Soviet citizens were welcomed to do so.

There was a dilemma for those who had intermarried during the war, but the government allowed some spouses to join their families if they wished to leave.

This was a gift from Papa Stalin in order to keep families together. Most of them chose to leave.

The authorities began registering Polish citizens and issuing travel documents and train tickets to Poland. It was done in alphabetical order, so we knew that it would take a while for our turn to come. The process of identification and verification of citizenship was slow, and people spent many hours and days waiting for their turn.

Some Polish citizens who could afford it bought train tickets on their own and began their trip back home. Some got as far as Poland and witnessed the ravages of the war. They got a sampling of the devastation on the way while passing through Russia and the Ukraine, but the shock of the Holocaust did not hit them until they actually arrived in Poland.

Some people wrote back to their friends and relatives in Dzhambul what they had seen and heard about the war years. It was hard to believe some of the stories that came back from Poland. Some of the letters skirted the truth or held it back altogether for fear of causing enormous pain to their next of kin. After all, every family repatriated by the Russians had left behind relatives and friends.

The true story of the Holocaust became known to us only after we were on Polish soil. Even then, it was too painful and too hard to comprehend how the "final solution" took place while the world was looking on.

Those people with travel documents and tickets would board trains for Poland whenever they became available. We had no money to buy tickets, so we had to travel in cattle cars, thirty to forty persons in each, just as we had come. Our trip back to Poland was paid by the Soviet government, a gift from Papa Stalin.

It took several weeks to register and process the people.

In the meantime, many Russian citizens who wound up in Dzhambul during the war tried to buy travel permits from the Polish citizens and leave the Soviet Union. I understand that there were some Polish people who sold their travel documents and stayed in the USSR. That was the gossip that went around. Maybe it was true.

There were quite a few intermarriages, and some spouses did not want to leave their families for reasons of their own, so they sold their permits. There were thousands of Soviet citizens who left the country at that time. The atmosphere was charged with anticipation and high emotions. Many people sold their belongings, if they had any left, in order to have some money for the trip.

Nobody knew what awaited them at the end of their journey. If my memory serves me right, our turn to leave Dzhambul came on the second transport, March 20, 1946.

One thing we requested from the authorities was that they allow us to travel together with our relatives. Our request was granted. We were given three days to get ready for the trip.

Mother packed our belongings into bundles, as we had no suitcases. I think we still had a beat-up wicker trunk. The bundles were made either of sacks or sheets.

Mother hated to part with anything, so we had quite a few.

The down quilts and pots and pans were our most valued possessions. I must say again that those down quilts saved us from freezing many, many times. Father yelled at Mother about why she had so much stuff.

Trust me, it was very little, but to him, it looked a lot. He never needed anything, and Mother, on the contrary, needed everything, or so she thought. She used to say that one never knows when an item might come in handy.

Father always made sure to pack his Holy Books; they were his most-prized possession.

We hired a horse and wagon to take us to the railway station. It was difficult to say good-bye to my schoolmates and other friends. We were hoping to meet again in Poland, but this didn't happen. Everyone went his own way.

After all, Dzhambul had a mixture of refugees who came from all corners of Poland, not counting the Soviet refugees who arrived during the war.

When we said good-bye to our neighbors and landlady, there was a lot of hugging, kissing, and crying. They were natives and envied us terribly.

They knew that as Russians, they would never be able to leave their country in search of a better life.

On the way to the railway station, we met many other people going in the same direction, doing the same thing. There was a question mark on everyone's face.

Short conversations were struck. People asked one another where they were from in Poland, what their destination was, where they were heading, if they were going directly home.

The answers were vague and as varied as the people themselves were. There was a common feeling among all the people—uncertainty and hope.

Some exchanged addresses in the hope of visiting or meeting sometime in the future.

They were sure that "home" would be much better than what they had endured these past six years.

That was not to be either, but a Jew must never lose hope.

There was a myriad of people milling around at the railway station. People were exchanging information, arguing, and discussing the war, politics, and everything else imaginable.

No one knew what tomorrow would bring and what we would find at the end of our journey. There were as many ideas as there were people on that platform.

In late afternoon, horse-drawn wagons arrived, laden with loaves of bread and white loaves of salty cheese, called brynza. The cheese was so salty that it was impossible to eat it without soaking it in water at least overnight.

These were the food rations we received for the road. Naturally, everybody prepared their own food and took as much as they could. We still remembered the journey to Siberia and the lack of it.

The cattle train car pulled into the station in the early afternoon, and soon after, a contingent of policemen arrived with lists of passengers in their hands.

The cattle cars were numbered 1 to 35. One policeman stood on a truck and, through a megaphone, called out the names of people and which car they were assigned to.

Ours was 22. Mother had commented on how orderly the process was. Our car must have been somewhere in the middle, because I remember that when train would make a turn, we would see as many cars ahead of us as behind us.

Our turn to load our belongings came toward dusk, when the men were gathering for evening prayer. The authorities didn't wait for prayers to be concluded and ordered the men to board as soon as their names were called. The train had to leave before midnight.

We were told that wherever the train would stop, they would give us an opportunity to refill food and drink but that we had to fend for ourselves—no more freebies. We were on our own.

We heard some people say, "Be thankful that you can leave."

Everyone scurried to fill whatever vessels they had available with water. We wound up together with our relatives and some close friends. Everyone was, or pretended to be, in a jubilant mood. Both sides of the cattle car were outfitted with two stories of large wooden shelves. Each family occupied enough space on the shelf to sleep and, if possible, stack some of their belongings.

The platform emptied very quickly, and as the last passenger boarded the train, the whistle blew and we were off.

Emotions were high. Some people laughed, some sang, and some cried. The men resumed their religious obligation and gathered for evening prayer in the moving train.

The passengers soon realized that there was no provisions made for a lavatory. Children could use a potty, but what about the adults? Every family had a potty for their small children and adults, if necessary. The first task for the men was to create a "bathroom." They found a saw and other tools among the passengers and cut a hole in the wooden floor in one of the corners of the wagon, near a window. They hung two blankets around it, and there it was, a makeshift bathroom. The inconvenience of it was the noise of the turning wheels and the wind, but they found a remedy for this problem very soon. Whenever the toilet was not in use, the hole was covered with a wooden box. It really helped a lot.

By nightfall, everyone was more or less settled in, and our monthlong journey back home began.

It took again four weeks to get us back to Poland. For some, the journey lasted even longer, depending where they decided to end it.

We all made it an early night, as everyone was exhausted from the day's activities and excitement. The first stop was during the morning hours on the edge of a nondescript small town. That first morning, we found out that we were being escorted by several soldiers, and they seemed friendly.

This time, we didn't see any weapons and didn't know if they had any or not. When someone inquired why we had the soldier's escort, we were told that since we were foreigners and didn't know the land, they were placed on the train to watch over us and be of help if necessary.

We quickly realized, knowing by now the Soviet mind-set, that there must be an ulterior motive.

The soldiers were actually placed mainly to make sure that no one defected or tried to antagonize the local population.

Stalin was never sure or satisfied with the loyalty of his countrymen. He did not trust anyone.

After all, we were foreigners and not too enamored with the regime after the stint in Siberia.

I'm sure that the soldiers also informed the authorities of any "wrongdoing."

As days went by, we passed many large and small towns, villages, rivers, endless steppes, lakes, and forests. One day, we stopped on the banks of Lake Balchash. It's a very large lake in the European part of Russia and is well-known for the abundance of fish and salt. We were told that we would spend most of the day at this stop. The terrain at the lake was flat and sandy. We could discern a village in the distance a few kilometers away. Some people, including my father, ventured out to the village. By noon, a few local women came to our train to sell freshly baked bread, and some offered cheese, milk, vegetables, and other staples. One woman even tried to sell a freshly killed chicken, but nobody bought it because we had no cooking facilities. We also never knew in advance how long we would stay in one place, so real cooking was out of the question.

Most women didn't want money for their products. They wanted to exchange them for other staples, like sugar, rice, thread, yarn, fabric, etc. One woman asked if we had shoes or clothes for sale.

In the afternoon, my father returned from his adventure with a sack of salt on his back. Mother got angry and scolded him for bringing so much salt.

What was she going to do with it? She wanted products she could use the salt for. When asked how much he paid for the sack of salt, Father said he gave the man a few cigarettes for the whole sack. Mother wanted to throw the salt out, but Father said he had a feeling it would come in handy.

Sure enough, a few days later into the trip, he bartered a whole loaf of bread for a glass of salt and a quart of milk for another. Though we knew from experience that the distribution of goods and services in the USSR was very disorganized, to put it mildly, Father's salt business brought the subject to the fore. As our train traveled farther and farther west from Lake Balchash, we received more and more value for the salt. Father was very proud and pointed out to Mother at every opportunity what a profitable deal he had made by buying the sack of salt when he did. He was not the only one on the train who bought a sack of salt for a pittance. Many other passengers did the same and were glad they did.

Most of us learned in the Soviet Union that you take or buy whenever you have an opportunity. One never knew when an item might come in handy. Mother lived by that rule—she horded. I was bitten by the hording bug.

The days dragged on, and the scenery changed. There were whole days or nights when we stood still in the middle of nowhere. The reason was usually a train going in the opposite direction, and we waited for the tracks to be freed up so it could pass.

The weather was getting balmier, and we could keep the door open and enjoy the views; with the door shut, we were like in a prison. There were only two small dirty windows high up on each wall. With the door fully closed, we could not see much and hardly had any air to breathe.

Some evenings, my older cousins and their friends would get together and sing Russian songs we all knew so well. That was my favorite pastime.

Whenever we stopped at a major station in a large town, we stocked up on *kipiatok* (boiling water), gathered information whenever possible, and always asked how far Moscow was.

We were told that we would be crossing Russia's most famous river, the Volga, passing Moscow, and maybe even stopping there. Everyone was looking forward to this honor. We did not know that the Volga River is not even close to Moscow.

We heard so much about the beautiful capital city, the Kremlin, the grand wide boulevards, the magical metro, and so much more. It was supposed to be the highlight of our trip. The excitement built up every day.

At school in Dzhambul, we were fed so much love and admiration for that city that I could not wait to experience it firsthand.

As we neared the region, we were informed by one of the accompanying soldiers that we would be passing Moscow during the night and would probably not be able to stop at any of the stations. Apparently, those were the orders they had received.

Naturally, we were all disappointed but were sure to see the bright lights of the Kremlin, where Stalin lived, and probably other important government buildings.

My cousins decided to stay up that night and witness the magic of Moscow.

I was right there with them. The night was warm and dark. No moon or stars were visible. We sat on the floor, our feet dangling out in the open door, and we sang away merrily in anticipation of the wonderful spectacle that awaited us. The hour was getting late, and people, who could not care less about Moscow, wanted to sleep and asked us to lower our voices or try to be completely silent. We reluctantly obliged.

It was really dark, so we couldn't read or do much else.

The hours ticked away, and there was no sign of Moscow or any other lights. I was getting tired, too, but fought the urge to go to sleep. I moved away from the open door and leaned against the inside wall of the car. My cousin assured me that in case I fell asleep when we were nearing Moscow, they would wake me up so I wouldn't miss a thing.

When I woke up and saw daylight, I was shocked. I remembered every detail of the anticipation of the night before. My cousins were fast asleep on their shelves, and the door was closed.

I began crying and screaming at them for failing to wake me up and depriving me of seeing Moscow, the city of my dreams. They woke up from my screaming. Their answers differed.

One said that the train bypassed Moscow and they never saw it. Another played on my nerves and described the colorful lights of the city, the tall towers of the Kremlin, the long bridge over the wide Volga River. He would have probably continued to torture me with many other fascinating descriptions, but my cousin Rachel stopped him and declared that the train never passed near Moscow. It was all lies and fabrications of their vicious minds. He was simply joking.

I lived with that lie and the disappointment of missing Moscow for decades. It truly bothered me all those years until my childhood dream was fulfilled thanks to my daughter's caring nature and her dear friends. She made it possible for me to see Moscow in all its glory, and Saint Petersburg, too, in 2008.

Arriving in Poland

We were very ignorant of the devastation the war had caused, human and otherwise. Not until we reached the European part of Russia, where the battles raged, did we witness the physical destruction of the towns and villages. We heard gruesome stories from the people we met at the train stations, but it was still hard to believe that humans were capable of such horrors.

The word *Holocaust* was not born yet. We had not heard of it yet, but as our train advanced into Polish territory, the shocking truth began to emerge.

One strange phenomenon was in evidence at every station; there were no Jews seen anywhere, which was very strange.

Before the war, Jews could be seen in most cities, big and small, at railway stations, and everywhere else. Christians came to the train stations to sell their wares or for curiosity's sake.

They were wondering, *Where did all these Jews come from? We thought Hitler got rid of them.*

This was an eye-opener for most of us.

One day—I don't recall what town it was—a woman came to the train to sell soap. These were oblong grayish bars of soap with an unpleasant scent. After the monthlong trip, many people needed soap. They were fairly inexpensive, so many people, including my mother, bought several cakes of soap from this woman. When she sold her entire supply, she told the next customer that she would run home and bring some more. The cakes of soap were of a gray/cream color, and each had the letters RJF prominently stamped on them. One curious woman wanted to know what the letters meant. She did not recall soap by that name from before the war, and none of the train passengers could figure them out.

They decided to wait for the woman who was selling them to come back and ask her. When she returned with a fresh supply of the same cakes of soap, the curious Jewish woman approached her and asked what those three letters, RJF, meant. The Christian woman answered without blinking an eye. "These are German words. Rein Juden fet." Pure Jewish fat. A shudder went through the assembled group. They knew exactly what it meant. The horror of the crime and the disbelief shook them to the core. They asked the woman to leave. She had difficulty understanding why all this sudden change of heart. These Jewish women were so glad to buy the soap, so why did those three German words upset them?

Maybe she didn't know and did not bother to find out. She must have known that the German word *Jude* means Jew. Some women began crying and really didn't know what to do with the soap.

An elderly man, seeing the commotion, came over to ask what the problem was. When he was told, his face turned white and he stood there dumbfounded.

He told the gathered women that the soap must be buried. They were holding in their hands human parts of victims of the German atrocities. These bars of soap must be buried according to Jewish law. There were very few other men around because they must have gone into town to gather information.

By now, there were much fewer wagons attached to the locomotive and much fewer people. As returnees got off the train, hoping to return to their homes, to their loved ones, the Polish authorities decided to consolidate the passengers and leave behind the empty cars.

By that time, we just about had enough of cattle cars and asked the Polish authorities to transfer us to regular passenger cars. I should not forget to mention the utter devastation we saw in each city we passed. Warsaw was completely decimated. We began to realize that our being in Siberia's labor camps and all the other hardships we had endured for the past six years were nothing compared to what we eventually heard and witnessed in Poland, especially the almost-total inhalation of the Jewish community. As time went by, we learned more and more about the atrocities the Germans and some Polish citizens inflicted on the Jews who remained.

We soon learned that the majority of the Jewish community of Rozwadów, save those few who hid or those who survived in the USSR, were murdered.

In Warsaw, we finally got on a passenger train that was going west. The family decided to settle temporarily in a town in the western part of Poland, find out if any family members were alive, etc.

When Poland was divvied up, a large chunk of former Germany now belonged to Poland. The family decided to settle in one of those cities until the whereabouts of our relatives who remained under German occupation in 1939 became clear.

It began to dawn on us that Hitler actually did us a favor by expelling Jews from certain areas of Poland, and Stalin saved many by transporting us to Siberian labor camps.

I am sure that their reasons at that time were totally different, but it worked in our favor because the majority of those who were expelled did survive.

We finally arrived in a city called Szczecin on my fifteenth birthday.

This would not be the end of my and my family's wanderings, but it was good enough for the time being. We had to contend with it until we could figure out what to do next.

A dream fulfilled in 2008

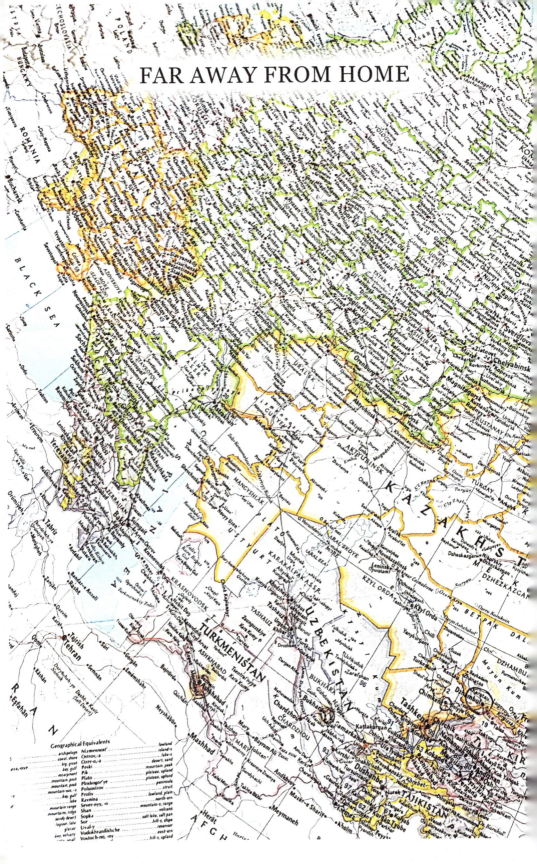

FAR AWAY FROM HOME

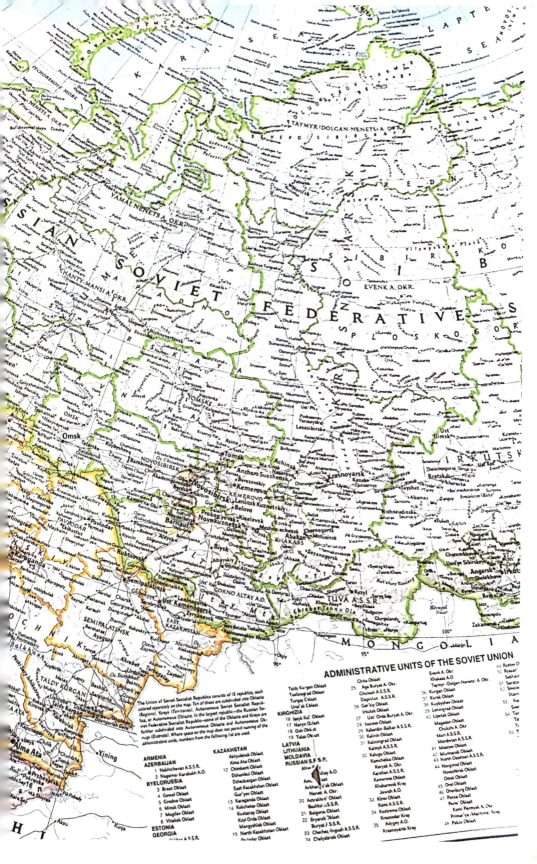

About the Author

Anna Pasternak was born in a village of Zbydniów in Southeast Poland called Galicia. Her happy and innocent childhood took 180-degree turn on September 1, 1939, the day Hitler invaded Poland and WWII began. Uprooted by the Nazi Army and ordered to go east, she and her family traveled on foot, horse and wagon, and cattle cars, winding up in a Siberian gulag (government labor camp) close to the Chinese border, suffering hunger, poverty, negative thirty degrees frost, and a disease that claimed six members of her family.

Freed from the Siberian wilderness in October 1942, the family traveled through Southern Soviet Republics, seeking warmth and a better life, all the time learning a new language, new customs, new cultures, new religions. They finally settled in Dzhambul, Kazakhstan, for the remaining four years of the war. In 1946, the family returned to Poland, finding absolute devastation, including that of millions of innocent souls, including next of kin they had left behind.

Anna returned to school way behind her age group but always strived to catch up.

As an adult, she continued to learn whenever and whatever she could (she tried to live up to the lessons her father had taught her in childhood): "Knowledge is the only thing no one can take away from you."

She arrived at America's shores in January of 1955, and the first thing on the agenda was to learn the language of her host country.

She tried her hand at several professions: nursing, teaching nursery school and kindergarten, sales, and singing. She recently retired from a long real estate career and moved to her ancestral home, Israel. Her passions are music, singing (opera), travel, art, architecture, and history. She has been married for almost sixty-one years to Herman Pasternak, and they have two children, Daphne and Zev, and two grandchildren, Eden and Daniel, to whom this book is dedicated.

CPSIA information can be obtained
at www.ICGtesting.com
Printed in the USA
BVOW05s0956011117
499252BV00033B/1501/P